COMMEMORATING

50 years
OF ASIAN AMERICAN
STUDIES AT SF STATE,
UC BERKELEY & UCLA

MOUNTAIN MOVERS

*STUDENT ACTIVISM & THE EMERGENCE
OF ASIAN AMERICAN STUDIES*

D0218124

edited by

RUSSELL JEUNG
KAREN UMEMOTO
HARVEY DONG
ERIC MAR
LISA HIRAI TSUCHITANI
ARNOLD PAN

Educational resources related to this book
can be found at: ucla.in/2ILk88H

MOUNTAIN MOVERS

Student Activism and the Emergence of Asian American Studies
1ˢᵗ Edition, 288 Pages, April 2019

Editors:
Russell Jeung
Karen Umemoto
Harvey Dong
Eric Mar
Lisa Hirai Tsuchitani
Arnold Pan

Printed in the United States of America

ISBN 978-0-934052-54-2
Library of Congress Control Number: 2019935627

ucla asian american
studies center press
www.aasc.ucla.edu

UCLA Asian American Studies Center
3230 Campbell Hall, Box 951546, Los Angeles, CA 90095-1546
aascpress@aasc.ucla.edu

CONTENTS

Introduction
Mountain Movers & the Emergence of Asian American Studies | *1*
By Russell Jeung

Discussion Questions | *24*

SF STATE

1

Origins
People, Time, Place, Dreams | *27*
By Malcolm Collier and Daniel Phil Gonzales

2

The Strike is Not Over | *57*
Irene Dea Collier, *Oral History*

3

Opening Doors for Organizing and Advocacy Work | *74*
Jeff Mori, *Oral History*

UC BERKELEY

4

UC Berkeley's Asian American Studies:
50 Years of Growing Pains and Gains | *90*
By L. Ling-chi Wang

5

Still Relevant Today:
Changing the World | *112*
Harvey Dong, *Oral History*

6

Stand Fast & Don't Go Quietly into the Night | *139*
Lillian Fabros, *Oral History*

UCLA

The Founding of the UCLA Asian American Studies Center | *158*
By Jean-Paul R. deGuzman

Back in 1969
Protests, Yellow Power, and the Emergence of Asian American Studies | *186*
Amy Uyematsu, *Oral History*

Living a Commitment to Service
Pilipino Students & the Beginning of Asian American Studies | *209*
Casimiro Tolentino, *Oral History*

NEW VOICES IN ASIAN AMERICAN STUDIES & ACTIVISM

Standing on the Shoulders of Giants | *223*
Holly Raña Lim, *Oral History*

Honoring Community Resilience & Resistance | *238*
Nkauj Iab Yang, *Oral History*

Sharing Leadership, Challenging Systems
A Grounded Perspective of Asian American Studies | *257*
Preeti Sharma, *Oral History*

Biographies | *271*

Acknowledgments

there are many people who are responsible for this publication. First and foremost, our gratitude goes to all of the "mountain movers" who took part in the movement for ethnic studies at campuses across the country. Without the collective actions of students, faculty and community supporters, Asian American and ethnic studies may not exist today. We also thank all of those who have shared their stories, some of which are featured in this book. The passing on of history is also a collective project.

THE EDITORS FROM SF STATE want to thank not only our featured interviewees, Jeff Mori, Irene Dea Collier, and Holly Lim, but also many others who contributed to the San Francisco State University content. Jensine Carreon, M.A., Asian American Studies (2018), helped conduct the interviews and meticulously transcribed them. Our faculty colleagues who were participants in the 1968 Black Student Union/Third World Liberation Front strike, Malcolm Collier and Daniel Phil Gonzales, wrote their account of the founding of Asian American Studies. This edited version first appeared in 2009 under the title, *At 40: Asian American Studies @ San Francisco State: Self-determination, Community, Student Service.* Richard Wada and Kenji Taguma also provided useful feedback and suggestions.

UC BERKELEY editors would like to express our sincerest appreciation to Lillian Fabros and Nkauj Iab Yang for their willingness to share their stories with us, as well as L. Ling-chi Wang for his detailed historical account of the founding of Asian American Studies and Ethnic Studies at UC Berkeley. Thank you to Elaine Kim and Jere Takahashi for their invaluable roles in the establishment of the Asian American Political Alliance/Asian American movement interview project, as well as Dharini Rasiah, Mike Tran, and Songvy Nguyen for their help with conducting and transcribing our interviews. Sine Hwang Jensen of the Ethnic Studies Library, Robert Javier of the Fremont Union High School District, Beatrice Dong, and Eastwind Books of Berkeley also provided important feedback and support throughout this effort. Lastly, we acknowledge our Asian American and Asian Diaspora Studies students and colleagues who inspire us with their tireless dedication to this invaluable program.

AT UCLA, we would like to acknowledge Jean-Paul R. deGuzman for his meticulous research in narrating the history of the UCLA Asian American Studies Center's founding, and Marjorie Lee for assisting in the assembly of original documents. Appreciation also goes to the UCLA Special Collections Library for making accessible additional materials. This would not have been possible without the willingness and generosity of Amy Uyematsu, Casimiro Tolentino, and Preeti Sharma, who shared their stories and memorabilia. We thank Susie Ling, Karen Ishizuka, Meg Thornton, and Valerie Matsumoto for conducting these and other interviews for the Collective Memories oral history project. We are grateful for the work of Janet Chen of EthnoCommunications, who coordinated and filmed the interviews of early founders, with the assistance of Emory Johnson, Christian Gella, Lian Mae Tualla, Marnie Salvani and Sarina Ngo. Our deep gratitude goes to Helen and Morgan Chu, Kenyon Chan and Carol Mochizuki for making this project possible.

The editors at all three campuses would like to thank HyunJu Chappell of Magna Citizen Studio for design and production, as well as Antony Wong for his artful copyediting.

MOUNTAIN MOVERS

Third World Liberation Front leaders marching down Bancroft Way in front of UC Berkeley, c. 1969, (from left to right): Charles Brown (Afro-American Student Union), Ysidrio Macias (Mexican American Student Confederation), LaNada Means (Native American Student Union), and Stan Kadani (Asian American Political Alliance).

PHOTO BY NACIO JAN BROWN

MOUNTAIN MOVERS

The Black Student Union and the Third World Liberation Front, a coalition of student groups, organized the longest strike at a U.S. academic institution at San Francisco State College (now San Francisco State University). The five-month strike culminated in the creation of the College of Ethnic Studies and policies for relevant, community-engaged curriculum.

Warren Furutani speaking at an anti-war rally at UCLA's Drake Stadium, c. 1970.

COURTESY OF UCLA ASIAN AMERICAN STUDIES CENTER, *GIDRA* PHOTO COLLECTION

INTRODUCTION

MOUNTAIN MOVERS AND THE EMERGENCE
OF ASIAN AMERICAN STUDIES

RUSSELL JEUNG

rene Dea was the village darling in her little farming town of Hoiping, China in 1948, just before the founding of the People's Republic of China. Often found singing at the top of her lungs on rooftops, she was a self-declared "spunky chatterbox." When she was two years old, her father in the United States sent for his wife and three children to reunite the family. Unfortunately, he had visa papers for two of his children, and Irene was the only girl.

Her mom took a photo of two-year-old Irene so that she could remember her soon-to-be left-behind daughter, and packed up all their belongings to make the journey across the Pacific. On the day they were about to leave, though, Mrs. Dea looked at Irene's little face and couldn't bear to leave her. She decided to remain in China with her three children, separated from their father.

After first moving his family to Hong Kong, Irene's father sent passage again for his wife and two of the children. This time, Irene's older brother remained behind and Irene, who had cut her hair and was disguised to look like a boy, took his place. Arriving in San Francisco in 1953, the Deas lived in a Chinatown hotel where they shared a bathroom and kitchen with five other families. Despite her harsh and crowded living environment, Irene felt fortunate that her mother had made the split-second decision to bring her to the U.S. She felt even luckier when they moved to a small, one-bedroom apartment, and they could have their own bathroom.

Even in Chinatown, Irene found her whole world had changed. She no longer could use her village dialect, Hoiping, because Cantonese was the main language spoken in Chinatown. At school, her teachers forced her to use English; it was sink or swim for her. Because of these drastic changes, Irene became reticent and withdrawn. The former chatterbox and darling of the village found herself muted in this new land, and her entire personality changed because of her migration experience.

Irene's school experience wasn't unique but commonplace for Chinese Americans.

She recalled that her white male teachers would yell at the Chinese American students at Galileo High School in the 1960s because they "would not speak up in class." Just as her teachers didn't understand her immigrant experience, her school curriculum was alien to her. She couldn't recall a single book that took place in China or Chinatown.

By the 1960s while Irene was in high school, Chinatown, like the rest of the United States, was swept in the changes of the time. Young Chinese Americans, like those in other low-income urban areas, drew attention to the deplorable conditions that they faced—substandard housing, dire health disparities, and lack of social services. Irene joined in the spirit of serving the community and nation by tutoring younger immigrant children almost nightly at the local YWCA. She would later go on to San Francisco State College (now SF State University), where she would join the Intercollegiate Chinese for Social Action (ICSA). Soon after starting school, she would join the student-led strike for ethnic studies with hundreds of classmates supporting the demands of the Black Student Union and the Third World Liberation Front

(TWLF). They were calling for an education that was relevant and accessible to the communities from which they came. She explained,

> When the strike came along, it just spoke to me. Everything that I had wondered about, everything that I cared about, everything that I was working on in the community—it all came together in the strike—all the experiences of my life, of having teachers yell at us, the way we were taught English.
>
> When the Black students said, "We need classes that reflected our own communities," it really spoke to me, because you could just see in our community—we needed services! My main concern was the community and the lack of services in the community: the inequality of services given to our community.

For Irene, the strike's demands synthesized all that she had experienced and felt as a student of color. They made up more than an ideological statement; the TWLF was a movement addressing the community that she cared about and the values she espoused.

What socio-historic factors shaped Irene to become a student activist and, eventually, move mountains in her community? Why did students like Irene feel such a need for Asian American studies that they organized and went on strike for over four months? The year 1968 was a watershed moment for students of color in the United States. At the height of the Vietnam War with no end in sight, students rallied at college campuses across the country to protest the mounting casualties of American intervention in Southeast Asia. The assassination of Dr. Martin Luther King, Jr. heightened urban tensions between African Americans and whites as well, and the nation convulsed with race riots in several cities. Challenging the twin evils of imperialism and racism, Asian Americans joined with other young persons in movements for peace, the environment, Black power and civil rights, and women's rights.

Not only did students like Irene participate in these broader movements, but they fought for themselves and the self-determination of their communities, that is, the right to have a say in the issues affecting their lives. Likewise, they supported the right for nations to have independence and sovereignty over their people and lands. They sought neighborhood preservation and healthcare, for decent housing and for needed social services. They wanted to see democracy lived in practice. Thus, the fight for ethnic studies was a call for an education relevant to contemporary social problems where they could learn to develop effective strategies for social change.

Mountain Movers: Student Activism and the Emergence of Asian American Studies details the founding of Asian American Studies (AAS) programs at San Francisco State University (SF State) and the University of California at Berkeley (UCB) and Los Angeles (UCLA). This book shares the life story of six individual students who sought and obtained educations to make a difference in their own home communities and in the larger world. It also features the stories of three younger students who benefited from ethnic studies and Asian American studies almost fifty years after both were established. They represent a new generation of leadership who carry on the legacy of community activism. Together, they are mountain movers who have made changes on campuses and in their communities through activism, community organizing, and solidarity with others.

To put the narratives of the nine individuals profiled in *Mountain Movers* into historic context, this chapter offers a brief historical background of Asian Americans leading up to the student protests of 1968. It then discusses the "twin evils" of racism and imperialism, and how they impacted Asians in the United States. These socio-historic forces set the stage for the

PHOTOGRAPH BY STEVE LOUIE, WEI MIN SHE AND ASIAN COMMUNITY CENTER PHOTOGRAPHS, AAS ARC 2015/3, ETHNIC STUDIES LIBRARY, UNIVERSITY OF CALIFORNIA, BERKELEY

Elderly Filipino manongs and Chinese American residents fought displacement from their homes at the International Hotel in San Francisco in the 1960s and 1970s. Asian American students joined the campaign to fight the evictions and redevelopment and to preserve low-income housing for the elderly.

According to the Densho archive, "This retrospective on a 1946 Japanese American Committee for Democracy march reminded young folk that Nisei and even Issei were also down for the cause." (Gidra, Dec. 1970)

founding of Asian American studies not only at the three California universities covered in this book, but for other campuses as well, including Merritt College in Oakland, the College of San Mateo, Santa Clara University, UC Davis, UC Santa Barbara, and California State University at Pomona and Long Beach. Early Asian American and ethnic studies courses were also fought for on East Coast campuses, such as Yale University and Hunter College of the City University of New York. In general, Asian American college students sought self-determination for themselves and their communities, and this demand required relevant curriculum in their schooling. After highlighting the roots of Asian American studies, this introduction concludes with a reflection on the fruits that Asian American studies has borne and new areas for growth.

THE HISTORY OF ASIAN AMERICANS BEFORE 1965

By 1968, Asians had been in the United States for over three generations. Chinese, Japanese, Filipinos, and Koreans were the first groups to arrive in significant waves starting with large-scale migration of Chinese after the California Gold Rush in 1849. Smaller numbers of arrivals reached the continental U.S. even earlier, including Filipinos, who had established a settlement in Louisiana as early as 1763. The early settlers, primarily male laborers, soon met racial hostility, political disenfranchisement, economic exploitation, and cultural stereotyping from the European American establishment. This pattern of racial subjugation would continue with each wave of Asian immigrants.

On May 19, 1979, the Korean American community rallies with Asian American student and community activists in Stockton, CA, calling for the release of Chol Soo Lee, an immigrant facing the death penalty for killing a man in a prison fight. The pan-Asian Chol Soo Lee Defense Committee organized support from campuses to Korean churches, building awareness and pressure on the courts, resulting in Lee's acquittal March 28, 1983, and eventual release.

In response, Asians in California resisted discrimination and oppression through protests and strategic maneuvers, through lawsuits and mass civil disobedience. Tens of thousands of Chinese refused to register as aliens when the U.S. Congress passed the 1892 Geary Act that extended the Chinese Exclusion Act. Japanese, unable legally to purchase land as non-citizens, bought farms under the names of their children until further laws prevented them from doing so. Filipinos, despite mob violence and police harassment, organized as unions and went on strike for fair wages and decent conditions in several notable cases.

World War II exposed the blatant hypocrisy of American democracy and its institutional racism when the U.S. government incarcerated over 120,000 persons of Japanese ancestry in concentration camps. Over six in ten internees were U.S.-born citizens, who were incarcerated for about four years under the suspicion of espionage and fear of their disloyalty. Not until 1988, after Japanese Americans lobbied for redress and reparations, did the U.S. government apologize for unjustly incarcerating its own citizens.

In the decade after World War II, Asian Americans remained scarred by the internment and by the anti-communist hysteria of the McCarthy era. Consequently, the U.S.-born generations of Asians, who grew up attending American public schools, generally felt pressure to integrate into American society by acculturating and assimilating. While African Americans protested for civil rights during the 1950s, politicians would pit them against Asian Americans, whom they framed as the "model minority": a racial group that stereotypically did not complain about the discrimination they faced, but simply worked hard to overcome it. This new stereotype con-

During World War II, Japanese Americans were held in temporary "assembly centers" before being taken to one of 10 concentration camps operated by the War Relocation Authority. Pictured is the Sacramento Assembly Center, which held nearly 5,000 Japanese Americans from the Sacramento area in 1942 prior to their transfer to Tule Lake concentration camp in northern California.

tinued the labeling of Asian Americans with dehumanizing, blanket generalizations.

In 1965, the Hart-Cellar Immigration and Nationality Act radically changed the demographics of the Asian American population. Following the principles for equality and social justice advocated by the Civil Rights movement, this act removed bans on immigration from Asian nations. Instead, it gave preferences for visas to family members of Americans and to professionals. As a result, the numbers of family reunion visas and professional visas for Asians to the United States skyrocketed, and increased the population of Asian Americans drastically. The demographic shifts in the community corresponded to social and political changes that also took place in the 1960s.

ASIAN AMERICAN STUDENTS IN THE 1960S: THE SOIL OF THE ASIAN AMERICAN MOVEMENT

Coming of age in the 1960s, Asian American students at universities developed a new, distinct consciousness as Asian Americans shaped by the racial and international context of the time. By 1968, when the Asian American population numbered about 1.3 million, 80 percent of Japanese Americans and about 50 percent of Chinese Americans and Filipino Americans, respectively, were born in the United States. Asian Americans had come to reach the same educational attainment as whites, but still earned substantially less because of racial discrimination. For example, in 1960 Filipinos earned only 61 percent of the income of whites with comparable educations. Japanese and Chinese also earned less than their white counterparts, making 77 percent and 87 percent, respectively. Among the 107,366 Asian American college students on university campuses in 1970, Chinese and Japanese made up the vast majority, with over eight out of ten Asian American students being of either Japanese or Chinese American descent.

ASIAN COMMUNITY CENTER ARCHIVES

These students arrived at campuses in tumult, as the nation was undergoing a political unrest over U.S. involvement in the Vietnam War and a cultural revolution over race, sexuality, and the role of authority. The assassinations of President John Kennedy, presidential candidate Robert Kennedy, and Dr. Martin Luther King, Jr. devastated the nation's morale. Yet young people continued to rise up. Urban race riots in Harlem, Philadelphia, Watts, Newark, Chicago, and Baltimore—just to name a few—erupted over discrimination, high unemployment, and police brutality. The Black Power movement, led by various groups including the Student Nonviolent Coordinating Committee, Nation of Islam, and the Black Panther Party, emerged in the latter half of the sixties. Coined by Black Panther leader Stokely Carmichael, the Black Power movement inspired racial pride and advocated for local community control, self-determination and economic development. At the same time, other social movements challenged the existing social order. At UC Berkeley, students engaged in civil disobedience over a university ban on political activity and initiated the Free Speech movement. The women's liberation movement emerged in the late '60s as organizations formed to confront society's sexism and to promote women's equality. Likewise, activists organized the

Above: Oakland High School students participated in the funeral for Black Panther Bobby Hutton, killed by Oakland Police in 1968.

At left: Huey P. Newton, who was a cofounder of the Black Panther Party in 1966, is seen speaking. Behind is Richard Aoki, who was an early member of the Black Panthers and became a leading member of the Asian American Political Alliance (AAPA) at UC Berkeley.

Asian Americans not only called for peace in order to bring troops home, but also protested U.S. intervention and imperialism in Vietnam, c. 1971.

environmental movement to protect the earth, stop pollution, and clean-up toxic environmental hazards in low-income neighborhoods and communities of color. Each of these movements, as well as their militancy, informed the Asian American movement.

In this movement, Asian Americans, who had individually become involved with the causes of the times, drew together to address their own racial status and identity. They confronted enduring stereotypes of the unassimilable heathen, the Yellow Peril, and the perpetual foreigner. This generation of students faced the model minority myth, that Asian American students were expected to be hard-working, studious, and quiet even in the face of discrimination. While many sought to assimilate to mainstream Anglo-American cultural norms, they soon recognized that they could not assimilate fully into the white mainstream.

The other racial model for Asian Americans was the Black Power movement, which rejected American racism and promoted Black autonomy, racial pride, and community control. For those African American activists, the ideologies of self-determination and cultural nationalism became realized through militant organizations, a flowering of Black arts and expression, and a reclamation of indigenous and ethnic histories. Some of the subsequent Asian American organizations, such as the Red Guard, modeled themselves partially after the Black Panthers, while others were more connected to diasporic movements, such as the Union of Democratic Filipinos, which was also involved in opposing martial law in the Philippines.

Students involved in the Asian American movement challenged the existing white/Black dichotomy of U.S. race relations that rendered Asian Americans mostly invisible to the broader society. Being neither Black nor white, Asian American students became conscious of their marginalized status as unequal racial minorities. They came to embrace a pan-ethnic identity as Asian Americans to reject the connotations of the oft-used group term, "Oriental." To be Oriental was to be traditional, objectified, and foreign. In contrast, the newly minted group identity of "Asian American," signaled a political and cultural collectivity with new possibilities and shared aspirations.

As a newly-formed group identity, Asian American consciousness was rooted in the communities from which they came. Actively seeking to reclaim their histories and to find their own voices, they sought out narratives from their ancestors and elders. They became engaged with their home neighborhoods, creating local programs to "serve the people" and to rally the masses. They also sought to forge solidarities across ethnicity, race, and national boundaries as they identified with other "Third World" peoples. This term recognized the exploitative relations in the global hierarchy where the least developed nations faced oppressive histories and conditions similar to historically marginalized communities in the U.S. Through the practice of supporting one another's movements and struggles, Asian American students built a collective identity and common cause to address racial injustices.

Additionally, Asian American students were deeply influenced by major international developments of the 1960s. The anti-war movement against U.S. military involvement in Southeast Asia reached its apex on campuses in early 1968; the success of North Vietnam's Tet offensive demonstrated that despite the onslaught of U.S. military might, the war could not be easily won. Asian American war protestors realized their paradoxical position. On one hand, they knew they were Americans, but they were being sent to fight an enemy that not only looked like them, but were in a subordinate position in the world order like they found themselves to be within boundaries of their own country.

Identifying themselves as part of the Third World, Asian Americans drew inspiration from the Bandung Conference held in Indonesia in 1955. This meeting of African and Asian nations, many who had just become independent from their colonized status, promoted international cooperation and independence from the United States and the Soviet Union—the First and Second World powers. The thought of Chairman Mao Tse-Tung of the People's Republic of China, Ho Chi Minh of North Vietnam, and Che Guevara of Cuba, each of whom advanced Third World-ism, became another source of ideology for some in the Asian American movement. Students came to embrace their analysis that racial discrimination in the U.S. was a product of colonialism and imperialism, such that people of color and Third World peoples faced a common oppression from Western nations.

So in this way, Asian American students in the 1960s responded to the twin evils of racism and imperialism. First, due to racism, Asian Americans found themselves marginalized since they were neither white nor Black. Furthermore, they were considered neither authentically American nor Asian. Often coming from ethnic enclaves, they recognized that their parents faced discrimination, segregation, and cultural stereotyping due to their race. Yet they continued to feel the pressure to discard their ethnic heritages and to assimilate into the white mainstream in order to pursue the American Dream. Second, in examining the wars in Southeast Asia, students came to question American intervention that violated the sovereignty of other nations for the sake of its national interests. And they opposed maintaining a long-term war that did not seem winnable. Instead of seeing other Asians as the enemy, students who joined the Asian American movement found solidarity with them in their common subjugation as Third World peoples, dominated by other Western nation-states and subject to exploitation by multinational corporations.

THE CALL FOR ASIAN AMERICAN STUDIES
ON WEST COAST CAMPUSES

As students became involved with both international and local issues, they began to call for a relevant education that could address these concerns. However, as Irene Dea expressed, they found a system of higher education that largely excluded students of color from admission and whose courses showed little reflection of their histories and experiences. In 1960, California enacted its Master Plan for Education that created a three-tiered college system. The University of California (UC) system was to admit the top 12 percent of the state's high school students, while the California State University (CSU) system was to accept the top 33 percent. The community colleges were to admit all others. Due to the creation of this stratified system, the percentages of Black students dropped at San Francisco State University from 11 percent in 1960 to only 5.3 percent in 1968. Students of color made up only 17 percent of the university overall.

In response to these educational disparities, students at SF State were the first to mobilize large numbers of campus and community supporters around demands for an accessible and relevant education. The Black Student Union (BSU), along with the Third World Liberation Front (TWLF) organizations, demanded special admissions for underrepresented communities. TWLF included three Asian American student groups: Intercollegiate Chinese of Social Action (ICSA, founded in 1967); Philippine Collegiate Endeavor (PACE, 1967); and Asian American Political Alliance (AAPA, 1968). Each of these groups had already developed community-based projects, such as youth development work in Chinatown, resistance to the I-Hotel evictions in Manilatown, and fighting redevelopment in Japantown. The TWLF organized itself around three goals: special admissions, development of Third World curricula, and hiring of faculty of color. Supporting the BSU and TWLF, members of these groups participated in a sit-in at the campus president's office in spring 1968, and won the establishment of an Educational Opportunity Program (EOP) office on campus and an increase in special admissions.

The next fall semester, however, SF State administrators attempted to remove a lecturer in Black Studies who was an advocate in the Black Power movement. They also broke their

San Francisco State College

STRIKE
DAILY

VOLUME ONE / NUMBER ONE / NOVEMBER 6, 1968 / JAMERSON PRINTING

MASS STRIKE CALLED

10 THIRD WORLD DEMANDS

1 THE BLACK STUDIES DEPARTMENT MUST BE GRANTED FULL DEPARTMENTAL STATUS IMMEDIATELY, WITH ALL BLACK STUDIES COURSES PLACED UNDER ITS JURISDICTION.

2 THE BLACK STUDIES DEPARTMENT WILL GRANT A B.A. IN BLACK STUDIES.

DR. NATHAN HARE, CHAIRMAN OF THE BLACK STUDIES DEPARTMENT, MUST BE GIVEN A SALERY SUITED TO HIS QUALIFICATIONS.

3 UNUSED SPECIAL ADMISSION SLOTS FROM THIS SEMESTER MUST BE FILLED NEXT SEMESTER BY THIRD WORLD STUDENTS.

4 ALL THIRD WORLD STUDENTS APPLYING TO SF STATE IN THE FALL, 1969, MUST BE ADMITTED.

5 TWENTY FULL TIME TEACHING POSITIONS MUST BE PROVIDED TO THE BLACK STUDIES DEPARTMENT.

6 HELEN BEDESEM MUST BE REPLACED AS FINANCIAL AIDS ADMINISTRATOR BY A THIRD WORLD PERSON WHO CAN MEET THE SPECIAL NEEDS OF THIRD WORLD STUDENTS.

7 NO DISCIPLINARY ACTION WILL BE TAKEN AGAINST STUDENTS, FACULTY, STAFF OR ADMINISTRATORS FOR THEIR PARTICIPATION IN THIS STRIKE.

8 THE CHANCELLOR'S OFFICE PROPOSAL TO RESTRICT STUDENT SELF GOVERNMENT AND AUTHORIZE THE
9 ADMINISTRATION TO DISSOLVE STUDENT PROGRAMS WILL NOT BE IMPLEMENTED.

10 GEORGE MURRAY MUST RETAIN HIS TEACHING POSITION.

STUDENTS ASKED TO WALK OUT

If you support the ten demands; if you object to being an instrument in the latest attack on George Murray of the Black Panther Party by the people who run this state; if you are appalled by the latest repressive measures of the Chancellor's office and the Board of Trustees; if you think you are entitled to some say over your own education and your own life; if you feel that Black people are entitled to the same things and have been forced to put up with a vicious system of institutionalized racism for too long; if you support the student programs or feel you have a right to demonstrate on campus; if you feel any sympathy at all for the attempt by Black people to liberate themselves from the rule of a racist power structure...then you support this strike. We call upon all students to boycott their classes, to participate as actively in the strike as they can, to stand together and make themselves heard. We need everybody.

THIS IS THE FIRST ISSUE OF WHAT WE HOPE WILL BE A CONTINUING DAILY NEWSPAPER. ANYONE AND EVERYONE WHO SUPPORTS THE STRIKE AND WANTS TO RAP ABOUT IT IS WELCOME TO CONTRIBUTE--POSITIONS, ARGUMENTS, POEMS, HUMOR, SATIRE, ANYTHING. WE'LL PRINT AS MUCH OF IT AS WE CAN. BRING YOUR STUFF TO THE OPEN PROCESS OFFICE IN HUT C OR CALL 469-1441.

Students had to keep fighting for Asian American and ethnic studies courses to be offered every year in the early period of the ethnic studies centers.

promise to use special admissions for 428 Third World students and shelved a proposal to hire for Black Studies. BSU and TWLF thus initiated a student strike on November 6, 1968 with the BSU making ten demands and TWLF seeking five additional ones, including community control over faculty hiring and curriculum development in the establishment of ethnic studies.

After a five-month strike, during which picketing students would be tear-gassed, beaten, and arrested, the TWLF gained a School of Ethnic Studies which included departments of American Indian Studies, Asian American Studies, Black Studies, and La Raza Studies. The first semester after the strike in the fall of 1969, students were able to take 17 different Asian American Studies courses, most focusing on the experiences of specific ethnic groups. The following fall, the school offered 44 courses, reflecting the hard work of student curriculum committees to establish these first-of-their-kind classes.

Across the San Francisco Bay, students of color at University of California, Berkeley were similarly fighting for ethnic studies, but faced formidable challenges. In 1966, African Americans and Latinos made up only 1.5 percent of the student body, with Asian Americans comprising 10 percent. Each of these racial groups had made demands for ethnic studies courses, but the university administration dragged its feet in implementing this curriculum.

In January 1969, the UC Berkeley Chinese Students Club, the Nisei Students Club, AAPA, and other organizations hosted the Yellow symposium at Pauley Ballroom, which included attendees from as far as New York to Hawai'i. SF State strikers George Woo and Laureen Chew called on the group to support the TWLF strike and to initiate their own ethnic studies programs at their campuses. On the campus at UC Berkeley itself, an experimental course for Asian American Studies in fall 1969 drew over 400 students, demonstrating the high interest for such curriculum.

Following the model of SF State, UC Berkeley students formed their own Third World Liberation Front and initiated a strike in January 1969. Like their counterparts, they sought a Third World College and "Third World control" over curriculum and programs. The UCB strike lasted three months, including a confrontation between 3,000 strikers and 1,600 law enforcement officers and National Guardsmen. Students subsequently won an Ethnic Studies department with four divisions to cover the history, culture and experiences of African Americans, Mexican Americans, Asian Americans, and Native Americans.

To the south, UCLA students were also caught up in the political moment and advocated for Asian American studies. In the fall of 1968, of the 29,000 students on campus, 12 percent were students of color and 1,700 were Asian American (5.8 percent of the student population). That year, students founded Sansei Concern, a student organization of primarily third-generation Japanese Americans, who sought to become active in the pertinent issues facing the Asian American community. Sansei Concern organized the "Are You Curious Yellow?" conference in fall 1968, prior to UC Berkeley's Yellow symposium, and that convening helped to galvanize a movement for Asian American studies classes, an Asian American studies research unit, and Asian American organizations such as *Gidra*, a community-based, student-run magazine.

Building from the momentum of this conference and related efforts to establish an Asian American research unit on campus, students and supportive faculty created the first AAS course at UCLA called "Orientals in America" in spring 1969. This class brought in an array of speakers and presenters, including representatives from community organizations such as the Yellow Brotherhood, the Oriental Service Center, the Japanese American Citizens League, and the Filipino-American Council.

While this course was offered through an experimental program, students and faculty were lobbying for an Asian American Studies program alongside African American Studies, Chicano Studies, and American Indian Studies. UCLA's Chancellor conceded to a research institute model, perhaps due to fear of student unrest that had already exploded at SF State and UC Berkeley. He envisioned the institute to be an academic research center that would examine Asian Americans in ways traditional to the academy. In contrast, students negotiated for, and eventually won, a center that would address the social problems in the community and courses that would engage students in community issues. By fall 1969, the UCLA Asian American Studies Center offered five courses: "Orientals in America," "Koreans in America," "Chinese in America," "Wartime Relocation Experiences," and "Comparative Analysis of Asian American Community Organizations."

THE FLOWERING OF ASIAN AMERICAN STUDIES

After the TWLF strikes at SF State and UC Berkeley and the creation of the Asian American Studies Center at UCLA, the struggle to establish Asian American studies continued as students sought to develop the curriculum that was relevant to their communities. At UCLA, in 1975, for example, the university did not approve Asian American studies courses for having enough intellectual merit. Again, the students and faculty had to organize to keep Asian American studies alive. To establish and maintain Asian American studies, students at each campus needed:

1) to create the curriculum and classes themselves;
2) to produce and publish Asian American works;
3) to establish further institutional relationships in local communities.

Since Asian American studies was a new field, it had very few published books and articles in 1969 and the faculty had to create their own readers from mimeographed articles. These new classes also had to be officially approved by the universities, and the students formed curriculum planning committees that ensured that the course content was relevant to Asian American communities and met university standards. At SF State, the faculty and students worked extensively so that Asian American studies courses fulfilled General Education requirements. The classes were purposively interdisciplinary to address the Asian American experience in a holistic manner. At UC Berkeley, classes addressed not only the significant social problems facing Asian American communities, but also examined the literature, arts, and creative expressions of Asian Americans. These courses revealed the diverse voices of many important Asian Americans who had been silenced or ignored in American mainstream popular culture. Likewise, Asian American history courses highlighted the contributions and struggles of Asians in the United States. Replacing a history of faceless victims, these classes instead revealed the resilience, activism and movements of past Asian Americans for a better life and a more just society.

Along with offering classes that were relevant in these ways, these early programs helped to lay the foundation for Asian American studies as academic field of study. At UCLA, students gathered oral histories, uncovered primary source materials, and collected existing publications about Asian Americans. The UCLA Asian American Studies Center published the first anthologies: *Roots: An Asian American Reader* (1971), *Counterpoint* (1976), and *Letters in Exile: a Pilipino American Reader* (1976). In 1971, it became home to *Amerasia Journal*, the first academic journal in Asian American studies.

Along with creating the curriculum and scholarly field, Asian American student activists remained engaged in an extensive array of grassroots organizations and bridged their campus-

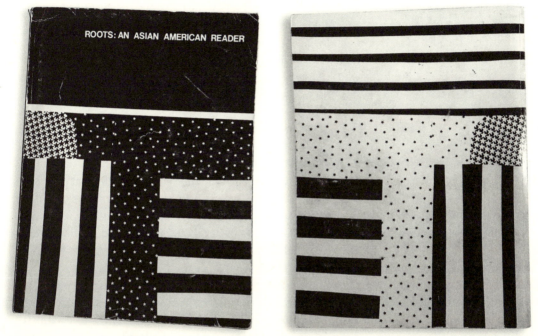

ROOTS: AN ASIAN AMERICAN READER

PHOTOS BY AMY UYEMATSU

In 1971 UCLA's Asian American Studies Center produced one of the first books in Asian American Studies, Roots: An Asian American Reader. It was co-edited by Franklin Odo, Buck Wong, Eddie Wong, and Amy Uyematsu (then known as Amy Tachiki). Roots has sold over 50,000 copies.

es to their communities. San Francisco State created a special program, the Nine Unit Block, where students got credit for working in the community. SF State student Jeff Mori credits this program for helping students apply their ethnic studies knowledge, providing direction for their future careers, and building networks of leaders in the Asian American community. His fellow classmates became future leaders in Asian American organizations. They included Gordon Chin (Chinatown Community Development Center), Steve Nakajo (Kimochi Senior Center), Tom Kim (Korean Community Center), Ed De La Cruz (West Bay Pilipino Services), Fred Lau (San Francisco Police Chief); and Anita Sanchez (San Francisco Civil Service Commission).

Just as SF State Asian American Studies Department produced community leaders and UC Berkeley established centers in the community, the UCLA Asian American Studies Center spawned several organizations that linked the university with the surrounding Asian American communities. Besides *Gidra* newspaper, it hosted Visual Communications, a visual arts organization, and Asian American Studies Central, which promoted ethnic studies both in higher education and at K-12 public schools. Activists involved at UCLA similarly came to lead many important local and national service and advocacy organizations.

THE FRUITS OF ASIAN AMERICAN STUDIES

The roots of Asian American studies and its flourishing as a field of study has borne fruit, evidenced by the accomplishments of its students, a growing diversity in the curriculum, and the strength of local Asian American community institutions. For the students, Asian American studies validated their identities as Asians in America. It allowed them to explore a common history and cause with fellow Asians. And it offered a space to develop solidarities within and across racial, ethnic, gender and other boundaries. Asian American studies was a hotbed where students could grow in their activism and leadership. On university campuses, Asian American studies institutionalized community-based learning and research that re-envisioned the role of the university. Finally, the Asian American community as a whole benefited, as students went on to apply their skills and experiences to establish needed community programs and services as well as local and national organizations. They also entered mainstream institutions and advocated on behalf of those whose voices were missing.

The 1960s student activists profiled in this book each helped to establish Asian American studies and to work on behalf of Asian American and Pacific Islander communities afterwards. UCLA student Casimiro Tolentino, hailing from central Los Angeles, tutored three nights a week across town in Venice, California while in school. He later worked as an attorney litigating unfair agricultural labor practices and served many community organizations, such as Asian Americans Advancing Justice-Los Angeles. Amy Uyematsu was raised in a white Los Angeles suburb but recognized how her high school history and civics classes failed to acknowledge Japanese American internment during World War II. While she worked at UCLA's AASC, she co-edited *Roots*. Eventually, she became a high school teacher herself, while gaining acclaim as a poet. SF State student Irene Dea tutored almost nightly in San Francisco Chinatown, and Jeff Mori organized youth in San Francisco Japantown while they were undergraduates. Later, Irene would lead the Association of Chinese Teachers and Jeff would become executive director of the Japanese Community Youth Center. Harvey Dong, whose family lived near Sacramento Chinatown, shared how UC Berkeley students established the Asian Studies Field Office, which housed an elderly drop-in center, the Chinatown Cooperative Garment Factory, a community meal site, and a bookstore in San Francisco's Chinatown. Eventually, that space became the Asian Community Center, funded by the seniors themselves. While earn-

As Alan Ohashi (at left) and project director Alan Kondo (at right) look on, fellow Visual Communications co-founders Eddie Wong and Robert Nakamura prepare a 16mm camera during a location shoot in Los Angeles' Griffith Park. Visual Communications created pioneering motion picture documentaries through the 1970s and early 1980s.

ing a Ph.D. in Ethnic Studies at UC Berkeley years later, Harvey began Eastwind Bookstore, promoting Asian American books in Berkeley. Similarly, UC Berkeley student Lillian Fabros grew up supporting Filipino farm worker organizing in Salinas, and later worked as a mental health organizer herself. Her work included staffing the Pilipino Organizing Committee in the low-income South of Market neighborhood of San Francisco.

Today, Asian American studies courses provide students with the theories, frameworks, language, and role models that help students acknowledge and claim their Asian American narratives and identity. Along with the student activists from the1960s and '70s, *Mountain Movers* profiles recent graduates of Asian American studies: Holly Lim, a Filipino American student from SF State; Nkauj Iab Yang, a Hmong American student from UC Berkeley; and Preeti Sharma, a South Asian graduate student from UCLA. Each grew up in communities quite different from the students of the 1960s. Holly Lim came from a multiracial, Southern California suburb, Nkauj Iab was raised in a low-income neighborhood in Sacramento, and Preeti came from a Caribbean diasporic community in south Florida. Nevertheless, each shared how Asian American studies gave them the words to frame their own experiences and that of their immigrant families. Not only did they learn about their own histories, but they also connected with fellow Asian Americans to draw inspiration and solidarity for their own community advocacy and research work. Today, Holly runs a leadership development program, and Nkauj Iab and Preeti are graduate students, in addition to actively contributing to the community.

These three Asian American Studies programs, like others across the nation, have played a critical role in making institutional reforms and advancing new fields of knowledge. They have created curricular changes and student-serving programs to broaden access for Asian American students. They continue to further research of Asian Americans and Pacific Islanders in the U.S. through their faculty and graduate programs. The legacy of programs like SF State's Nine Block Program continue to shape the curriculum, as SF State Asian American Studies majors all do community internships as part of their coursework. UC Berkeley hosts the premier doctorate program in Ethnic Studies. UCLA's Asian American Studies Center continues to publish *Amerasia Journal* and other important publications, while the Asian American Studies Department offers both master's and undergraduate degree programs.

While ethnic studies and Asian American studies programs have altered the landscape of the university and while students and faculty continue to play prominent roles in society, much work remains. Many campuses across the country have yet to incorporate ethnic studies into their curricular offerings. Many courses still lack the diversity of critical perspectives that such scholarship provides. Asian American and ethnic studies faculty still face discriminatory treatment in a field that continues to push intellectual boundaries. A major issue is the underrepresentation of newer immigrant and refugee populations in many universities; in particular, groups, including Southeast Asians, South Asians, and Pacific Islanders, face a lack of faculty representation, which impacts teaching and research. Asian American studies continues to experience growing pains as the field strives to expand the tent to be more inclusive of the diversity reflected in our populations.

This book is written in hopes that it provides useful historical context as well as interesting stories that can paint a clearer history of Asian American studies as a product of the militancy and vision of the Civil Rights and Black Power movements. The stories here remind us that ethnic studies, like any change born of conflict and struggle, is something that people are often forced to defend over time as it becomes part of our institutions. It is the students, faculty, and community partners that continue to establish and grow these programs in the service of our communities and our increasingly, interconnected world. Just as students and community advocates of the sixties and today have placed themselves in the timeline of history, may this history lay a foundation for future activism, engagement, and innovation.

Latinx students mobilize at the TWLF 50th Anniversary Rally on the Mario Savio Steps at UC Berkeley on January 22, 2019. Jesus Barraza of Dignidad Rebelde designed the anniversary poster.

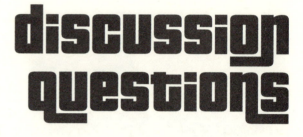

discussion questions

FOR ALL CHAPTERS

FOR LEARNERS

1 What were the key historical factors that led to the emergence of the Asian American movement?

2 What conditions, movements, and people inspired students to become involved in the Asian American movement, and, more specifically, in the creation of Asian American studies?

3 Why and how did students mobilize to establish Asian American organizations during this time? What were the challenges they encountered in doing so, and how did they overcome them?

4 In their strikes and struggle to establish Asian American studies, what resistance did the students face? What does this reveal about society at the time? How did they persist and eventually establish ethnic studies?

5 Once Asian American studies programs were created, what roles did students play to help establish and sustain the curriculum and programs? Why would it be necessary for students to keep active in developing and sustaining these programs?

6 What do you believe has been the impact of Asian American studies at these schools? Has Asian American studies had a lasting impact beyond these schools?

7 Can you relate to the educational experiences of the students in this book? Why or why not? What gaps in your educational experiences today still need to be met in light of this book?

CHAPTER 1

ORIGINS

PEOPLE, TIME, PLACE, DREAMS

MALCOLM COLLIER & DANIEL PHIL GONZALES

Two days after Bloody Tuesday, faith-based leaders and community members joined over 2,000 students marching across 19th Avenue on December 5, 1968. As San Francisco police responded with violence and arrests, an officer choke-holds Ecumenical House director Rev. Gerry Pedersen after he comes to the aid of students who appealed for non-violence.

Asian American Studies at San Francisco State was the product of efforts by Asian American students, faculty, and community members to effectively address pressing academic and community issues. Although our backgrounds and motivations were varied, we shared common concerns and goals. As participants in the development of this first curricular program of its kind, our purpose here is to present a retrospective on the origins of Asian American Studies at San Francisco State.

Beyond the influences of the Civil Rights and Black Power movements of the 1960s, and concurrent domestic and international movements, the founders of Asian American Studies had personal experiences with particular forms of racial and ethnic antagonism, restriction, and exclusion suffered by Asian American communities. While we had similar perceptions of inequities in American society, our ethnic and class origins were diverse, and so were our motivations. Adherence to a single, sanctioned political paradigm was not a requirement for participation in our activities, but a critical awareness of the contradictions of America, and a deep concern for the practical needs of Asian American communities, were expected from all involved.

A SEARCH FOR EQUITY

he development of a Third World perspective that recognized relationship among race, class, and access to political power led Asian American student organizations to form alliances with each other and with other Third World groups, assisted by some faculty and community leaders. These alliances were intended to address pressing community issues, provide mutual aid, and increase community-centered political power. The most immediate motivating factor was a broad frustration with academe because of its racial and class inequities, and its gross irrelevance to the needs of Third World students and their communities.

Most of us—then students—involved in the creation of Asian American Studies at San Francisco State began our formal education in U.S. schools in the late 1940s and early 1950s, a time of ultra-conservative sociopolitical conformity associated with the Cold War and McCarthy era. For Asian Americans and "non-whites," there were extreme pressures to assimilate toward the idealized white Anglo-Saxon Protestant cultural model. In the 1960s, the influence of the Civil Rights movement and the growth of the so-called counterculture began to weaken the social rigidity that marked the 1950s. When we arrived at San Francisco State College (now San Francisco State University) in the mid- to late 1960s, we found a campus awash in a ferment of experimentation and new ideas. However, like most of our earlier formal schooling, the existing college curriculum was largely disconnected from the lives of our families and communities.

At San Francisco State, we met others from our communities and engaged in discussions about our social, economic, and cultural circumstances with a depth that we had never done before. At the core of these discussions was a developing articulation of the needs and desires of our communities that we were both witnesses to and participants in.

We were becoming aware that existing institutions did not effectively meet these needs and desires. We shared a hope—soon frustration—that higher education would provide us with increased knowledge to address issues important to our communities. As we learned to describe our circumstances, hopes, and expectations, we searched the college for language courses, history classes, literature classes, and courses in different branches of the social sciences for content and meaning relevant to our experience.

We found little.

We found no Pilipino language course; Mandarin classes, but no Cantonese classes; and literature courses that did not include readings from Asia, let alone anything written by or about Chinese, Japanese, or Filipinos in America. Asian studies provided little that informed Asian American students about our places of ancestral origin. Whatever our varied backgrounds, even our limited knowledge of our own family stories, made us aware that THERE MUST BE HISTORIES of Chinese, Japanese, and Filipino Americans in the United States, though we usually lacked detailed knowledge of these histories. We found that courses in the History Department contained little regarding Asians in America.

Those of us with interests in social work and teaching knew from our own observations that there were few Asian Americans in those fields. We envisioned using our college educations to become trained professionals, equipped with the skills necessary to address the issues of our communities. The hard reality was that even these programs—ostensibly designed to prepare students for real world circumstances—had virtually no awareness of our communities, nor did they provide the knowledge that we so much desired. There was an absence of even the most fundamental reference to the existence of Asian Americans from the general curriculum, just as it had been missing in our earlier schooling.

In blunt contradiction to the daily recited pledge that described the United States as "one nation, under God, with liberty and justice for all," formal education at all levels presented students from cultural minority groups with extremely limited access to information about either their historical, or contemporary, circumstances. Apparently, our histories, cultures, and communities were not part of the American "all?" White students were provided multiple opportunities to obtain knowledge about their place in American history, culture, and society—but we were not. As our understanding of the extent of these omissions grew, so did our feelings of exclusion. This was an obvious violation of the principles of democracy that we were taught as children and adolescents, and that we wanted to believe.

Beyond the issue of equity, there was also the pragmatic question of how can a society that claims to be democratic and pluralistic, operate as such, if the full range of its sociocultural character is not recognized and addressed? The evidence presented in our academic setting pointed away from "liberty and justice for all," and toward cultural dismissal and racialized restriction instead.

We felt the college should do better.

By 1968 youth in Chinatown and other immigrant communities were growing and faced a lack of educational and employment opportunities. They began demanding better housing, schools, healthcare, family support, and a political voice, over the objections of the much older Chinatown community leaders.

COMMUNITIES

Our desire for change was, ultimately, shaped by our community circumstances. A variety of historical realities and new trends were shaping our communities in the late 1960s.

Starting in the late 1950s and accelerating through the 1960s, Chinese American families were moving out of San Francisco Chinatown and into other neighborhoods at a steadily increasing rate. Many of these families were comprised of second generation parents with third generation children, but some were also families formed by the arrival of wives and children after the war. These migrations were also related to the gradual opening up of public sector employment to Asian Americans and others in the same time period, as well as to the decline in legalized housing discrimination. Yet even as some long-term residents moved out, new immigrants moved into Chinatown in ever larger numbers, which led to a rapid increase in the numbers of new immigrant children in local schools and on the streets.

The pressures brought by the growing population began to expand Chinatown to the west and the north. New immigrants were joining some students' mothers in the sewing factories unknown to Chinatown outsiders—and new immigrant-owned businesses were opening up on Stockton Street. Immigrant youth were joining existing street organizations or forming their own peer groups that were often misidentified as gangs. By 1968, immigration had major impacts on Chinatown: housing shortages, increased traffic congestion, new businesses, crowded schools, the need for more jobs, youth and family problems, and health concerns to name just a few. The old, familiar Chinatown struggle for survival took on new dimensions, in part because they were going unaddressed by both traditional Chinatown organizations and government agencies.

Concurrently, political tensions festered below the surface of the community. Chinese American students were very much aware of familial fears of the immigration authorities. They knew that their family names were often changed and false. They knew that there was tremendous danger to being labeled "communist" and that silence, not protest, was a virtue.

What history lay behind these fears?

The structure of the Chinese American community had been long dominated by conservative elements that suppressed progressive movements; however, their often crude tactics were losing their effectiveness by the mid-'60s. These conservative elements had declining influence on both the families that were moving out and the new immigrants moving in. Their inability to address the changing needs undermined their power. The federal "War on Poverty" was starting to bring money into the community that could provide needed services as well as new bases of power. These resources from outside further weakened the old power structure that was politically disinclined, as well as poorly prepared, to make use of these new opportunities. The new generation of college-educated Chinese Americans, both American-born and immigrant, began to take social service roles in Chinatown. By 1968, they were agitating for wider response to the pressing needs of Chinatown, and would later provide some of the community support for the student strike at San Francisco State.

Certain issues were affecting all three of the city's larger local Asian American communities. In the mid- and late 1950s, the San Francisco business and political elite spawned a major redevelopment plan that targeted the Fillmore District, a heavily Black populated area, an older Japanese American community, and Central City where there was a large and growing Filipino American population.

While the core area of Chinatown successfully resisted redevelopment, powerful corporate interests threatened encroachment of Chinatown and Manilatown on Kearney Street. The

200 persons rally with the Committee Against Nihonmachi Evictions (CANE) to protest a high rise hotel development by Japan's Kintetsu Corporation and San Francisco's Redevelopment Agency which threatened to displace many low-income Japanese Americans and small businesses in 1974. Like the I-Hotel tenants, CANE successfully mobilized thousands of people and forcibly occupied several buildings slated for destruction to protect their community.

Two hundred Filipino students, faculty, staff, and community members, along with lead artists James Garcia and Christina Carpio, unveiled the Filipino Community Mural in 2003 at SF State University's Cesar Chavez Student Center.

expanding financial district endangered low income housing and small businesses at the precise moment when the need for more housing and community-based businesses was growing. Single-room-occupancy (SRO) housing in those communities, including the International Hotel (I-Hotel), which housed both Filipino and Chinese American residents, was inadequate for the large families arriving from the Philippines as a result of the Immigration and Nationality Act of 1965 (Hart-Cellar Act).

While Chinatown expanded north and west to accommodate new arrivals, new immigrants from the Philippines concentrated heavily in the Central City/South of Market and the Inner Mission District. By the late 1960s, the area had become a very visible and dynamic Filipino community with issues that paralleled those of Chinatown. The City's redevelopment project very quickly razed buildings that included SRO hotels and four- and six-unit flats.

This sweeping demolition affected the Kearny Street population most directly, decimating the Filipino manong/bachelor community within a few years. The symbolic center of this change was the I-Hotel, located on Kearney, between Jackson and Washington Streets, on the eastern border of Chinatown.

Filipino American students, whose political consciousness had been wakened by the Civil Rights and anti-war movements, and the struggles of farm, hotel, and restaurant workers, turned their energy to the plight of the manongs of Kearny Street and the needs of the recent immigrants residing in Central City. These activities further encouraged student interest in Filipino American history. Manongs and manangs told stories from the 1920s and 1930s about work in the fields of Hawai'i, California, and Washington, and the canneries of Alaska, as well as those about their service in the U.S. military during World War II. The students heard accounts of their elders' experiences with prejudice and how they responded. They learned about union organizing, and about making good times from bad ones.

The same forces that threatened Chinese and Filipino American communities were at work in Japantown as well, which was still recovering from the damages of wartime relocation to American concentration camps. Redevelopment demolition in the Fillmore was in full swing in 1968, displacing Japantown residents along with the Black community. Combined together with the movement of many Japanese American families into the Richmond District and outlying suburbs in the 1950s and 1960s, the City's redevelopment process raised major questions about the future of the Japanese American community in San Francisco. Would it survive?

These circumstances also raised questions among younger Japanese Americans about their history in America. In particular, they were beginning to seek complete discussion of the World War II internment that many of their families had endured. Questions about the camps were met with silence or terse dismissals by the generations that experienced them. Why? Many Sansei (third-generation) Japanese Americans were frustrated by the lack of meaningful responses and looked for additional sources about their Japanese American history.

On a certain level, the Asian American students of the time were following in the footsteps of their own parents and communities. When Chinese and Filipino American men worked hard and long enough to raise the funds to bring wives and families from Asia after World War II, they were laying a very emphatic claim to a permanent place in America. However conservative some of their politics, they knew about the struggles of their predecessors, as well as their own. They were asserting their rights and challenging the old order by establishing families, seeking new avenues of employment, and moving into neighborhoods where racial covenants meant to exclude them. They too were concerned with equity and inclusion. Some went further by forming and joining labor unions, and taking public stances on community issues. Seen in the context of this dynamic, it is not at all surprising that many of their children would be concerned and active as well.

Students and youth linked arms with allies from throughout San Francisco on August 4, 1977, to defend the I-Hotel tenants from evictions after nearly ten years of resistance. Organizers like Pam Tau Lee, who lived in Chinatown SROs (single room occupancy hotels) several blocks away, used their knowledge and skills to improve housing, employment, and environmental health and safety conditions in their communities. Front row from left: Lynn Yokoe, Craig Wong, Pam Tau Lee, unknown, Karen Wing, and Carol Friedman. Behind Karen is Sharon Lew.

IT'S OUR HOME - WE
NO EVICTIONS! WE WON'T
The residents, small shop
community organizations of th
stand united against all a

PHOTO BY CHRIS FUJIMOTO

After the strike, students from SF State and other campuses joined artists, labor organizers, and other communities facing evictions in Chinatown, Manilatown, and Japantown. Over the next decade, some joined revolutionary organizations while others formed new grassroots community groups like Kearny Street Workshop, Chinese Progressive Association, Asian Community Center, and nonprofits like Chinatown Community Development Center.

ARTWORK BY RACHAEL ROMERO, SF POSTER BRIGADE, 1977

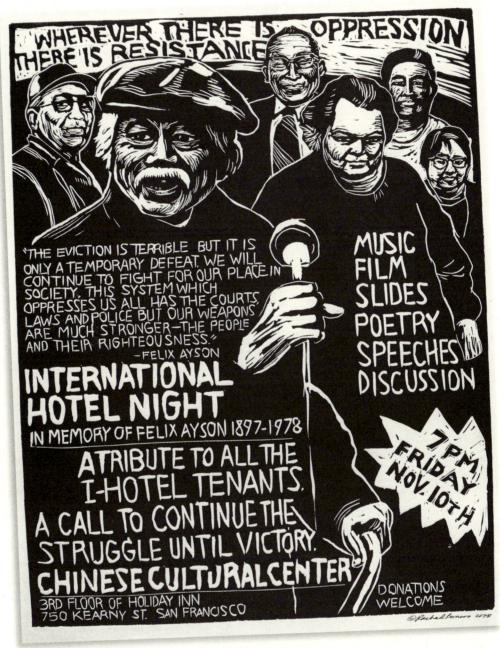

WHEREVER THERE IS OPPRESSION THERE IS RESISTANCE

"THE EVICTION IS TERRIBLE BUT IT IS ONLY A TEMPORARY DEFEAT. WE WILL CONTINUE TO FIGHT FOR OUR PLACE IN SOCIETY. THIS SYSTEM WHICH OPPRESSES US ALL HAS THE COURTS, LAWS AND POLICE BUT OUR WEAPONS ARE MUCH STRONGER—THE PEOPLE AND THEIR RIGHTEOUSNESS."
— FELIX AYSON

MUSIC
FILM
SLIDES
POETRY
SPEECHES
DISCUSSION

INTERNATIONAL HOTEL NIGHT
IN MEMORY OF FELIX AYSON 1897-1978

A TRIBUTE TO ALL THE I-HOTEL TENANTS.
A CALL TO CONTINUE THE STRUGGLE UNTIL VICTORY.

CHINESE CULTURAL CENTER
3RD FLOOR OF HOLIDAY INN
750 KEARNY ST. SAN FRANCISCO

7 PM FRIDAY NOV. 10TH

DONATIONS WELCOME

ARTWORK BY RACHAEL ROMERO, SF POSTER BRIGADE, 1978

International Hotel Night, 1978. Woodcut print by Rachael Romero. SF State students formed new arts organizations like Kearny Street Workshop to inspire, unite, and "serve the people!" They were part of a new Asian American "cultural revolution" that helped shape community consciousness to build respect for our cultures, languages and historical struggles.

STUDENT ORGANIZATIONS

n conversation, we discovered that our questions, and growing anger, were collective matters, not simply individual issues. This realization led to the formation of new activist student groups rooted in, but extending beyond ethnic community experiences.

Three Asian American student organizations formed in 1967 and 1968: the Intercollegiate Chinese for Social Action (ICSA, 1967), Philippine (later Pilipino) American Collegiate Endeavor (PACE, 1967), and Asian American Political Alliance (AAPA, 1968). The Alliance had a largely, but not exclusively, Japanese American membership at San Francisco State. Unlike preexisting student groups, these were politically-charged organizations.

Most of the Chinese American students in ICSA were second generation: born in the United States, the children of families formed by the arrival of wives from China, and who sometimes were accompanied by older children. These wives joined their husbands who had come earlier, often twenty years or more, usually as "paper sons." Some ICSA members, however, were third, fourth, and even fifth or more generation Chinese Americans. Some were born in China, having come to San Francisco in the 1950s.

Despite these generational differences, almost all ICSA members had longtime family connections to America, either directly or through a history of split families. This variation of the extended family structure occurred when two or more generations of fathers, grandfathers, and great grandfathers had lived much of their lives in America while their wives and children were forced to remain in China due to restrictive U.S. immigration laws. Through these multi-generational connections, ICSA members had a basic awareness of a longer Chinese American history in America, although usually a limited specific knowledge of it.

Most ICSA members were local, and many lived in San Francisco Chinatown for all or most of their lives. Several came from small towns in northern California with very old Chinese American histories like Isleton, Weaverville, and Marysville. Most had parents who worked in sewing factories, restaurants, and small stores, or ran small businesses. Only a few had parents with better paying jobs in mainstream employment. All were the first generation in their families to attend college, most were working their way through school, and many living at home in their local community.

PACE members had somewhat similar backgrounds: most were children of men with earlier histories in the United States who, because of changes in immigration laws in 1946 and their U.S. military veteran status, were able to bring their wives from the Philippines and start families after World War II. In 1968, there was a near even distribution of PACE members born in the Philippines and those who were second generation. Many had fathers or other relatives who belonged to the manong generation—men who arrived between 1899 and 1935.

Like their Chinese American counterparts, PACE members too had an awareness of the earlier Filipino American bachelor society experience. Most were also working their way through college and from well-established Filipino American communities throughout Northern California, ranging from Salinas Valley in the south to Stockton and Central Valley in the east. Their activism was informed by the farm labor movement which was started by groups with Filipino leaders and majority members (the Agricultural Workers Organizing Committee), who were later joined by the better-known Mexican American union (the National Farm Workers Association), to form the United Farm Workers of America (UFW). Students were also intensely curious about the colonial history of the Philippines, and the impact of America's relatively recent colonial control on Philippine and Filipino American culture and society.

AAPA was mainly, though not entirely, a Japanese American organization. Unlike PACE and ICSA, most AAPA members were Sansei with family backgrounds of more varied socio-economic status, and almost all of their families had experiences with the World War II American concentration camps. They didn't have as many older members as PACE or ICSA, but like the others, AAPA members were largely from Northern California and had community concerns that reflected their backgrounds. Their somewhat more Americanized backgrounds, and more differentiated social origins, may partially explain why the Japanese American students—sometimes individually, sometimes collectively—took slightly different positions from the other Asian ethnic organizations. AAPA members seemed often more ideologically grounded and more likely to espouse a pan-ethnic Asian American perspective than the other groups.

COURTESY OF ASIAN AMERICAN STUDIES, SFSU

In 1969, SF State Asian American Political Alliance leader Penny Nakatsu and others not only played a critical role in the strike, but also helped build the Asian American Studies Department as a new pan-Asian political force connecting the campus with their communities.

The three organizations saw themselves as community focused, and not just simply traditional campus student groups. Prior to the 1968 Third World Liberation Front Strike, ICSA was primarily engaged in a variety of social service endeavors. These included academic tutoring programs, social and recreational work with youth groups, and issue-based community advocacy intended to draw attention to needs in public housing and the development of more social services in Chinatown. Consequently, many ICSA members were more involved with the community service element of the organization than with on-campus activities. AAPA members were developing community-based activities related to redevelopment and issues associated with wartime internment, and also involved in disseminating the very new concept of *Asian American*.

PACE was actively supporting the I-Hotel resistance to eviction that began in 1968, advocated for community opposition to the destructive effects of business-oriented development, and encouraged intergenerational political activism and organized youth groups. Some PACE members developed a critical perspective of the Philippine government, particularly the Marcos administration—well before the 1972 declaration of Martial Law—when the Marcos family enjoyed tremendous popularity in the Philippines and among Filipino communities the world over. When anti-Marcos critics, including some members of PACE, began to voice their criticisms publicly, they were labeled communist-inspired radicals by the conservative leadership elite of their own ethnic community.

Community activism had substantial formative influences on all three student organizations, which, despite the overlay of ideological rhetoric, were shaped by the pragmatic needs and immediate issues of their respective communities. ICSA, PACE, and AAPA members tended to identify as community people who were going to college, and not college students returning to the community. This shared self-concept would continue to affect the operating values and direction of their activism.

IDEOLOGY

he public language of those involved in the strike, including many from the Asian American student groups, was often phrased in the ideological style of the time, with references to Mao Zedong, Frantz Fanon, and Malcolm X. This language, together with the radical nature of some of their demands, masked the actual diversity of political perspectives within each of the three Asian American student groups. There existed a shared Third World perspective: an identification of racism as a major problem in American society and a strong emphasis on development of social consciousness, but the ideological modalities expressed by the student organizations differed.

The demand for an Asian American Studies program with Chinese, Filipino, and Japanese American components reflected an element of cultural nationalism that was largely driven by the desire for more knowledge about their own communities that had been previously denied to them. This produced a clear anti-assimilation perspective, which conflicted not only with the pressures to acculturate in the United States, but also with universalistic tendencies within Marxism that promise superficial recognition of cultural minorities while limiting their access to power. Asian American ideological perspectives were correspondingly complex.

Some members of the three groups saw themselves as revolutionaries, influenced by international Marxism or domestic militant socialist groups. Others were inspired by the Civil Rights Movement and related traditions, by political movements in Asia, by local activism around issues affecting their own communities, or by their family's values.

None of the three groups forced a strict orthodoxy on their members, but instead tolerated a range of eclectic personal political perspectives. The core standard for each was a commitment to community and to the particular goals of the organizations. At San Francisco State, whatever the rhetoric, the reality was that the dominant ideological perspective was idealistic, democratic pragmatism.

THE CAMPUS

San Francisco State College of the late 1960s was a place where traditional, academic practice was constantly questioned. In addition to the Civil Rights movement, the counterculture challenged both conventional standards of behavior and concepts of knowledge. By 1968, the anti-war movement was gaining strong momentum. The world-renowned Experimental College has been oft-cited as the most evident expression of this ferment. Proponents saw the Experimental College as an officially sanctioned venue for innovative teaching methods, and for the presentation of content that was not in the standard curriculum. While the College was primarily concerned with the alternative educational interests of the white cultural majority, it was also the setting where a few courses that clearly served as precursors to ethnic studies were first offered. Equally important, the Experimental College established precedents for university recognition of new areas of study, and the legitimacy of providing funding and academic credit for such offerings.

The campus was primarily a teaching institution: faculty tended to see teaching as their primary activity. Asian American and Third World activists saw several major deficiencies among these positives. Despite a few classes on aspects of Black and other ethnic experiences in the Experimental College, the openness of the campus to experimentation on subjects of interest to white students and faculty greatly contrasted with the general lack of attention to content related to American Indians, Asian Americans, Blacks, Latinos, or Mexican Americans.

Additionally, the Black student population, which approached 12 percent in the late

Muralist David Cho, with Albert Yip, worked with the pan-Asian student organizations at SF State to design the Asian & Pacific Islander Mural, dedicated April 30, 2004, at the Cesar Chavez Student Center.

The artists and community salute not only leaders but also Asian American resistance organizations and movements: Japanese American Redress and Reparations, the Third World Student Strike at SF State, Chinatown's Red Guard Party, and the Revolutionary Association of the Women of Afghanistan.

PHOTO BY NACIO JAN BROWN

The SF State student leaders quickly built support from diverse grassroots community, labor, and workers rights organizations. The Community Strike Support Coalition included the Pacific Heights ad hoc committee Supporting SF State Strike, SF State American Federation of Teachers (AFT) Local 1352, San Jose State College AFT Local 1362 and Japanese Americans Concerned Supporting Striking Students.

*Philippine American Collegiate
Endeavor (PACE) and TWLF
leader Robert "Bob" G. Ilumin
addresses the December 5,
1968, mass rally as Dr. Juan
Martinez stands by.*

1950s and early 1960s, had declined to under 4 percent by 1965. The number of U.S.-born or schooled Latino students was very small, and certain groups of Asian American students were also underrepresented. Third World student groups began to examine course titles, content, and the admissions process—interests that would lead to the first major confrontation with San Francisco State administration.

EOP AND THE PRELUDE TO THE STRIKE

Higher education in California was governed by a statewide Master Plan for Higher Education. This template defined a three-part structure for higher education: the University of California (UC) system, the California State College (CSU) system, and the community college system. The plan held very positive aspects, not the least of which was a substantial philosophical and financial commitment to the idea that higher education should be available to anyone who wanted it. Adversely, it created a hierarchical structure, with the UC system on top and community colleges at the bottom. We came to the conclusion that the plan fostered maintenance of a social class system in which many Black and other minority students were being shunted into community colleges and often dead-ending there.

Through our research, we discovered a category called Special Admissions. Special Admits were students who did not meet standard grade point average and Scholastic Aptitude Test (SAT) score requirements but were admitted on the basis of special qualifications—most frequently athletic abilities. It occurred to us that, if there could be special admissions for good athletes, why couldn't there be special admissions for students who come from underrepresented communities—especially when their lack of full academic qualifications was often the result of schools being poorly funded and operated?

Asian American student groups joined other Third World student organizations to form the Third World Liberation Front (TWLF). The TWLF pushed for expanded special admissions for minority students and the provision of associated support programs for such students to succeed academically. Buoyed by federal funding via the Economic Opportunity Act of 1964, similar programs were being proposed nationwide as Educational Opportunity Programs (EOP).

College administration dragged its feet on these requests and student groups organized a major sit-in of the campus president's office in late spring of 1968. This was the first-ever coordinated effort by the TWLF and provided a training ground for the later strike. The end result, after some confrontations with police, was the establishment of a campus EOP, including expansions in special admissions and a variety of special classes, tutoring, and support services for new EOP admits in the fall of 1968.

THE STRIKE

From our perspective, the strike, though an important element, was only one part of the origins of Asian American Studies (AAS). The glamour and excitement associated with periods of open conflict like the strike often obscure the reality that any new vision only becomes successful with subsequent implementation, and involves long and arduous effort. Dwelling too long on the strike might tend to obscure the importance of what followed. It is not the purpose of this essay to recapitulate the history of the strike but rather to clarify its character and describe its impact on the subsequent development of Asian American Studies at San Francisco State. To that end, we will address selected aspects of that crucial moment in the origin of AAS and other units in Ethnic Studies on the campus. It should be understood that

The Third World Strike created new relationships and alliances as it brought together Chinese American community leaders like Alan Wong and African Americans like Black Panther Party Minister of Information Eldridge Cleaver.

TWLF SF STATE COLLEGE STUDENT DEMANDS

1. That a School of Ethnic Studies for the ethnic groups involved in the Third World be set up with the students in each particular ethnic organizations having the authority and control of the hiring and retention of any faculty member, director, and administrator, as well as the curriculum in a specific area of study.

2. That 50 faculty positions be appropriated to the School of Ethnic Studies, 20 would be for the Black Studies Program.

3. That in the Spring semester, the College fulfill its commitment to the non-white students by admitting those that apply.

4. That in the Fall of 1969, all applications of non-white students be accepted.

5. That George Murray and any other faculty person chosen by non-white people as their teacher be retained in their position.

(George Murray was an English Department lecturer who was dismissed for his participation in the Black Panther Party. SF State Strike Committee: On Strike: Shut It Down. 1968. p.3.)

the strike was a chaotic affair, and the logic and order of its history is most often a much later reconstruction.

As the fall term opened in 1968, the skeleton of an agenda shared among the student organizations in the TWLF directly addressed the deficiencies of San Francisco State. The immediate triggers of the strike were disputes over treatment of Black lecturers, including English instructor George Mason Murray, working in support programs for EOP students. The Black Student Union (BSU) and TWLF quickly articulated a wider range of issues that reflected the collective anger caused by the inability of the institution to deal with the needs of minority students and communities. These concerns were presented as a series of demands, ten from the BSU and five from the TWLF.

The most important of these demands was the creation of a School of Ethnic Studies for all of the ethnic groups involved in the Third World Liberation Front, and that it be set up with the students in each particular ethnic organization having the authority and control of the hiring and retention of any faculty member, director, or administrator, as well as the curriculum in a specific area of study. At that time, a "school" was a separate academic administrative unit within the larger San Francisco State College. What was being sought was the establishment of an academic unit with a substantial degree of autonomy over its internal processes. This demand for a free-standing school flowed from the TWLF's core principle of self-determination. More importantly, the demand demonstrated that TWLF member groups understood the need for as much independence as they could acquire within the larger college structure. Ultimately, a partial agreement to this demand by the administration made the development of Ethnic Studies programs, especially Asian American Studies, unique in comparison to related efforts at other colleges and universities.

Third World Liberation Front activists and supporters created art and images that countered the dehumanizing depictions of their communities in the mass media and U.S. culture.

The strike was not simply a confrontation between students and authority—whether the authority was in the form of campus administration or the police. On one hand, the administration repeatedly called in large numbers of police to maintain order, but on the other hand, prior to the imposition of Samuel Ichiye Hayakawa as college president, the administration also bowed to faculty pressures from the American Federation of Teachers (AFT), and allowed campus-wide debate on the issues. The debates included several massive convocations where the TWLF and other groups were able to present and explain their demands to overflowing audiences at San Francisco State's largest venues.

Students in the TWLF learned to detail their demands to a wide range of groups and coordinated those presentations with each other. The larger student body and faculty were thus afforded the opportunity to gain a better understanding of the issues and the players. These extended and repeated discussions drew many students, as well as a number of progressive faculty, into active participation with the strike. Some faculty participants, like James "Jim" Hirabayashi (later Dean of Ethnic Studies), believed that the participation of the teacher's union had a significant impact on the behavior of the administration, both during and after the strike, with positive results for the development of ethnic studies.

Although appropriately called the Third World Student Strike, not all Third World students supported it. For a variety of reasons, many continued to go to class and, conversely, the greater number of students who did strike and walk the picket lines were white, as were the great majority of faculty who supported the strike demands.

NISEI AND SANSEI STUDENTS!

ARE YOU COMPLETELY UNINVOLVED, DISINTERESTED?

Are you concerned about the strike, the closing and opening of the campus, or are you just sitting back and waiting it out???

Do you believe the strike demands will be met???

Do you CARE???

Do you understand the 15 BSU - TWLF demands?

Do you have some specific questions regarding the strike and the demands?

Do you see yourself as benefiting from a school of Ethnic Area studies, specifically in terms of Japanese-American courses?

Would you like to hear and perhaps participate in a discussion of the issues and problems of the Campus crises (including the subject of Hayakawa) by Japanese-American faculty and students at San Francisco State College and active members of the Japanese American Community.

Most likely the strike demands will not be met right away, so the strike activities will be a prolonged one. It is urgent that we as Japanese-American students begin to discuss and clarify NOW the very vital questions that are being posed by the campus conflict.

FRIDAY NIGHT, DECEMBER 6, 1968 --   7:30 p.m.
UNITED CHRIST PRESBYTERIAN CHURCH at POST AND
OCTAVIA STREETS, SAN FRANCISCO.

IT IS URGENT THAT ALL JAPANESE-AMERICAN STUDENTS
OF SAN FRANCISCO STATE COLLEGE ATTEND THIS DIS-
CUSSION!!!!   (BRING YOUR PARENTS)

The SF State Asian American Political Alliance organized a large open community meeting on a Friday evening, December 6, 1969, a month after the start of the strike, to educate the Japantown community and broaden their base of support.

Many Bay Area communities were also very much involved. At the start of the strike, the TWLF immediately moved to seek outside support. ISCA, PACE, and AAPA held forums intended to cull support from individuals and organizations in their respective ethnic communities. Some of these meetings, especially those held in Chinatown, drew large crowds and significant press coverage. Community leaders and student strikers themselves, presented the strike to the public as being far more than a student-versus-college administration affair. Growing numbers of leading community figures began to show up on the campus picket lines. Several unions also publicly supported the strike and sent members to join the picket lines. The intent, which was successful, was to define the issues to the public in larger political terms, and to prevent the students from being isolated and vulnerable to police attacks.

The college administration and the TWLF both had many internal disagreements. Neither had full control of their supporters' actions. As the strike continued, it attracted people with agendas, ranging from political to personal, who wanted to be seen and heard. Some were confrontation groupies with little real interest in the goals of the TWLF. The resulting chaos was further aggravated by an intense and often aggressive, militaristic police presence, given encouragement from politicians, particularly San Francisco Mayor Joseph Alioto and California Governor Ronald Reagan.

For students and faculty, the tactical reality of the strike required the display of a unified front. The TWLF's internal unity, tactical discipline, and cooperation with elements of the Students for a Democratic Society (SDS) were, however, real. The TWLF experience was positive in many respects, providing important practical lessons and an exciting sense of collective effort and success that many participants remember with considerable fondness, and which have continued to shape their political perspectives to the present. The camaraderie and productive interactions with people from different student groups enriched inter-group understanding and provided very valuable lessons in the building of a political movement. Collaboration among the students and community activist groups, however conflicted and imperfect, demonstrated a potential for future collective actions.

Conversely, it sometimes seemed that the operative word in Third World Liberation Front was "front"—behind which discord, mutual misperceptions, and other problems festered. As one participant, Penny Nakatsu, put it shortly after the strike, "underlying all this effort was a faith that by 'acting as if it were so' the myth (of unity) would at some imperceptible point cease to exist and merge into the realm of reality." Underlying this facade was a pattern of recurring contradictions and disunity among the groups which this participant attributed to incomplete political consciousness and an overemphasis on self-determination. Each group had its own agenda and frequently had only limited understanding of the positions of the other groups. For example, the BSU tended to see themselves as the vanguard, and consequently, did not always coordinate their activities with the rest of the TWLF, even negotiating separately for Black Studies resources during the settlement of the strike.

There were also obvious and serious gender issues. The leadership of TWLF and the public leadership of the various student organizations were overwhelmingly male, with some of the men not treating the women with respect. This led to conflict and frustrations for the women activists during the strike over the general failure to address their concerns and to recognize their full contributions.

The gains of the strike also came with substantial costs. Many strikers and some community supporters were arrested, spending varying amounts of time in jail and in court. Others were beaten by the police. One unfortunate member of ICSA was overlooked in the chaos following a day of mass arrests, and languishing in jail for weeks as his relatives refused to bail him out while the student organizations assumed he had been bailed out by relatives.

After the strike ended March 21, 1969, Asian American students, staff, and faculty began writing curriculum, recruiting new faculty, and institutionalizing the new Asian American Studies Department (AAS) and School (now College) of Ethnic Studies. Pioneering AAS faculty depicted in the photo included social scientists, playwrights, poets and writers, psychologists, historians, educators, sociologists, social workers, and community activists.

This is just one example of the tensions with family that some members of ICSA, PACE, and AAPA experienced as they were ostracized for their activism. While the student organizations received some community support, they were also subject to extreme criticism from many other segments of their communities who encouraged the authorities in their attempts to suppress the strike by whatever means necessary. Many students, both strikers and non-strikers, lost academic progress, delaying their graduation. Male strikers ran significant risk of losing their student deferments and being drafted; some were able to regain their deferments while others had difficulty doing so.

The larger campus itself also paid a price. The Experimental College did not survive—as some striking faculty suspected that it was a specific target for defunding by the Hayakawa administration. A procedure for offering experimental courses was institutionalized, but the spirit of experimentation and alternative approaches to learning was stifled. Many strikers have commented that much of the larger, dynamic, and positive energy on campus faded after the strike. The reasons were varied, but an important factor was that the strike created schisms in many of the traditional departments between those faculty who supported the strike and those who opposed it.

TWLF Chairperson Al Wong speaks (2nd from left) with other Asian American strike leaders (from left) Mason Wong, AAS moderator Ben Kobashigawa, Betty Inouye (Matsuoka) (seated behind), Penny Nakatsu, and Rich Wada at the 40th anniversary of the strike October 29, 2008. Al Wong and Mason Wong helped build Intercollegiate Chinese for Social Action (ICSA) while Al Wong continued teaching in Asian American Studies and served as Associate Director of the Upward Bound program.

RELEVANCE AND LEGACY OF THE STRIKE TODAY

The goals during the strike were both simple and ambitious. On a broad scale we wanted the college to become a place in which Asian American history, culture, and communities would be accepted as legitimate areas of study at the university level. We saw this as an issue of equity. This was a dream, a push for inclusion and redefining what is American. We wanted Asian Americans to be seen as Americans, not at the price of assimilation, but through a change in the conception of America that was broader and more varied in its character. If college is intended to provide students with an understanding of their society and culture, then it should include ours. The pragmatic aspect of our dream was that we believed if Asian American students could be provided with a solid understanding of Asian American realities, past and present, that they/we would emerge both better individuals and better prepared to help provide for the needs of our communities.

We were seeking a change in the focus of the college, and of academia in general. We wanted a connection between the college and communities, believing and hoping that such connections would lead to long-term benefits for the communities and, secondarily, the college. We wanted the college to serve their communities, not to remove or rescue students from their communities.

And so, how relevant are these concerns today? In some arenas, little has changed in the intervening years. The overall content of American schooling remains as resolutely ignorant as ever. It has regressed and tragically continues in that direction.

Neither has there been an improvement on a college level beyond the confines of Asian American studies programs. While Asian American populations have exploded and spread across the country, the pressures for assimilation are as high as ever, and the notion of who and what is genuinely American has only slightly expanded. An appropriate understanding and inclusion of Asian American issues and experiences within the curriculum of many traditional departments has remained fragmentary or shallow since 1968. Given this reality, and the fact that most students still arrive at college with little or no knowledge of Asian American history, strong, community-conscious Asian American studies programs at the college level are even more important than they were forty years ago.

On a larger stage, the goal of a more inclusive concept of American is as important today as it was then. The hostility and exclusion experienced by Chinese, Filipino, and Japanese Americans in the past is now, in a period of increased phobia and security concerns, visited on all new immigrants and many ethnic groups. While the residential, employment, and social opportunities for many Asian Americans have substantially improved since the establishment of Asian American Studies in 1969, the price of acceptance continues to be a significant degree of assimilation and a casting away of important aspects of ethnic, familial, community, and individual culture and identity.

The strike was settled on March 20, 1969, with many but not all of the TWLF's demands met. The most important success however was the creation of an independent School of Ethnic Studies that housed four separate programs: American Indian Studies, Asian American Studies, Black Studies, and La Raza Studies. As a consequence of this victory, AAS was able to establish and manage itself with more autonomy concerning curriculum and faculty hiring than most other Asian American studies programs nationwide.

Another legacy of the strike stems from the fact that three separate student groups, each primarily associated with a particular Asian ethnic community, represented Asian American interests during the strike. The AAS curriculum at San Francisco State developed strong ethnic-specific content and perspective. The internal governance structure for AAS that evolved after the strike reflected these distinct, ethnic-specific interests.

Beyond the immediate creation of the Asian American Studies program, the most important product of the strike for Asian American communities was a generation of students who participated in it and the subsequent creation of the AAS department. Their experience provided them with organizing skills, a shared commitment to community, increased political sophistication, and self-confidence. These young Asian Americans had learned that sustained, organized action could produce substantive results, and that coalition efforts—while difficult to build and maintain—can be effective and important in establishing a coherent intellectual foundation for action. Many of these students went on to become important leaders and political players in their own communities, in large part, because they were willing to challenge authority and had the discipline to move new ideas from concept to reality.

NOTE: *In addition to direct personal knowledge, this essay draws on minutes of the General Planning Group and individual planning groups, position papers, and a variety of other departmental documents. We are also indebted to communications with Jim Hirabayashi, George K. Woo, Penny Nakatsu, Jeffery Paul Chan, Bette (Inouye) Matsuoka, Laureen Chew, and Richard Wada. The views presented here, however, are those of the authors and we are solely responsible for any errors and oversights.*

PHOTO BY ERIC MAR

Hundreds of students and community supporters rallied on May 9, 2016 at San Francisco State University in support of student hunger strikers demanding adequate funding for the College of Ethnic Studies, a stop to the gentrification of the university, and the decline of the African American student population on the campus.

THE STRIKE IS NOT OVER

IRENE DEA COLLIER

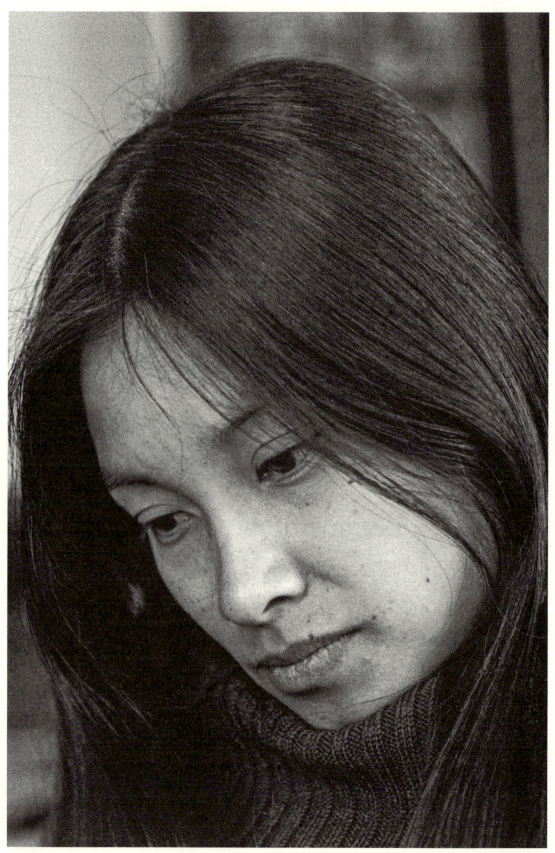

COURTESY OF MALCOLM COLLIER, 1974

FAMILY UPBRINGING IN HOIPING, CHINA

I was born in 1948, in Hoiping in Guangdong Province, China. At that time, the government was being taken over by the Communists. My father had already been to the United States as a boy when he was 12, but later returned to the village as an adult. My grandfather had been to the United States and worked as a cook for one of the businessmen in San Francisco's Chinatown, and also returned to China, because he was quite ill with diabetes.

My father had just returned a year before I was born, and I had an older brother that was born ten years before me, before my father left to America.

Growing up in Hoiping, I was one of the darlings of the village. Everyone thought I was "real spunky." They had stories of me singing at the top of my lungs from the rooftops. When I was about two years old, my mother and father thought this wasn't a good place for us. My father had returned to the United States by then, and my mother was raising me and my younger and older brothers by herself. Worried about China's new government, my father sent her passage for "paper" children—papers for two kids. The trouble was they had three.

My mother was going to leave me behind, but she told me later that because of my spunkiness, everyone wanted me to stay. When they were just about to leave, she looked at my little face and said, "I can't do it. They're too little! I'm going to stay in the village." So my father lost the money he had paid for the passage.

But by the time we were five, we had to leave. Mother could still only get passage for two children. We all left China and got to Hong Kong, hoping to find her brother living there. But there was some miscommunication and he didn't come to get us. So there she was—stuck with three children with no place to go. But a very kind old woman said to us, "You can sleep in my bed and I'll find your older brother."

My mother had his address, and eventually, my uncle came and brought us to his house. My mother still had to decide which one of us to leave behind. Because my brother was 15, she left him behind, hoping to bring him later. She took us, the two younger ones, to America. She left my older brother with my uncle. Everyone said, "We'll get him later, somehow."

COURTESY OF MALCOLM COLLIER

Dea Collier at age two with her mother and baby brother in Toisan, China. The photo was taken by an itinerant Chinese village photographer circa 1950.

I've always felt so grateful to my mother, because usually you bring the boys and you leave the girls behind. My fate could've been very, very different. I feel very fortunate even though we had to leave my brother behind and it was another ten years before we would see him again.

We came to America in 1953 and lived in a small SRO (Single Room Occupancy) housing unit on Grant Avenue for about a year. We had no toilet of our own. We had to share it with five other families. We also had no kitchen. When I was five and my brother was four, my mother had to go to work as a seamstress and left us home alone.

The good thing about those days was the Chung Mun family association provided help and bought clothes for us. My father was the darling of the family association because he was very handsome and articulate. He worked at a hardware store and at different enterprises that members of the family association had.

My father was quite active in the family association and well-known in the community. Years later, in the '80s, people wanted to build a school near our village in China, and my father raised $180,000 from all the people in his family association. They built a middle and high school with a dormitory and a chemistry lab that my father was very proud of.

CHINATOWN: THE SPUNKY CHATTERBOX BECOMES SILENT

When I first came to this country, it was a shock to me, because I was placed into American school right away. We mostly spoke Hoiping at home. They gave me a new name: Irene. Everyone spoke a totally different language. I did not understand one single word. Suddenly, the whole world changed. Also, in Chinese school, they didn't speak Hoiping. They spoke Cantonese. My brother and I didn't know what the heck was going on both in American and Chinese school! Nobody was speaking what we spoke. Nobody understood us. That was a great shock to us.

In China and at home, I was a very spunky chatterbox, but once I got to America, I stopped talking. I refused to talk in class and I became very quiet at home. I didn't really talk again until after college. When I was called upon to speak in public, I couldn't do it. So you can see a very big shift in personality because of the language policies. It was always "sink or swim" in the American school.

I grew up in Chinatown and lived there all my life until I got married in 1972. I always lived on Stockton Street opposite the Ping Yuen housing projects. It was a segregated neighborhood, but in some ways, I really think it was good for us, because we grew up with neighborhood friends. These were friends and people that I knew for the rest of my life. We went to school together. Everyone was poor, but we never felt poor because everyone was in the same boat as you.

I went to Old Saint Mary's Chinese Mission, a K-8 Catholic school. It was a mission school at that time, because they wanted to save us "pagans." They didn't charge any tuition. The curriculum was Catholic, so we learned about saints and different stories from the Catholic faith. There were no stories about Chinese people. We had one Chinese nun who was a third grade teacher there. Everything was in English and everything was a Western-style program.

ASIAN COMMUNITY CENTER ARCHIVES

The 1968-69 SF State strike not only brought young people together in political struggle demanding "Power to the People"; it also created close human and social connections among activists like the Colliers.

In fourth grade, the school inserted a half-hour of Chinese into the curriculum. It was just tacked on. We were angels in American school, but the worst kids in Chinese school! We were disruptive and didn't pay attention to the teacher. That kind of helped me later, when I became a teacher, to understand how language curriculum needs to be really infused. It can't just be tacked on, as much as the parents wanted it, and the teachers saw a need for it. It just doesn't work like that.

American school was taught by nuns. One nun really tried to teach us about the Chinese and the railroads. But again, because it was tacked on, it didn't do anything for us. We never understood. "Yeah, we built the railroads. So what?" This really helped me to understand how curriculum was much more complex than just introducing the subject.

I was always a good student. Once I got into Francisco Middle School for ninth grade, it was totally different—mostly Chinese students! But then we came face-to-face with more middle-class Chinese people. The teachers at Francisco were pretty good. But when I got to high school, that was when things changed. I went to Galileo High School. At that point, we had teachers who were mostly men. They would yell at us because we would not speak up in class.

We also had some very good literature teachers who taught us about the backgrounds of the authors, what the authors were trying to do, and the social situation of the society in which he or she lived. Those classes really helped me and developed a love of literature in me. We learned so much. But looking back, couldn't we have had one book that took place in China or in Chinatown? We had none, nothing about people of color.

By the late 1960s the whole school exploded with many immigrant Chinese students. We were the first class that elected Chinese American student body officers and a homecoming queen! We were resented by the non-Asians because Galileo was seen as the Italian school, where several generations of Italian kids' fathers and mothers had gone.

SAN FRANCISCO STATE: FINDING LOVE OF KNOWLEDGE, THE COMMUNITY, AND MALCOLM

knew that my parents couldn't afford the tuition and the books, so I always had to work throughout high school. Tuition was about $50, and books were $5 each. Still, it was a lot for us, because I was only paid 75 cents an hour to work in the Chinatown curio shops. I saved up my money and paid for my own tuition because I didn't want to ask my parents to work any harder than they already were for money.

When deciding where to go for college, I thought about applying to UC Berkeley. It was very prestigious, but I still had to work, and taking public transit there was too difficult. When I came to San Francisco State College (now San Francisco State University), the first thing that I noticed was the green lawn! There were plants and flowers here, and a huge library full of books, full of knowledge. I wanted to go in there and learn everything I could learn!

My first class was Psychology. There were mostly women, but only a few Chinese kids in my class, maybe about six of us. It was an encounter group, which is what they had in those days. We had to turn to the person next to us, introduce ourselves, and to talk to them. Well, the person I sat next to was Malcolm, who later became my husband! Who would've thought that the first person you meet in your first college class is someone that you're destined to be with for the rest of your life? Fate, I suppose.

Malcolm was very nice, but I thought, "God, what an odd character he is!" I knew some white people, but had never been friends with any all through my life. I only had Chinese friends. And then suddenly this guy comes up to me, dressed oddly—wool shirt—unlike anybody else. I think he thought I was odd too, because I was dressed like a Chinatown kid. Two oddballs sitting next to each other. He was very easy to talk to—much easier than some of my

Chinese friends. And right away, because he had grown up in New Mexico speaking Spanish, he asked me, "What language do you speak at home?" He understood right away the challenges of growing up as a Chinese American!

I really loved literature because I had some very good high school teachers. But my college literature teacher was like some of my worst high school teachers. She would say, "You people all need to talk. You're bumps on a log if you don't talk, so talk." Instead of seeing a piece of literature as an expression of people's feelings and thoughts, she forced us to analyze literature, taking everything apart like a chemistry lab experiment.

I took an intro anthropology class, and who would be sitting next to me again? It was that odd guy! He plopped himself next to me and started appearing in a lot of my classes years later. Was it by accident or by design? I guess it was by design and I didn't know.

I became an anthropology major because it was one of the few classes that taught about non-white people. In my geography class, we had a very good teacher who used a relevant study of Africa. We were just yearning to learn about people from other cultures and other parts of the world. That was the only class that did it for me. History was mostly a European perspective. In my "History of Immigration" class, the professor went on and on about Europeans. When my classmate asked, "What about the Chinese?" The professor said, "The Chinese are only three percent of the national population, so they represent a very insignificant group." His teaching and most of the curriculum at SF State was just a continuation of the high school teachers that made us feel insignificant.

WORK AND ACTIVISM

In Chinatown, not only did I have to work to make money so I could go to college, but I also volunteered at the Chinatown YWCA. I tutored immigrant kids who needed help, almost every night, partly just to get out of the house to have a little bit of freedom. During the summers, I worked as a day camp counselor helping immigrant kids integrate with predominantly African American kids from the Western Addition.

I had always worked in the community as a volunteer. At that time, President Kennedy inspired many of us to go into public service with his signature phrase, "Ask not what your country can do for you. Ask what you can do for your country." That shows how important leaders are in setting the tone. We had a growing number of community social workers, like Alan Wong, advocating for more services for the Chinatown community.

The first year and a half at SF State, I participated in a social Chinese American student club. But I was never comfortable because I felt that there had to be more to life than just going to dances and parties.

When the Third World Liberation Front strike came along at San Francisco State in November 1968, it just spoke to me. Everything that I had wondered and cared about, everything that I was working on in the community—it all came together in the strike.

Immigration laws had changed and suddenly, we had this whole group of new people who needed services. With all the experiences of my life, of having teachers yell at us, and the way we were taught English. . .when the Black students said, "We need classes that reflected our own communities," it really spoke to me, because you could just see in our Chinatown community—we needed services.

Some of the UC Berkeley and SF State students were in the Red Guard, a radical youth organization. They really looked up to the Chinese government. It was political—Marxism. But I grew up in a communist government and saw what it was like. So, my motivation was never that. I knew what Marxism and communism were on a very practical level. My main concern

PHOTO BY NACIO JAN BROWN. 1968

George Woo speaks at a SF State strike rally. Woo was a leader of the Intercollegiate Chinese for Social Action, a member organization of the Third World Liberation Front. He also served as the spokesperson for the Wah Ching, a Chinese American youth gang that advocated for better living conditions in San Francisco, particularly Chinatown. He became Chair of Asian American Studies and is now a Professor Emeritus.

was the community and the lack of services given to it.

Chinatown at the time had a budding group of young social workers—Alan Wong in particular, Buddy Choy, and Larry Jack Wong. All those people supported the strike. When they needed money for social work and organizations in the community, the students supported them, and they came out to support us. There are famous pictures of Alan walking the picket line. I have to hand it to the community people. When we were not eligible for federal funding because Chinatown was not considered a poverty area, Alan fought tooth and nail to have it included in Lyndon B. Johnson's War on Poverty. He took people to the SROs and public housing, and tours through Chinatown. But because he did those things and it appeared in the paper, his life was threatened. This was no laughing matter because people were putting their lives on the line!

We had a lot of student gangs—high school and young people; they weren't in college. They had some legitimate gripes. They were concerned about the community and angry that Chinese people were getting no services. But they were also involved in some illegal activities, too. George Woo was asked to be their spokesperson because they didn't feel that their English was good enough. George was not a member of the gang but was always labeled as one. He was very bilingual and could present their viewpoints in English and Chinese. That was very courageous of him to do that, so I'm sure he took some heat for many, many years after that.

As George always said, "The line between legitimate and illegitimate business is very thin." A lot of the legitimate businesses were also operating illegitimate businesses and the gangs would sometimes be the lookouts. There was money passing back and forth all the time.

During the strike, I participated by not going to class, and went to the demonstrations instead. I was never really active in the ICSA (Intercollegiate Chinese for Social Action), or Third World Liberation Front (TWLF), because by then, Malcolm and I had become involved and it was difficult for me. At that time, ethnic consciousness and concerns about your own community were so strong. In some ways, it was very ethnocentric. Our relationship was not seen as totally on the up-and-up. It was also hard because both of us participated in the strike and were committed to the principles of it. I did support ICSA though by tutoring for their program while I remained active in the community.

GENDER ROLES AND FAMILY EXPECTATIONS

Gender roles during the strike were very sharply defined. ICSA leader Mason Wong was very charismatic, and a leader, because he could get along with people. Among the women like Laureen Chew and Dorothy Yee, Laureen was very flamboyant. But at that time, she didn't perceive herself as a leader. Yet she became a leader as a result of the strike. It helped develop her. It changed us. The women's movement was just kind of starting, but we saw it nationally as a white women's movement. It really didn't seem to touch us. At home, we knew who made the decisions—our mothers did. But publicly, it was always the men. In our organizations, the men did the public work. But the women—Laureen and Dorothy— were pretty strong too. Laureen participated in disrupting classes, which I never had the nerve to do. That's the way it was.

The Black Student Union (BSU) was the first group that disrupted classes and made demands of the university. It was very powerful to see a group of people demanding classes about themselves. This expanded into the Third World Liberation Front, which was not an organization but coalition of many different ethnic groups. The BSU had a list of ten demands which were on the news all the time. The TWLF grew out of that and the spokesman was Ron Quidachay, who later became a judge in San Francisco.

Mason and a couple of the men did a lot of negotiating and working with the other TWLF groups. I guess the TWLF was kind of sexist because the women handled the community end, while the men handled the campus groups. But we didn't see it as sexism in those days. Our moms were very strong women—my mother, Laureen's mother, Dorothy's mother. They ran the family. It was always like that. The dads would ask, and the moms would respond with their opinions. And mom's opinion ultimately was the family decision.

It kind of was like that in ICSA too. The men wouldn't always ask, but whenever they did, they respected our opinions. On the surface, it looked very sexist, because the men were out in front. We, the women, were out in front in the community. So I think sexism isn't really the right construct for us. Even sexism within the Chinese family—people always see it as Black and white, but it's always the yin and yang, where the struggles are always shifting all the time. Sometimes you're on top. Sometimes you're on the bottom. Each yin has a yang, and each yang has a yin. Both of them form a complete body. That's what it was. It wasn't two opposing segments just butting heads all the time. It was more fluid.

My parents and my family didn't really know about my involvement in the strike. They knew I was tutoring and going out every day, but they didn't know I wasn't going to class, that I was walking the picket line. My dad could speak some English, but my mom spoke none. She never learned. When they found out about my involvement after the Strike had ended, they hit the roof! They were mad! I received several F's that year because I did not go to class. They said, "Don't do that again!" Laureen's mom knew. Laureen was very open with her mother, who was very upset when Laureen got arrested. And Dorothy's mother knew. But I think Dorothy's mother was a little bit more knowledgeable about the ways of this country. My mother was a village girl—no clue.

ESTABLISHING ASIAN AMERICAN STUDIES

The Strike was very suddenly settled after the professors got involved. It would've been over much more quickly and we would've gotten a lot less, or maybe nothing, if the professors hadn't stepped in and said, "We're going to go on strike too—because we want a raise!" It was them taking advantage of the situation.

People usually don't understand how those first Asian American Studies (AAS) classes were formed. They were brilliant, and ICSA leader and later, AAS faculty member, George Woo, must have had a hand in it. There were history, community, identity, and literature classes. There were also Cantonese classes, which ate up a lot of time. All of us wanted these classes to prepare us to go back into the community as teachers, social workers and community leaders. That was the original intent of AAS.

Asian American Studies also offered an unusual class on Chinese art. It was not Chinese art just for art's sake. It was Chinese art to get at the underlying assumptions and influences in the way that we were thinking, and the way that we approached problem solving. The first group of teachers included Him Mark Lai, Phil Choy, Jeff Chan, and Bill Woo. The whole thrust of AAS at that time was to develop people who would go back to the community to address the issues of poverty, which was different from the other schools with ethnic studies. Berkeley was much more focused on a global phenomenon and more Marxist in nature. Ours was never that. It was to give us enough knowledge so we could function as good leaders in the community.

But many of us were already in the community. I took a class from Phil Choy who suddenly started talking about things that my parents were always kind of talking about. My dad had come as a young kid through Angel Island. He was imprisoned there. He always talked about the "Wooden House." I had no idea what it was until Phil Choy brought it out into the open.

SCHOOL OF THIRD WORLD STUDIES

Structure, organization and personnel for planning the School of Third World Studies.

The planning committee for the school is orientated toward developing the school from a Third World perspective; meaning organizationally the division of the planning committee into three major areas. The areas are as follows: Black Area Studies, Native American Area Studies, and Asian American Area Studies. The division of specific area studies within the major areas occurs on the basis of ethnic origin. In other words, within the general area of a total Third World race; African, Native or Asian, the area study of Filipino peoples is to develop within the division of Asian area studies.

Each of the Organizations in TWLF will have a planning committee involved in developing the specifics for their area study. The organization of each planning committee is as follows:

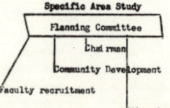

Specific Area Study

Planning Committee

Chairman

Community Development

Faculty recruitment

Librarian

THE ETHNIC STUDIES PROGRAM PLANNING COMMITTEE
JOB DESCRIPTIONS

I. Committee Chairman

  A. Curriculum Development: The assistant in charge of curriculum development is responsible for action leading to the creation and development of courses most pertinent to the goals of the department. Basically, this assistant must function in the processes of:

    1. Course foundation: the description, evaluation and explanation of chosen curriculum

    2. The transition: the establishment of a method of inter-relationship curriculum and the reservation of allowances for experimentation

    3. Growth: the process of academic objectives as defined by departmental goals.

II. Assistant for research development and librarian

The responsibilities of the assistant for research development include:

    1. The intense survey for and conscientious accumulation of data that relate to the general functions of the department.

      a. literature (e.g. texts, books, periodicals, etc.)

      b. all other possible sources of material for further development of department in cooperation with other assistants within the department.

    2. The refinement of such general data into particular information concerning specific areas of study. (i.e. behavioral sciences into sociology, psychology, history)

    3. The evaluation of materials by:

      a. the determination of the validity of obtained research infor-

In the aftermath of the strike on March 21, 1969, SF State students and faculty began the process of planning and designing Asian American Studies courses, recruiting faculty and staff, and ensuring a democratic structure of decision-making.

You couldn't come into the U.S. unless you were interrogated, and could also be sent back to China. He talked about all these restrictive covenants, taxes, and discriminatory laws that were passed.

One of the first Asian American Studies classes was taught by the first Dean of the School of Ethnic Studies, Jim Hirabayashi. All the students from the activist groups were in that class. Malcolm signed up it, and of course, that created a lot of controversy. A lot of people did not want him there. A lot of people were thinking, "This is an ethnic movement. Why are we having a white person here?" Jim knew Malcolm and his family, because he was an anthropologist and had worked with Malcolm's father, who also was an anthropologist. George Woo, PACE leader and AAS professor Dan Gonzales, and Jim Hirabayashi all accepted and advocated for Malcolm, who eventually became a very important and respected member of what became the AAS Planning Group. This group created the early AAS curriculum and courses like the "Nine Unit Block" that allowed students to receive academic credit for applying classroom knowledge to active involvement in community organizations and struggles.

NINE UNIT BLOCK AND BUILDING COMMUNITY ORGANIZATIONS

I was the secretary of the Nine Unit Block. George Woo was the director, but we had to have a tenured faculty member from another department be the official one. The Nine Unit Block was an attempt in those days to fast-track people through the college, and to have people from other departments co-teach classes with Asian American Studies. Students would get nine units of credit and meet once or twice a week. We had people from Social Work, Geography, and Psychology each teaching. The students were expected to work in their respective communities for over twenty hours a week. There was a Chinese section, a Filipino section, and a Japanese American section, each directly involved with creating leaders for our communities. It was one of the most successful programs and fulfilled the dream of Ethnic Studies—developing leaders. Out of that, we had: Gordon Chin, who later built the Chinatown Community Development Center and contributed greatly to San Francisco's affordable housing issues citywide; Jeff Mori in the Japanese American community; Ed de la Cruz, founder of West Bay Pilipino Community Multi-Service Center; and Fred Lau, who later became San Francisco's police chief.

Everybody worked in the community to develop nascent community organizations.

I can't even mention how many community leaders came out of the Nine Unit Block.

Even though it only lasted for two years, it was just enough time to get those people their bachelor's degrees. After that, they went directly into the community—most of them. And we're very proud of that.

THE ASSOCIATION OF CHINESE TEACHERS

The Association of Chinese Teachers (TACT) was founded in 1969 by people like Ruby Hong and other educators. The mainstream educational approach to teaching children was to use "sink or swim" English teaching methods. You just plop them into the classroom and they had to learn how to survive. I knew as an immigrant that that was the worst way to teach a child. You received punishment for speaking Chinese and weren't encouraged to use your language in any way. Schools were beginning to start supporting English as a Second Language (ESL) and later on, they thought, bilingual education was even better. But there was great resistance to ESL techniques—to pull out a child or to integrate exercises for immigrant kids.

TACT was founded on the premise that the Chinese were not being included in the educational policy process. It became an advocacy organization for some of our young teachers. The way I got involved was the same way everyone gets involved: somebody asked me, "Do you have a few minutes to spare? Come to a meeting!" And that's what I did. I went to meetings and they said, "We need a treasurer. Just keep track of the money coming in." I agreed. Later on, they asked me to become secretary, and then president. At that time, I had two kids and said, "I will only become president if you take my children for one day, so I can spend some time with my husband!"

THE BILINGUAL SCHOOL MOVEMENT

was second director of the bilingual Wah Mei School. A lot of our community leaders felt that the school district wasn't going to meet the needs of our students, so we started our own school in 1974. We became a preschool because of the growing need for childcare. Women were joining the workforce and needed more care for their children. Wah Mei was only a half-day program. Parent leaders wanted to start it for their own children who weren't being exposed to anything ethnic. Built into the description of the directorship was a requirement to be an advocate. So I did a lot of advocacy for bilingual education and children's rights.

We had a state-funded preschool program because income levels were very low. Wah Mei could have made a lot more money and bought its own site if we got rid of that program. The director had to spend ninety percent of their time dealing with reporting requirements, site requirements, and food requirements. People thought, "Why don't we just get rid of that program and just have private kids? We could make a lot more money." But I fought very hard against that idea. We needed to be a mixed-income school, so I expanded the program. I got a full-time daycare and childcare program. I wrote a proposal and we received an additional $80,000 per year and started the full-day program. Again, it was low-income. We added the private kids later and they just integrated with the low-income kids. For a mix of children's language learning abilities, mixed-income was better.

As TACT president and director of Wah Mei, I was involved in creating and advocating for the first Chinese Immersion Program, a bilingual school. I sat on the original committee and we did a lot of work lobbying the school board, getting parents to speak at school board meetings, and drawing up the plans. I also sat on the hiring committee of that program. We got it through the school board. But once we got the program approved in principle, we had to worry about the philosophy of it. I was only there for the groundwork during the very early days. The first set of teachers always dropped in at Wah Mei whenever they needed some encouragement.

UNITED EDUCATORS OF SAN FRANCISCO

Dea Collier was active not only in Chinese and Asian American community groups but also her union, United Educators of San Francisco.

When I became TACT president, we fought with some school board members who wanted to disband the San Francisco [Unified] School District's bilingual program. Former Chinese

Above, *Irene Dea Collier speaking on Asian images in children's books in 2016.*

Below: *As the director of Wah Mei School and leader in the Association of Chinese Teachers (TACT), Irene Dea Collier led community campaigns for bilingual education and educational rights.*

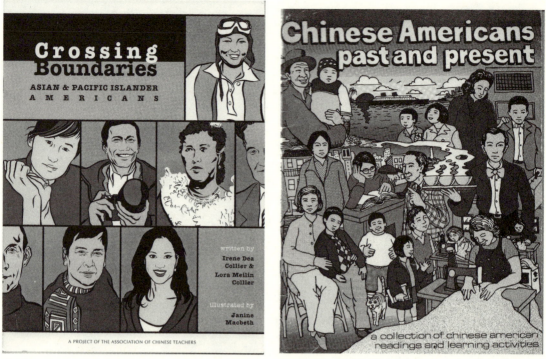

Irene Dea Collier worked with other educators, including her daughter Lora Meilin Collier, and the Association of Chinese Teachers to produce relevant curriculum materials for teachers, community groups, and school districts.

for Affirmative Action director Henry Der and I were always speaking out at school board meetings, talking about the need to include a Chinese American curriculum. I had already written *Chinese Americans Past and Present (1977)* with Don Wong; a set of short stories about the history of Chinese Americans in the United States. The act of speaking out at the school board meetings got so bad that they called us the "Chinese mafia." They were not used to seeing Chinese people speaking out.

ETHNIC STUDIES CURRICULUM DEVELOPMENT

worked hard to develop a lot of curriculum, and that's what I'm still doing today. It's so depressing to hear about racism and oppression. We needed stories for kids to show them how Asian Americans fought racism and oppression.

I wrote *Crossing Boundaries: Tools for Teaching APIA Histories* (2010) with my daughter, Lora, for fifth to eight graders. Jim Hirabayashi is one of the people that we chose to feature because he was the one who shepherded the School of Ethnic Studies. Nobody expected the School to survive more than three years. Jim didn't let that happen. Everyone thought we would self-destruct and never follow any of the college guidelines for maintaining classes like course outlines, reading lists, getting grades done on time. People like Jeff Chan and Dan Gonzales had to write them for other Ethnic Studies departments. They went to the library to research the information so that they could turn in a credible college outline and reading list.

They spent a lot of time at the library reading these horrible texts. At that time, there weren't that many resources. In support of the strike, they did the hard work to develop the Asian American and ethnic studies curricula.

Walking the picket line and disrupting classes may seem very glamorous when they write stories or make films about the strike. That is the part that they focus on. What nobody writes about or understands is the development of curriculum: all the hours spent in the library, all the hours trying to meet the requirements of the college. A lot of people put in a lot of time, going over and above, for our department and others as well, so that Asian American and Ethnic Studies could survive. Jim had to go around and sweet talk everyone. It just wore on him.

I also have to give a shout-out to people like AAPA (Asian American Political Alliance) member and AAS staff Betty Matsuoka, who willingly typed up everything and did so with a smile. She did a lot of work for the faculty and never complained. That's commitment. All these people worked hard so that the Ethnic Studies, now the College of Ethnic Studies, could survive. Those first three years were rough.

LESSONS FOR FUTURE GENERATIONS

The strike is not yet over. It's still ongoing. We continue to do this work. We're still fighting the fight. We're still trying to figure out how to do this. And fifty years later, we're still doing this.

In some ways, we've lost our focus in Asian American studies. It has become a program of Ph.D.s instead of its original focus on educating and training working community activists. There are scholarly works available now, but there is a great de-emphasis in preparing students to go back into the community. I hope that AAS is preparing students to think about helping the community in whatever way they can, no matter what their profession is.

I'm really disappointed however that we're not pushing more students towards social service occupations and getting them more involved in the community as part of their coursework. Some AAS faculty seem to care more about footnotes than they do about the community.

In the past fifty years, we've had Asian American mayors, police chiefs, people in elected offices—things have changed somewhat. But we need more. We need more people to help out in the community. The original purpose of ethnic studies for me was to serve as a conduit to serve the community, and I hope that will be the case over the next fifty years.

Fifty years after the strike, gray-bearded Professor Emeritus George Woo speaks to an Asian American Studies class at San Francisco State in 2017.

SCREEN CAPTURE FROM NOVEMBER 2018 VIDEO
OF *50 YEARS OF ASIAN AMERICA: REFLECTIONS
ON THE 1968 SFSU STRIKES*, ASIAN AMERICANS
ADVANCING JUSTICE - ASIAN LAW CAUCUS

ICSA leader Dr. Laureen Chew speaks, along with AAPA's Penny Nakatsu and PACE's Juanita Tamayo Lott, in November 2018 on how the strike changed her and the educational system. On January 23, 1969, Chew was swept up in a mass arrest on campus and served 20 days in jail. She went on to become a teacher, actress (Dim Sum and Chan Is Missing), bilingual education leader, Professor of Education, and Associate Dean of the College of Ethnic Studies.

OPENING DOORS FOR ORGANIZING AND ADVOCACY WORK

JEFF MORI

FAMILY BACKGROUND

my mother's family came from Hiroshima. Her father came to San Francisco in 1896. He landed in Seattle and worked his way down to the Bay Area after a couple years. He figured out way back then that, "This is going to be an international city!" At that time, he couldn't marry outside his race. My grandmother was a picture bride and arrived shortly after the 1906 earthquake. My mother was born somewhere around Oak and Divisadero Streets.

My father's family came from Fukuoka to San Jose. His father had landed there and was planning to return to Japan to farm. He had sent my father and his younger brother to Japan for seven years as children to learn the business. Of course, the family never went back to Japan again.

Both of my parents came from large families—seven children in each. I was born in Oakland because my dad worked at Peralta Hospital there and childbirth was free at the time for employees. I think my mother got the better end of his conscience and we moved back to San Francisco shortly after 1953 to be with her family. Both sides of the family were very close, all living around the area of Steiner and McAllister Streets.

Before they were evacuated during World War II, my grandfather worked as a domestic servant and had side businesses. He bought a large ten-room house near Alamo Square. My grandmother secured all of her possessions in the basement when they evacuated. This one guy my grandfather worked for liked him a lot and said, "I'm going to rent your place out and I'll pay your mortgage. You will be back. I'll write to

COURTESY OF NICHIBEI FOUNDATION

Jeff Mori used his Asian American Studies knowledge to strategically build organizations such as the Japanese Community Youth Council (JCYC) and Asian American Recovery Services (AARS).

you and we'll figure it out if you're not coming back and whether we have to sell your place." So they were really lucky.

When they came back after the war, it was truly interesting because nobody took anything in the house, and my grandmother still had all of her important possessions. Also at that same time, a lot of Japanese families stayed with my grandparents when they were getting resettled since there was plenty of room in their home.

Growing up, my uncles bought the six-unit apartment building on the corner. Three of our cousins' families lived there. Around the corner at 1285 McAllister, where my parents and I lived, next to my grandfather's house, I had other aunts and uncles who also lived there raising their children. So we all grew up a very close family.

At that time, Alamo Square was considered part of the Fillmore District, even though it was at least three-quarter miles away from Japantown. It was still a relocation place for a lot of Japanese folks who lived there before the war and came back to the same neighborhood up and down Steiner Street, all the way to Bush and Pine.

My grandfather did a lot of things—worked, saved his money, and started various business ventures. A lot of them failed in the earlier years. He opened up a cleaners, but that didn't work out and so he ended up working other side jobs. Some way, however, he would be was able to work. As the family grew up, all the kids worked and contributed to the household.

When Japantown was in its earlier years, my dad had this little storefront where he sold tofu. The tofu was really a front for selling sake. After a while, his friends told him, "You should keep making tofu, because your sake is terrible!" So he ended up starting the business, and when his sons were old enough to do it, Azumaya became a family business. It remained successful because they were able to find large manufacturing plants elsewhere before redevelopment moved them out of the area. It was the first Asian foods on Safeway shelves. And twenty years ago, my uncle sold the business to Vitasoy.

My father was the oldest son in the family, and internment camp broke his father. I remember having a good time with my grandfather in the early years because he treated me really good. He would always take me to the corner store to buy me candy. I was the first Mori son from my father, who was the oldest son in his family as well. I was also the only son out of ten female cousins.

The camps had different impacts on our families. My mother and father didn't get married until they were in their thirties. Even though they dated quite a bit, my father had family responsibilities to take care of. He wanted to be a doctor, but because he had to be there to support the family, he had to made sure that all his siblings at least finished high school. I found out years later that one of the reasons why the family was so close was because his father hardly worked after camp and drank quite a bit. There was spousal abuse in the family, but my father was there to intervene whenever it occurred.

In our families, the only Japanese you could hear spoken was when we did things with our grandparents. My aunts and uncles all spoke to them in Japanese, but then over the years, it became more broken Japanese, and then English-Japanese. We were never encouraged to necessarily speak Japanese at home, but were encouraged to try to take some classes, which didn't work for me, especially when it was only on Saturdays.

It was really amazing at that time because all of my friends were Sansei (third-generation). I think the camp experience told that generation, "If you're going to make it here, you have to speak English. Don't speak Japanese in order to assimilate faster."

As I was growing up, my father was very patient with me over the years because I was a good student until I went to middle school. Even though I was having way too much fun, I still went to class, and so middle school was a great experience.

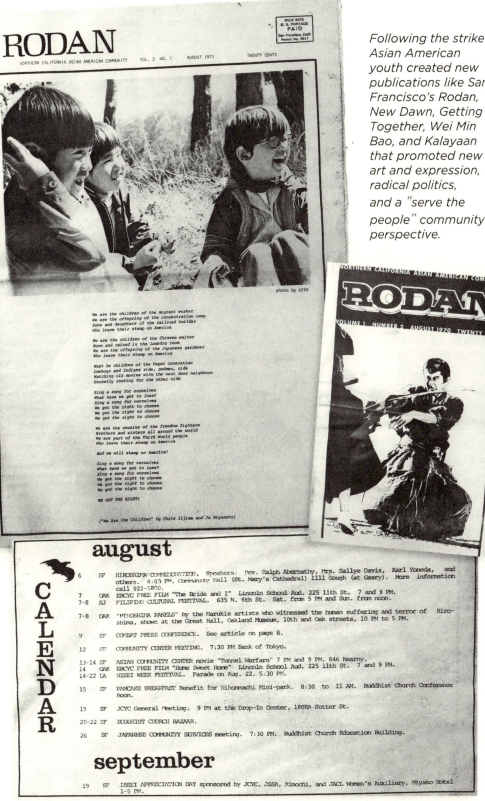

RODAN

NORTHERN CALIFORNIA ASIAN AMERICAN COMMUNITY   VOL. 2 NO. 1   AUGUST 1971   TWENTY CENTS

BULK RATE
U.S. POSTAGE
PAID
San Francisco, Calif.
Permit No. 9817

photo by KITS

We are the children of the migrant worker
We are the offspring of the concentration camp
Sons and daughters of the railroad builder
Who leave their stamp on America

We are the children of the Chinese waiter
Born and raised in the laundry room
We are the offspring of the Japanese gardener
Who leave their stamp on America

Must be children of the Pepsi Generation
Cowboys and Indians ride, redmen, ride
Watching old movies with the next door neighbors
Secretly rooting for the other side

Sing a song for ourselves
What have we got to lose?
Sing a song for ourselves
We got the right to choose
We got the right to choose
We got the right to choose

We are the cousins of the freedom fighters
Brothers and sisters all around the world
We are part of the Third World people
Who leave their stamp on America

And we will stamp on America!

Sing a song for ourselves
What have we got to lose?
Sing a song for ourselves
We got the right to choose
We got the right to choose
We got the right to choose

WE GOT THE RIGHT!

["We Are the Children" by Chris Iijima and Jo Miyamoto]

Following the strike Asian American youth created new publications like San Francisco's Rodan, New Dawn, Getting Together, Wei Min Bao, and Kalayaan that promoted new art and expression, radical politics, and a "serve the people" community perspective.

NORTHERN CALIFORNIA ASIAN AMERICAN COMMUNITY

RODAN

VOLUME 1   NUMBER 2   AUGUST 1970   TWENTY CENTS

august

6   SF   HIROSHIMA COMMEMORATION. Speakers: Rev. Ralph Abernathy, Mrs. Sallye Davis, Karl Yoneda, and others. 8:00 PM, Community Hall (St. Mary's Cathedral) 1111 Gough (at Geary). More information call 922-5800.

7   OAK   EBCYC FREE FILM "The Bride and I" Lincoln School Aud. 225 11th St. 7 and 9 PM.

7-8 SJ   FILIPINO CULTURAL FESTIVAL. 635 N. 6th St. Sat. from 5 PM and Sun. from noon.

7-8 OAK   "HIROSHIMA PANELS" by the Marukis artists who witnessed the human suffering and terror of Hiroshima, shown at the Great Hall, Oakland Museum, 10th and Oak streets, 10 PM to 5 PM.

9   SF   COMBAT PRESS CONFERENCE. See article on page 8.

12   SF   COMMUNITY CENTER MEETING. 7:30 PM Bank of Tokyo.

13-14 SF   ASIAN COMMUNITY CENTER movie "Tunnel Warfare" 7 PM and 9 PM. 846 Kearny.

14   OAK   EBCYC FREE FILM "Home Sweet Home" Lincoln School Aud. 225 11th St. 7 and 9 PM.

14-22 LA   NISEI WEEK FESTIVAL. Parade on Aug. 22, 5:30 PM.

15   SF   PANCAKE BREAKFAST Benefit for Nihonmachi Mini-park. 8:30 to 11 AM. Buddhist Church Conference Room.

19   SF   JCYC General Meeting. 9 PM at the Drop-In Center, 1808A Sutter St.

20-22 SF   BUDDHIST CHURCH BAZAAR.

26   SF   JAPANESE COMMUNITY SERVICES meeting. 7:30 PM. Buddhist Church Education Building.

september

19   SF   ISSEI APPRECIATION DAY sponsored by JCYC, JSSA, Kimochi, and JACL Women's Auxiliary. Miyako Hotel 1-5 PM.

JAPANTOWN AND AFRICAN AMERICAN INFLUENCES

Part of that whole movement of African Americans from the South changed our communities. They had very strong alumni, like my middle school woodshop teacher Maxwell Gillette. On the day John F. Kennedy was assassinated, Mr. Gillette explained to us that the president was just shot. He also talked about the promise of Civil Rights and brought many of his friends who were professionals in the South to teach. So I always make sure to talk to him.

My family lived in the Western Addition. We went to Golden Gate Elementary School and were among the few Asians there. By that time, after World War II, it became heavily populated with African Americans coming from the South and others just arriving to San Francisco who thought, "This city is a lot better than where I came from. I'm going to stay here." Then slowly my family bought homes out in the Richmond District. That's when I moved and attended Argonne Elementary, Presidio Middle School, and George Washington High School.

African Americans had a huge influence on my life. I didn't think about it very much when we moved to the Richmond District which was a whole different experience. It was whites and Asians there. Years later I'd come back to the Western Addition when I got recruited to work at the Japanese Community Youth Council (JCYC). There was a lot of involvement and openness to African Americans working with us, who were doing the same things we were with housing issues and redevelopment.

ASIAN COMMUNITY CENTER ARCHIVES

Buttons of Wei Min She and Leway, two Chinatown youth organizations

Yoritada "Yori" Wada, director of the Buchanan YMCA, and a woman named Toshi Koba, who worked at the Booker T. Washington Center, used to run both African American and Japanese clubs. Yori was such a key part of the human service network in the Western Addition that other African Americans would check, "Are you working with Yori?" He taught me at a very early age how you "make an influence in politics by doing three things: You donate money, you raise money, or you get a lot of volunteers to help out. Then, ultimately it's the vote that's the equalizer."

The Japanese Community Youth Council (JCYC), formed in 1969, and was the only group in that neighborhood other than religious groups and African American nonprofits that worked together in coalitions. Yori brought us together on a regular basis to do youth employment programs.

The youth councils got paid to do outreach and organize youth within all the neighborhoods. While the councils in most of the areas faded or transitioned to other service organizations, JCYC amended our bylaws and functions over the years and decided to keep the name. That's why it's still called a "Youth Council." But it was very far from that. JCYC was youth involved, but functioned with a board of directors. It's a service agency that moved to educational nonprofit status after we got into the federally funded TRiO programs with other Asian groups back in the early '80s. These programs helped low income students of color get into college and offered learning and career support. They now also have two Upward Bound programs as well.

FROM WASHINGTON HIGH TO SAN FRANCISCO STATE

I went to Washington High School in the late 1960s. I was a terrible student, but managed to graduate in 1969. By that time, the Black Panther Party, San Francisco State College's Educational Opportunity Program (EOP), and Youth for Service were all organizing on the campuses. There were a small number of us who felt discontent that the school would have world history classes but there wasn't any history on Asians within that; instead it would be all European history. That became a struggle and an issue. And so we got together and formed an Asian Students Coalition at Washington.

I felt like I didn't fit in a lot at that time and started cutting school, which became a habit. I had some friends, and I liked to smoke a lot of weed. I later started to settle down a little bit more in my junior and senior year when the Coalition started meeting. We had to be more responsible if we were going to organize and push things. There was a lot of activity going on. The generation just before me was actively involved in the Japanese community. But by the time I went to high school, it was the Chinese gangs that were predominantly active—the Wah Ching primarily, very well organized.

When we started organizing, however, the community came out to support us. I got a big boost in confidence when I saw Edison Uno, leader of the Redress and Reparations movement, come in the first time to educate my teacher and the principal about discrimination and the inclusion of history of Asian Americans.

Our group were mostly Japanese Americans but pushed the issue of Asian American studies. It was a pretty good movement. By the time I graduated from Washington, there was an accredited Asian American studies program taught by a student from SF State. In my senior year, I was actually five units short of graduating because of cutting classes. But the dean gave me a break and I graduated.

I wasn't planning to go to college, but when the Third World Strike's Richard Wada, leader of the Asian American Political Alliance, came to Washington to recruit for San Francisco State's EOP program, he encouraged me to apply. But my grades were so bad that I got rejected even from EOP! Then, in 1971, somebody introduced me to Dean Charles Stone of San Francisco State College. He said, "People speak highly of you, kid. So if you go to College of San Mateo for one year and you get a C average, get 18 units, I'll let you in." He gave me a note. I came back to him later and said, "Dean Stone, I barely got that C average." But he said, "Good enough for me." Then I showed him his note, he signed it and said, "Admit. Go to the registrar." I went to the registrar and I got admitted to the college.

The Asian Student Unions were organized statewide. We had a lot of youth-led conferences up and down California and were connected to the UC and State College systems. I first met Los Angeles leader Warren Furutani when he was the outreach organizer for the Japanese American Citizens League's FOX (Field Office Auxiliary) Program. He had three or four people around the state that he could hire part-time. One of the founders of JCYC, Rev. Ronald Kobata, referred me for the job. This was before I took the job as the executive director of JCYC. I worked for Warren part-time and got to know him. We would drive up and down the state with groups of people, like the Yellow Brotherhood in Los Angeles.

was the original chairman of JCYC when we invited eleven organizations to participate. Over a two-year period, before incorporating, we decided to open a drop-in center on Sutter Street. We paid a dollar a year in a redevelopment building for a 15-room Victorian, and decided to form a meeting place. Prior to that, we were meeting in churches. SF State provided the student manpower to supplement our community efforts. At the same time, UC Berkeley also set up a field office and helped to pay for our utilities and phone bills. We had a very tiny budget.

Rev. Kobata of the Buddhist Church of San Francisco was very much into community movement before he became a minister. He was the main impetus to form the Youth Council—to involve young people in a new way in the community. It was part of Lyndon B. Johnson's Great Society, and the back-to-the-community movement from Asian American studies and social work. Even though it was the end of the Vietnam War, a lot of us were getting ready to get drafted for not going to college. Young attorneys like Dale Minami and Don Tamaki, founders of Asian Americans Advancing Justice-Asian Law Caucus, came in and offered draft counseling. We met a lot of other Asian American leaders through a broader network.

The Council had a big debate about our future structure. A lot of people wanted to move more towards the direction of a political advocacy group because we were publishing a community newspaper called *Rodan* for a while. The FBI started coming around more often and we knew they were asking questions about people because *Rodan* reported on community and political news. This newspaper became international, because it was hooked up with the Red Guard, Leeways, and other youth organizations.

Then there was a political split between us. Some wanted to be politically active and others said, "We should organize within the community and build community through services and networks that don't exist currently." That's why JCYC does what it does, because it expanded on what was existing—summer day camp and after school programs. Through the years, we got into youth development, substance abuse prevention, education, and youth employment. It was the time and place for that. Yori Wada always told us that when we applied for funding, the city had five districts. There was only a certain amount of money for summer youth jobs. Yori advised us, "don't apply for more than 1/5, because 1/5 is going to be divided among all the communities in San Francisco." And that's what we did for years.

AT SAN FRANCISCO STATE

wanted to study psychology, sociology, or social welfare as an Asian, because I thought those would be applicable to the community service work we were doing. I took classes in all three areas through the Asian American Studies Department's Nine Unit Block program with other Asians and community organizers, allowing me to focus and apply my education. The Nine Unit Block program and Asian American Studies opened a door for people to think differently about what they could do in society within the framework of their education—not just to choose to be a doctor, lawyer, or accountant. This created a pathway for people to think about what they could do without being questioned or criticized by the generation that wanted us all to be doctors and lawyers. Half of my class of 12 people was working at JCYC at the time. They weren't all Japanese: communities were overlapping.

The program gave us time to do more organizing and it was pretty amazing to have your work being validated by professors. Social Welfare professor Kenji Murase was involved with supporting JCYC. We would meet with the three professors once a week and do twenty hours

Above: *From 1973-1980 the Committee Against Nihonmachi Evictions resisted evictions and the redevelopment of a four-block area of San Francisco's Japantown by uniting, educating, and organizing students, artists, seniors, small businesses, and religious leaders.*

At Left: *Artist Wes Senzaki joined the Committee Against Nihonmachi Evictions in 1974 and with CANE members rehabilitated an empty storefront at 1852 Sutter Street. On October 1, 1977, they founded the Japantown Art and Media Workshop, and working closely with the Chinatown-based Kearny Street Workshop, they taught art classes, supported hundreds of groups, and produced art for their communities.*

Two hundred people rally with the Committee Against Nihonmachi Evictions (CANE) to protest the demolition of a Japantown historical site.

of community work. Asian American Studies professor George Woo got federal government support for mental health in the early '70s for ten years to recruit more Asian social workers. This Asian Social Work Training Program also expanded to UC Berkeley, Laney College, and SF Community College to recruit social workers to be involved in the community. Stan Yee was actually the staff member for that program. He was a coordinator. Stan was not necessarily an academic, so it was a combination of Kenji pushing him from the academic side and Stan pushing with his community experience side. That combination really delivered a program. We cranked out a lot of social workers in that period and established infrastructure for a lot of the community agencies at that time.

Kenji would come out and ask, "What are you all involved with right now? What are you doing? Are you planning? Are you organizing? Are you building organizations? Are you doing community outreach?" We discussed the practical application of organizing, with whole sections about how to establish a nonprofit and be accountable for it. It was all very applicable. We were all undergrads, so we weren't doing counseling, yet. We also received a broad practical education from Psych 101. People chose their fields and trades after that. What we were taught in the classroom influenced the direction of what was going on.

In addition, EOP counselor Sue Hayashi was really accessible to folks. We were doing a lot of recruitment right out of the office. Former EOP Director Randy Senzaki and CSU East Bay President Leroy Morishita also came out of that era. The Nine Unit Block program opened up fields for people that Asians weren't traditionally involved with. When I came to campus, Asian American Studies had contemporary arts and community issues classes that overlapped with our fields. These were the beginning classes that people took that also met general education requirements. It was so good, because you didn't have to sit through other boring classes. George Woo had a big influence on strategically expanding the Asian American Studies general education requirement classes as part of the college. I always wondered how George did that. He didn't seem like he had the personality to go in there and ask politely. Richard Wada explained that, "George was the only one that read the college guidelines and manuals for the development of curriculum."

I had a field day because I felt like I belonged on this campus, having teachers who looked like me, and having people who had an open philosophy about being Asian American and what we could be doing at the time. It was pretty encouraging because a lot of them volunteered back in their community at events and activities. There was a really strong correlation between campus and college.

Because of the student demands from the Third World Strike, the School of Social Welfare was also involved in helping the Ethnic Studies Department. The whole impact of the strike was felt throughout San Francisco and the Bay Area within all the community organizations that grew and thrived. The healthiest nonprofits were Asian and grew out of that time. I almost dropped out of school at San Francisco State because working in the community became a priority over education. But the founding Dean of the School of Ethnic Studies, Jim Hirabayashi, was a great supporter and assisted me and others in graduating.

DEVELOPING JAPANESE AMERICAN ORGANIZATIONS

JCYC was a drop-in center, but you had to walk up two flights of stairs to get to our front door. Neighborhood leader Steve Nakajo was a big supporter of JCYC in the beginning, and we remained life-long friends. As the years went on however, it didn't look like the Council was going to be able to serve seniors coming to our funky youth center. Steve and some other folks started Kimochi, but originally ran a service escorting seniors from the Japanese movies back to their homes safely.

From there, Kimochi started to grow and became an organization itself. When we had the opportunity for funding through United Way, we applied under the name United Japanese Community Services (UJCS). UJCS was our fiscal agent and we split the money between JCYC, Kimochi, and Japanese Community Services, which was primarily services for the immigrant population. Nihonmachi Legal Outreach joined later. When we moved up to Pine Street, Nihonmachi shared our office space for years before they grew and left.

Within the arts community, we had the Japantown art movement, a sister organization to Chinatown's Kearny Street Workshop. Students were sent down to volunteer and would crank out silkscreen posters. There were festivals and activities. Japantown's Nihonmachi Street Fair was formed out of Steve Nakajo's SF State class in 1974. One of his students gave him an idea about how we should have an intergenerational fair in Japantown, and that's where it started, as a class project of Asian American Studies.

SERVING AND NETWORKING WITH THE BROADER ASIAN AMERICAN COMMUNITY

In 1981, representation on the San Francisco Recreation and Parks Commission became a big issue for the Committee for Better Parks and Recreation in Chinatown. The Committee was looking for an Asian appointment because there had been no Asian on that commission since it was formed in 1887. I applied for the position, and a lot of my support came from African American San Francisco Supervisors Doris Ward and Willie Kennedy; both supported me because of my work at the time in the Western Addition. Congressman Phil Burton wrote a support letter. Gordon Chin, director of the Chinatown Community Development, also put in a good word for me with the mayor. I got appointed and served for eight years.

Years later, when JCYC's funds were threatened, we received support from Chinatown leaders. I was never really that close with Chinese community leader Rose Pak, but when we were getting cut, she said, "They're not a Chinese organization, but they serve Asians." And so she helped us fight the cut backs.

A few years later, Mayor Art Agnos helped me get a big federal grant that included organizing nine neighborhoods. He made a personal call to the director of the Office of Drug Prevention which helped us win a $2.4 million grant for four years. When the program got terminated, we reached out to other community organizations, because we figured out it was better to work together and create a pie than get no pie at all!

ESTABLISHING ASIAN AMERICAN MENTAL HEALTH PROGRAMS

We started growing our mental health programs and expanding services for Asians city-wide. The mental health movement came on early in the '70s, and we were sending people to D.C. to lobby for our needs. When the Asian American Studies program started at San Francisco State, it wasn't just to have ethnic studies classes; it was about topics of concern. It's not just about learning about an issue, but getting people into the fields to address those concerns. The northeast section of San Francisco had the largest concentration of Asian therapists, but it still wasn't enough compared to the whole need that existed. It wasn't until folks expanded from the northeast that mental health centers started to get all-patient programs, and have youth-family prevention centers.

A lot of the coalition building was through the API community. The Filipinos, Japanese,

Koreans, and Chinese were concerned about mental health. I don't think the Vietnamese community was large enough to make that an issue. We came together around the community's needs and addressed urgent issues like AIDS, as well. RAMS (Richmond Area Multi-Services) took the lead and when they saw what we did with the youth employment program—how we expanded—they said, "Let's try this again with Asian mental health." And we did. We increased the program positions of Asians at the public health centers, and we equally increased the contracts that went out to Asian organizations.

We got everybody together, talked to the city employees of public health and then the nonprofits. We figured out that we were going to try to get these permanent positions at these centers, and then to try to increase the capabilities and capacities of CBOs (community-based organizations).

FOUNDING ASIAN AMERICAN RECOVERY SERVICES

In the mid-'80s, we had all these Asians getting into car accidents, but they weren't drunk. Chinatown Youth Center director Myra Chow pulled together a task force to investigate and discovered kids were falling asleep from taking Quaaludes—very popular, not only with young Asians, but [also among the gay population]. We received $10,000 from the health department for our coalition of youth organizations and mental health service providers. The task force recommended starting Asian American Recovery Services (AARS). We were looking for a youth residential treatment and outpatient program, but we had to settle for an adult residential treatment facility.

Later, I was recruited by AARS to be the director. Because of my work experience, the board asked me to manage and grow the agency—expanding it from 60 employees to 160 employees in seven years, including the San Francisco drug court. David Mineta was my deputy director, and he eventually went on to work for President Obama as the Deputy Director of Demand Reduction in the Office of National Drug Policy Control.

LESSONS LEARNED: MENTORING

Asian American studies helped me to learn that organizing and advocacy work was all about the politics. Asian American studies' creation at the time opened the doors for advocacy and people not to be afraid about coming out and working on issues, which wasn't happening en masse except for when we all started coming out around the Vietnam War. There was a vacuum of leadership on these issues, but there was enough of the older generation who helped put up some barriers of security for us while we protested and advocated.

The most important thing is to work and find mentors. Not just one mentor, but those who talk to each other, like the connection between a professor and people in the community they know. For you to find a mentor you're comfortable with is very important. At the same time, you have to take responsibility of mentoring other people along the way as well.

That's something that I'm proud of now. While some of agencies have a hard time with succession, I was able to leave JCYC in capable hands. At 46, I went to work for Mayor Willie Brown, and recommended Jon Osaki, who was 29 years old and running one of our programs. The board was going to do a national search, and I said, "What for?" So they hired Jon and he's still there today. Then when I left AARS at the age of 63, I recommended Tony Duong, a 29-year-old Vietnamese who was handling our finances.

Mentors should be chosen and not just given to people. A mentor must be comfortable

Jeff Mori and his wife Sandy, a co-founder of Kimochi, Inc., a pioneering senior service organization in San Francisco, have been an influential duo that have built and led community organizations. They have created new alliances and held City Hall acountable to the needs of Japanese Americans, youth, seniors and low income people.

knowing what they're thinking and what they want. Then that growth can take place. It's also important for the younger generation to share with other folks coming along the way too. That's part of the responsibility of growing our community, and continuity, so that there's a historical perspective and continued commitment. Programs have to come in with a vision of young people and have opportunities for them to grow a lot faster.

Things have changed so much over the years since the strike. We're dealing with a different era now where lot of young Asians don't even know what the Civil Rights movement was about. I think that is really the foundation of Asian American and ethnic studies—us being included in the history of education and the planning of education.

Today, San Francisco has a critical mass of Asian Americans. When I started organizing, Japanese were the largest API group at that time. But that changed dramatically over ten to fifteen years. There are more Vietnamese and Koreans, with Japanese the smallest population now. The Chinese community still is ever-changing however. I think that's why some of the issues that the Chinese American community is dealing with right now are multilayered, because of its generations of new people coming in—which isn't the case with a lot of the other Asian communities.

For today's Asian American studies classes, we should evaluate how our community has changed and developed. We're currently at a whole different level—there are Asians in politics, mainstream business communities and leaders in their fields. We used to build nonprofits. Now we need to connect with them more and bring some of them in to be guest speakers or lecturers to discuss about bigger issues around the Asian American and Pacific Islander community in different fields. The world has changed from when I attended school at SF State—we didn't have laptops or cell phones. It was a whole different way of communicating back then, and so new opportunities are now opening up for today's Asian American students.

Sheriffs confront TWLF Strikers. The Third World Liberation Front (TWLF) strike began at UC Berkeley on January 22, 1969. After one week of informational picketing, the strike escalated with the sealing off of the Sather Gate entry to the main campus. Campus police, the Alameda County Sheriff's Department, Highway Patrol, outside police agencies, and eventually, the National Guard, were sent in to quell the strike activities.

UC BERKELEY'S ASIAN AMERICAN STUDIES

50 YEARS OF GROWING PAINS & GAINS

L. LING-CHI WANG

During the late 1960s, African American studies, Asian American studies, Chicano studies, and Native American studies programs were creating a lasting and profound impact on teaching and research in institutions of higher education across the nation, fundamentally changing how Americans understood their history and identity. Emerging at the time of the Civil Rights movement, anti-Vietnam War protests, and counterculture movements, the beginning stages of these programs in 1969 were traumatic and painful: they were established by the university administration only after two months of militant protest and a lengthy—and at times, violent—strike, led by the Third World Liberation Front (TWLF), a coalition of students of color.

What follows is a brief account of what Ethnic Studies at UC Berkeley (UCB) and one of its four programs, Asian American Studies, encountered as new interdisciplinary fields of study being established at a leading research university that had systematically excluded minority experiences and their contributions from its teaching and research since its beginnings. Founding Ethnic Studies was a monumental and continuing project undertaken by a small handful of untrained but determined young scholars in a historic first step towards diversifying American studies in an institution of higher education in the U.S.

ASIAN AMERICAN POLITICAL ALLIANCE
AND THE RISE OF THE ASIAN AMERICAN MOVEMENT

The historical convergence of two separate developments in the late 1960s—one on the UCB campus and the other in San Francisco Chinatown—helped generate what eventually became known as the Asian American movement and the establishment of Ethnic Studies and Asian American Studies in the fall of 1969. On campuses such as UCB and San Francisco State College (now San Francisco State University or SF State), self-awareness and political consciousness among Asian American college students were on the rise, under the influence of the anti-war and African American Civil Rights movements. At around the same time, a parallel but different kind of political consciousness was also erupting: growing alienation and anger were brewing among the teenagers and young adults in San Francisco Chinatown, where they realized their community needs and problems were being ignored, and their personal and future growth was shut out by persistent racial isolation, discrimination, and failed leadership.

First, the awakening and active participation of Asian American students in the TWLF strikes at UCB and SF State shattered the popular stereotype of Asian Americans as the quiet, hard-working, docile, and subservient "model minority," who, unlike other minorities, were willing and able to help themselves in spite of racial exclusion and discrimination. These students also began to understand the racial dimension of American involvement in the escalating

ASIAN-AMERICAN POLITICAL ALLIANCE

We Asian-Americans believe that American society has been, and still is, fundamentally a racist society, and that historically we have accomodated ourselves to this society in order to survive.

We Asian-Americans believe that heretofore we have been relating to white standards of acceptability, and affirm the right of self-definition and self-determination.

We Asian-Americans support all non-white liberation movements and believe that all minorities in order to be truly liberated must have complete control over the political, economic, and educational institutions within their respective communities.

We Asian-Americans oppose the imperialistic policies being pursued by the American government.

Asian American Political Alliance (AAPA) statement of purpose, April 1968. The character "East" is adopted by AAPA.

*International Hotel tenant delegation to
San Francisco City Hall. Pictured: Yee Tung,
Frankie Delos Reyes, Claudio Domingo,
Anacleto Moniz, and others.*

PHOTOGRAPH BY STEVE LOUIE, WEI MIN SHE
AND ASIAN COMMUNITY CENTER PHOTOGRAPHS,
ETHNIC STUDIES LIBRARY, UC BERKELEY

*Banner across Kearny Street: "Workers
Unite to Fight Evictions! Fight for the
I-Hotel and Victory Building!" The Victory
Building was a single room occupancy
building with mainly Chinese tenants. It was
located next to the I-Hotel. Both properties
were purchased by 4-Seas Investments
who proceeded with eviction orders. The
banner was hung illegally by the Workers
Committee to Fight for the I-Hotel & Victory
Building. It was removed by the City and
replaced by protestors multiple times.*

asian experience / yellow identity

From: Asian Students of Chinese Students Club and Nisei Students Club 509-600 Eshleman Hall, University of California, Berkeley, 94720, 642-4216

Bring this, your invitation, to the 1st Asian Experience in America, Sat. Jan. 11, 1969, 9:00am-4:30pm Pauley Ballroom, ASUC Building UC Berkeley.

theasianexperienceinamerica/identifiedyellowqueriesqueuesfriendstheasianexperience/yellowidentity

False religions delude the land with a ceaseless clamor.
I would strike the barbarian tribes but the time comes not,
When will the great roc rise and southward soar?
Long have I waited the wind of his ten-thousand mile wings.
        Date Masamune 1567-1636

Get out of my road and allow me to plant these bamboos, Mr. Toad
        Miura Chora 1729-1780

Where, before me, are the ages that have gone?
And where, behind me, are the coming generations?
I think of heaven and earth without limit, without end,
And I am alone and my tears fall down.
        Chen Tzu-ang 661-702

the asian flu in america, blackheads all; gardeners, cooks, laundrymen and toshiro mifune; the golden race, america the beautiful, glittering ghettoes, second class citizens with visiting rights; chinatown, manilatown, little tokyo relocated concentrated, beautification, hallelujah christian colonies; submissive females, passive males, mellow yellows, that strong silent type; run run shaw, made in japan, p.r. 95%; japanophiles, sinophiles, you likee chop suey, chop chop, me no savee; white paper, brown paper, yellow paper, black paper, red paper, if i were god i'd make everybody white; third world liberation front, all men are brothers, love is a many splendored thing, black eyed blondes; we all live in a yellow submarine, antiqueue law, call me yellow, no vietnamese ever called me a nigger, let's call a spade a spade, a jap a jap; buddhaheads transcendental meditation, jesus is a'comin so get yourself ready for a hard day's night; reparations for the opium wars, christianity the whole world over, the asians get what they deserve, they breed like rabbits anyways; that fat jap, that skinny chink, chinatown my chinatown, my little houseboy, sayonnara suzie wong; Free University for Chinatown Kids, Unincorporated

An invitation to the "Yellow Symposium," held on January 11, 1969. Sponsored by the Asian American Political Alliance (AAPA), Chinese Students Club (CSC) and the Nisei Students Club (NSC), the conference was widely attended and concluded with a resolution in full support of the TWLF Strike at SF State. Also, more AAPA chapters were organized with many local Asian American organizations becoming AAPA chapters.

Yuji Ichioka speaks in UC Berkeley's first Asian American Studies class called Asian Studies 100X, "Introduction to the Asian Experience in the U.S."

AAPA NEWSPAPER 1969

and genocidal war in an Asian country, Vietnam. American GIs were sent there to turn the country into a killing field and, in the process, they themselves also became the casualties of the same war.

Second, people in Chinatown, young and old, felt trapped in overcrowded, dilapidated, and unsanitary quarters; an endless cycle of poverty; and widespread labor abuse in sweatshops and restaurants. While the newly enacted 1965 Immigration and Nationality Act (Hart-Cellar Act) immediately repealed the legacy of Chinese exclusion and opened the doors for separated families finally to be united, the conditions of Chinatown went from bad to worse. Since most of the new immigrants were poor and non-English-speaking, they had to settle in already crowded and run-down housing in the Chinatowns of San Francisco and Oakland, with little or no social support network. Compounding these problems, thousands of non-English-speaking children entered the ill-prepared and rigidly-run San Francisco public schools, alienated and dropping out. And yet, no one, including the Chinatown establishment and City Hall, seemed willing and able to step in and take the lead in addressing these mounting problems. These conditions felt increasingly like a time-bomb, ready to explode at any moment. These unfolding horror stories stirred the conscience of college students as never before and prompted them to raise questions about their own responsibilities to their communities in the absence of relief and political leadership.

During this time, in May 1968, two UCB students, Japanese American Yuji Ichioka and Chinese American Emma Gee, convened the first informal gathering by word-of-mouth in a Berkeley apartment at 2005 Hearst Street, to discuss local and national issues affecting them as Asians. It was at this meeting that all of the unsettling personal, social, cultural, and political concerns became crystal clear for the participants, who reached the consensus that they must act collectively in order to change the conditions of Asian people on campus and in society. Thus, the Asian American Political Alliance (AAPA) was born on the UCB campus, the first Asian American political organization in the nation. Members chose to name their organization beyond the national origin of Chinese, Japanese, Korean, and Filipino ethnicities. They pointedly rejected the prevailing use of the term "Oriental," which they considered derogatory, dehumanizing, and racist. Instead, they created the term "Asian American" to identify themselves. It was a defiant self-designation for a new collective identity and a shared destiny. Thus was born an Asian American political moment in the U.S.

At about the same time in February 1968, the problems in San Francisco's Chinatown burst open as Chinatown youth spoke angrily, loudly, and clearly at a town hall meeting at the Chinese American Citizens Alliance (CACA). The youth spokesperson, George Woo, denounced the community leadership and government for their indifference and negligence. Woo demanded prompt action and warned of impending outbreaks of social disorder like the riots sweeping across the country. A seed was planted. It was not until August 17 that sustained organizing began. On that day, a forum on Chinatown problems, sponsored and organized by the Summer Youth Program, an anti-poverty summer program, was held in the basement of Cumberland Chinese Presbyterian Church. For the first time, college students from AAPA, Intercollegiate Chinese for Social Action (ICSA) at SF State, and other organizations around the Bay Area met to learn about the myriad of problems in Chinatown and discuss what needed to be done about them. With prior planning, the all-day session ended with the students joining forces with a newly formed group, Concerned Chinese for Action and Change (CCAC), made up of young Chinese American professionals led by attorney Gordon J. Lau; together, they embarked on a provocative and noisy march down Grant Avenue during the height of Chinatown's tourist season. The march ended with a mass rally in historic Portsmouth Square in the heart of Chinatown. Speaker after speaker denounced slumlords, sweatshop operators, greedy restaurant owners, the deplorable conditions in Chinatown, racism, and City Hall.

The Saturday demonstration was unprecedented and its impact reverberated in Chinatown and across the Bay Area. Mainstream media covered the rare public airing of Chinatown's problems, deeming the sight of militant Asian Americans loudly condemning racism and discrimination as unbecoming of the "model minority." Airing one's dirty laundry in public was considered shocking, shameful, and disgraceful by the Chinatown establishment. The Chinese Six Companies, formally known as Chinese Consolidated Benevolent Association, quickly issued a rare "manifesto," castigating the demonstrators as "outside agitators" and "undesirable immigrants." Regardless, that day bridged the chasm between campus and community; college students and community activists found unity in purpose, courage, and power.

At the end of the summer, students returned to their campuses and started mobilizing their participation in various protest events and community service projects. In Berkeley, subgroups of Asian students came together to plan a day-long symposium entitled the "Yellow Symposium." Hundreds of college and high school students from around the country attended presentations on the history of Asians in the U.S. and community issues by scholars and community leaders. They also heard an emotionally charged report about the on-going TWLF Strike at SF State by Penny Nakatsu. Professor Paul Takagi of Criminology and the Board of Educational Development (BED) agreed to sponsor an "experimental" class on Asian American history in January 1969. Four graduate students were recruited to work as teaching assistants—Richard Aoki of Social Welfare, Alan Fong of Anthropology, Bing Thom of Architecture, and myself, L. Ling-chi Wang of Near Eastern Studies— and led the class with the help of several guest speakers from the community. None of the four TAs had knowledge about or experience with the subject matter. Nevertheless, they taught the class with a strong instinct and shared conviction that Asian American Studies must be created, and that the community urgently needed it. The course was officially labeled Asian Studies 100X, "Introduction to the Asian Experience in the U.S." The "X" stood for "experimental." About 120 students enrolled in the Winter Quarter course off campus in solidarity with the ongoing TWLF Strike on campus.

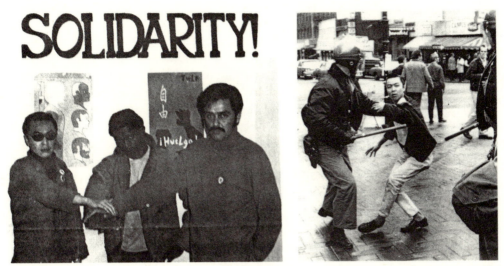

SOLIDARITY!

ASIAN COMMUNITY CENTER ARCHIVES (ABOVE AND BELOW)

Above left, Richard Aoki of the Asian American Political Alliance, Charles Brown of the Afro-American Student Union, and Manuel Delgado of the Mexican American Student Confederation join hands in solidarity as part of the Third World Liberation Front at UC Berkeley.

Above right, Richard Aoki, an early member of the Black Panthers, was arrested in 1969 for strike activities at the Bancroft Way and Telegraph Avenue intersection.

At left, a July 28, 1968, community panel announcement featuring speakers from the Black Panthers, Alianza, Hwa Ching, Philippine American Collegiate Endeavor (PACE) and Leway, a Chinatown self-help youth organization.

TWLF STRIKE FOR ETHNIC STUDIES

The Asian American Studies Program at UCB was born out of collective demands for an autonomous Third World College made by the TWLF. The coalition included representatives of the Afro-American Student Union (AASU), Asian American Political Alliance (AAPA), Native American Student Union (NASU), and Mexican-American Student Confederation (MASC). As oppressed minorities in the U.S., the groups pledged to stand united with each other, an act of multiracial solidarity unprecedented in the history of the U.S. When demands and negotiations for an autonomous Third World College fell through, the TWLF at UCB, like their counterparts at SF State, also called for a strike that began in mid-January and ended in early March 1969. The strike was disruptive and, at times, violent. The campus was occupied by the National Guard, State Highway Patrol, County Sheriff, and Berkeley City Police. Many students were hurt and arrested during this turbulent time.

The TWLF declared in fliers distributed on campus: "We recognize that the racist power structure does not give us power willingly. . . .We of the Third World now stand together in the fight for educational freedom in this racist society." The core principle advanced by the TWLF was the right of self-determination: to establish an autonomous Department of Ethnic Studies with the power to shape its own curriculum and appoint its own faculty.

The TWLF Strike resulted in the establishment of an *interim* Ethnic Studies Department in fall 1969 with four autonomous programs. The intent of the *interim* status, as stipulated by the Academic Senate, was to leave open flexibility to evolve gradually the department into a college with four departments and undergraduate and graduate programs—each with its own faculty, curriculum, administration, and budget. Student strikers also demanded incorporating the principle of "educational relevance"—the TWLF wanted the curriculum to be "meaningful and useful to the communities" from which minority students came, and to which they planned to return to serve upon graduation. While the TWLF respected traditional boundaries of academic disciplines, they also insisted that the new Ethnic Studies Department must be interdisciplinary rather than compartmentalized in their study of minority experiences in the U.S.

After nearly two months of intense conflict and campus debate, on March 4, 1969, an urgent meeting of the Academic Senate convened to discuss the merit of ethnic studies and how it should be established. Faculty attendance was record-breaking, with over 500 members attending. Chancellor Roger Heyns pledged his commitment to the formation and implementation of an Ethnic Studies Department with four separate programs in it.

"It is the sense of the Berkeley Division of the Academic Senate that it favors the establishment of an Ethnic Studies Department *reporting directly to the chancellor* and recommends that early appointment of its chairman. *Its structure should be of sufficient flexibility to permit evolution into a College*," read the resolution that was introduced. "The Division applauds the efforts already being made by its committees in this direction and encourages all interested parties to cooperate with them and the chancellor in this effort."

The resolution passed by a vote of 550 to 5. The virtually unanimous vote was historic and reflective of the faculty's strong, if not anxious, desire to end the disruptive strike, establish the department, and return the campus to "business as usual." The chancellor and the senate made a promise that ended a painful strike and the TWLF gained partially what it had demanded. Landing on the Normandy beach on D-Day was one thing; winning Europe was the challenge ahead.

CLASH OF VISIONS AND PRINCIPLES

The very existence of Ethnic Studies at UCB immediately generated strong resistance from its inception. Who should determine the contents of the Ethnic Studies curriculum and the qualifications of its faculty? Since the founding vision, mission and principles of TWLF were fundamentally at odds with the established academic policies and practices, how should the inevitable conflicts in values and standards between Ethnic Studies, on the one hand, and the chancellor and the entrenched Senate, on the other hand, be negotiated and arbitrated? The decision-making power on budget, faculty hiring, and curriculum rested exclusively in the hands of the administration and Faculty Senate, who knew next to nothing about the field of ethnic studies about to be created. How much freedom and flexibility should the new and inexperienced department be granted to recommend faculty appointments and submit course proposals?

Clashes between the Ethnic Studies Department and the administration and Senate were inevitable, frequent, and intense in the early years. Once the TWLF Strike was over, the side with power almost always prevailed. Only rarely did the powerless win in daily battles. When conditions in the department became intolerable, students decided to use their collective power and disrupt business-as-usual through protest marches, building occupations, and hunger strikes to force the University to take their grievances and demands seriously through negotiations and compromises.

At UCB, every department is expected to be competitive with its peer institutions in the U.S. and across the world. Six independent reviews of the Ethnic Studies Department have been conducted over the past fifty years and are important records of conflicts and compromises between the department and the University. From these reviews and their recommendations, we can see clearly the clash between the TWLF principles, and the traditional policies, values, and standards of the University. Furthermore, the University used these reviews to steadily erode the TWLF principles which Ethnic Studies and its programs sought to maintain, in order to bring them into full compliance with university norms and values and assimilate them into the academic mainstream. Struggling for incremental progress, and fighting for its integrity and survival, is the story of Ethnic Studies. It would be wrong to deny significant gains made over the past fifty years and equally wrong to proclaim the TWLF mission accomplished. As we shall see, the vision and promise remain elusive and the future of Ethnic Studies uncertain still. The remainder of this essay outlines the history of Asian American Studies in the context of the development of Ethnic Studies at UCB.

THE COLLINS REVIEW

Chancellor Albert Bowker appointed Professor O'Neil Ray Collins of Botany to chair the first review committee of the Ethnic Studies Department, from 1969 to 1973. Constant struggles occurred with the UC administration over the level of budget and resource allocation; and the Academic Senate over curricula, course approval, and the degree programs. Campus administration took advantage of the inexperienced faculty and staff and erected bureaucratic obstacles at every turn.

Fortunately, student, staff, and faculty commitment to the project and its founding principles provided guidance and helped overcome the many obstacles. The enrollment in Fall Quarter of 1969, for example, was 990 in 34 courses. During Winter Quarter of 1970, enrollment grew to 1,579 in 51 courses; in Spring Quarter, 1,927 in 67 courses. A total of 4,496 students enrolled in Ethnic Studies courses in the first year, which was a far cry from the administration's exaggeratedly low projection of 200 students. Most of the early courses fell into three broad categories: service courses (reading, writing and community languages); history and identity; and community issues, all of which were aligned with the TWLF principles. But ES faculty were all part-time lecturers and its curricula rather unstable.

The Collins Committee report came out in 1973. Using long-established academic criteria to judge the department's performance, the report was supportive but critical. Its major recommendations, not surprisingly, were clearly aimed at undermining the founding principles of Ethnic Studies:

1. Strip the power of the faculty to recommend faculty appointments,
2. Separate each ethnic program as an independent department
   and move each separately into the College of Letters & Science (L&S),
3. Reduce, or eliminate, the community studies component
   of the curriculum, especially in Asian American Studies, and
4. Remove students from participating in the decision-making process.

All of these recommendations challenged the department's founding principles of autonomy, educational relevance, and solidarity among racial minorities. Sensing the handwriting on the wall, the Ethnic Studies faculty unanimously voted on October 1, 1973 to reject the committee's recommendations on the grounds that they would severely undermine the development of the department and its programs. The administration made no official response. Instead, it took the review's recommendations and quietly worked through various Senate committees.

DEPARTURE OF AFRICAN AMERICAN STUDIES

Our first crisis erupted in December 1973 when a faction of the African American Studies faculty decided to use the Collins report to work secretly to split from Ethnic Studies and move the program into the Division of Social Sciences in L&S as its own department. The major reason for this move, according to internal documents, was to gain "intellectual legitimacy" on campus and "credibility" among students. Chancellor Albert Bowker aided and abetted the move, effective July 1, 1974, although procedures for, and approval of, the transfer were incomplete. The abrupt departure of African American Studies from Ethnic Studies was a mortal blow to the solidarity among the four programs since the TWLF strike and precipitated the most serious existential crisis since the department's founding.

Could the Department and the remaining three programs survive without African American Studies? What about the College of Third World Studies? The departure of African American Studies left the other programs paralyzed and distrustful of each other, the budget decimated, and leadership and power dismantled. Both Ethnic Studies faculty and students were left angry and uncertain of their future. The faculty denounced the decision and students demonstrated against the move, calling for a boycott of African American Studies classes. The boycott fizzled after two years. During the boycott, the administration assured the faculty not to worry about decreases in course enrollment; they should instead spend their time doing research.

After the initial shock and outrage, the faculty, staff, and students of the remaining three programs eventually came together for a postmortem and response. A task force, under the leadership of Ronald Takaki of Asian American Studies, was appointed to rethink the future of the department and remaining three programs, develop a long-range plan for its renewal, and work out an effective counter-strategy for its survival and growth. It became clear that the principle of solidarity had no substance and there was no integration in administration, curricula, and faculty among the programs. A few months of intense soul-searching and planning led to a plan to reorganize the department's administration and curricula, and to share faculty.

The task force recommended a sweeping strategic plan to move incrementally towards a college, as promised by the University in 1969, and to help new faculty achieve tenure. This plan included a new series of courses on the comparative experiences of racial minorities, and most importantly, the creation of a new undergraduate comparative ethnic studies curriculum and degree program. All full-time faculty must take part in teaching these new comparative courses. In short, these reform measures provided substance and teeth to the principle of solidarity that was absent since the department began.

From 1975 to 1983, the department steadily grew. All the new courses and four degree programs gained permanent approval. However, the department conceded to the virtual elimination of community studies from its curriculum and capitulated to UC-established criteria for gaining faculty tenure. As a result, the faculty make-up changed significantly and the commitment to its founding principles was placed on the backburner.

Unfortunately, these new department reforms pitted academic interests against community ones within each program. For example, in 1976 and 1977, a painful political struggle within Asian American Studies erupted publicly between Asian American students and faculty. Some of the new faculty being hired knew little about the founding principles and mission of Ethnic Studies and had little or no ties to its communities. In fact, by early 1980, other than a few select faculty with long personal ties to and projects in the community, both the department and programs eventually ceased to have any institutional or structural links with the communities out of which the field of ethnic studies had emerged and to which it owed its existence. There was a trade-off between gains and losses.

Before we proceed to the next period, we need to pause briefly to mention a looming issue which occurred on the UCB campus in the 1980s that foreshadowed a larger issue involving Asian American admissions into competitive research universities in the twenty-first century. The arrival of the baby-boomers in colleges and universities also signaled the arrival of highly motivated and competitive Asian Americans. UCB, as a prestigious public research university, was the first choice for many Asian Americans because it welcomed them at a time when it was acceptable for comparable private and public institutions to exclude them. In the late 1970s and early 1980s, Asian American enrollment skyrocketed rapidly at a time when the research universities were under mounting pressure to admit minority students who had been historically discriminated against. The Office of Admissions decided to slow down Asian American admissions by secretly changing several admissions criteria and procedures targeting Asian American applicants in the entering class of 1984 without public knowledge and authorization. That decision precipitously caused a huge drop of 21 percent among Asian Americans between 1983 and 1984.

The drop immediately caught the attention of Asian American faculty and community members. A high-profile community group, the Asian American Task Force on University Admissions (AATFUA), was organized to deal with the administration. Judges Lillian K. Sing of San Francisco and Ken Kawaichi of Alameda county co-chaired the task force. After five years of acrimonious legislative hearings, state auditing, and faculty investigations that uncovered wrongdoing, Chancellor Ira Michael Heyman reversed the changes and apologized publicly in 1989. In 1990, Chang-lin Tien was appointed Chancellor of UCB, the first Asian American to head a research university. The admissions issue attracted national attention and added a new dimension to the ongoing national debate on affirmative action, even though AATFUA was concerned only with the unfair treatment between whites and Asians and strongly supported affirmative action.

THE BRINNER REVIEW

n stark contrast to the Collins report, the second external review, led by Professor William Brinner of Near Eastern Studies in August 6, 1980, found that the Department and its four programs (Asian American Studies, Chicano Studies, Native American Studies, and the newly established undergraduate Comparative Ethnic Studies) had become strong, stable, and comparable to other departments on campus. The review also noted that Ethnic Studies and its programs had become a valuable intellectual asset to the campus, which by then had become increasingly racially diverse.

The Brinner Committee found the Department deserving of greater institutional respect and support, including additional faculty positions, the establishment of a Ph.D. program in Comparative Ethnic Studies, and a better and more spacious library facility. In a surprising but welcome move, the committee recommended the creation of a new Division of Ethnic Studies in L&S, into which all the Ethnic Studies programs would be housed. In return for moving its programs into L&S under the new Division, the review committee urged the administration to increase the power, prestige, and autonomy of Ethnic Studies by granting all of its programs departmental status.

The new Division, headed by a dean, would have five departments: Afro-American Studies, Asian American Studies, Chicano Studies, Native American Studies, and Comparative Ethnic Studies. The recommendation in effect called for the reunification of African American Studies with Ethnic Studies under the new Division, thus making Ethnic Studies equal in rank with the other four sister Divisions: Social Science, Humanities, Physical Science, and Biological Science. If the recommendations were to be accepted by the UC administration, it would move Ethnic Studies one step closer to becoming a college, the original vision of the TWLF.

Initially, the administration enthusiastically embraced the report and foresaw the important role Ethnic Studies would play in the changing student demographics. However, the leadership of the largely conservative Faculty Senate responded negatively. It moved swiftly to discredit the Brinner report by appointing an *ad hoc* Executive Committee to review the review. The *ad hoc* committee chose to ignore the Brinner report and its recommendations on May 27, 1981. Instead, the new committee proposed the further breakup of the Department by urging each program to separately become a department and move into the Division of Social Sciences. It also opposed giving additional faculty positions and more space to the overcrowded Ethnic Studies library.

The Faculty Senate's negative response did not deter the Ethnic Studies Department from using the Brinner Committee recommendations as a road map for new initiatives. Professor Barbara Christian and I, as chairs of African American Studies and Ethnic Studies, initiated our first joint faculty meeting in six years. Two concrete cooperative projects were established: co-sponsorship of the first Ph.D. degree program and a proposal to establish a campus-wide Ethnic Studies breadth requirement for all undergraduates. Through this joint effort, the first cohort of seven graduate students entered the Ph.D. program in 1985.

The Ethnic Studies breadth requirement proposal faced stiff political challenges, going through two years of intense campus scrutiny. A Special Senate Committee on Education and Ethnicity was appointed to study the proposal. After two years of extensive campus-wide meetings and negotiations, the University reached a compromise on May 28, 1989: a new breadth requirement for all undergraduate students called "American Cultures." The new requirement aimed to teach students about how the U.S. was a country made up of Native Americans and immigrants from all continents, nations, and cultures of the world—all of whom contributed to the creation of a new and unique nation. In short, the requirement called for new understandings of new American identity and history and the diversification of the curriculum across disciplines. Since its institutionalization, no less than 400 courses have been certified across the campus. By far it has been one of the most profound curricular innovations in American higher education and an enduring contribution ES can be proud of.

STRUGGLE AND SURVIVAL

In April 1989, a small but influential group of mostly senior faculty, in uncharacteristically blunt language, circulated a paper on campus denouncing the administration's support of diversity programs such as affirmative action, Ethnic Studies, American Cultures, and Women's Studies. They claimed that such programs existed at the expense of "educational and scholarly standards." What really troubled these aging white senior faculty was the rapid demographic shift from a predominantly white to a predominantly minority student body. These minority students considered the University, its faculty, and curricula out of touch with the experiences and intellectual interests of post-World War II baby-boomers and post-1965 immigrants from Asia and Latin America. Under the leadership of Chancellor Ira Heyman, the enrollment in all four Ethnic Studies programs grew rapidly as minorities became the majority within the undergraduate population, a result of the effectiveness of the University's affirmative action program. The racial and gender mix of the UCB faculty had likewise changed, though not fast enough. The white male faculty felt increasingly marginalized, sensed a loss of power and control of *their* institution, and decided to openly resist the change. Needless to say, they remained securely in control of both the administration and the faculty senate.

In 1991, Ethnic Studies once again came under review by another external committee. It was co-chaired by Professors Carol Stack of Education and Gwen Kirkpatrick of Spanish and Portuguese. In May 1992, the committee gave the Department a favorable evaluation and recommended additional faculty positions, an organized research unit (ORU), and a new facility for its library. However, it backed away from the Brinner recommendation of an L&S Division of Ethnic Studies. The Department also found itself caught between a rock and a hard place. Ethnic Studies obviously needed more faculty and financial resources at a time when it also faced a 10 percent mandatory budget cut caused by the 1990 recession. On July 28, 1994, Provost and Dean of the College of Letters & Science Carol Christ decided to move Ethnic Studies which had been located in the Office of the Chancellor since 1969 into the L&S Division of Social Sciences to become a downsized Department of Comparative Ethnic Studies, and consolidated the management and staffing of all of its programs. In effect, Ethnic Studies found its original four programs severely weakened and in the process, its autonomy and identities. She even hosted a lavish reception at the Faculty Club to welcome Ethnic Studies into the embrace of L&S. The faculty was left with two options: resist or surrender. They opted for the latter. With that, the TWLF dream of a college was dashed—the Faculty Senate's historic promise broken and its future vulnerable and uncertain. It is no wonder that the faculty and staff were left demoralized.

The administration was well aware of a number of senior faculty fast approaching retirement age when the decision was made to force Ethnic Studies and its programs into the Division of Social Science in L&S. The first wave of retirements had already started: Ronald Takaki, Mario Barrera, Carlos Munoz, Jr., Margarita Melville, and Gerald Vizenor. Not too far behind was the second cohort made up of myself, Elaine Kim, Sau-ling Wong, Norma Alarcón, Alex Saragoza, Beatriz Manz, and Patricia Hilton. The first wave hit Chicano Studies the hardest, while the second hurt mostly Asian American Studies. Time and attrition were on the side of the administration, if the intention was to slowly weaken Ethnic Studies and its programs.

In response to the lack of classes offered by Chicano Studies in Spring 1999, a group of mainly Chicanos and others, including Asian Americans, whites, and African Americans, without prior warning, occupied the entrance to Barrows Hall, which housed the offices of Ethnic Studies and its programs, on the afternoon of April 14, 1999. Soon, they were joined by students from other programs and Ethnic Studies graduate students, who also challenged the dwindling number of faculty. To these students, the administration was letting Ethnic Studies die by way of attrition.

The students sent Chancellor Robert Berdahl a set of demands in support of Ethnic Studies and other issues affecting campus climate and minority student life. Among the demands were:

1. Increased funding for Ethnic Studies and each of the programs within Ethnic Studies, while maintaining respect for the autonomy of each Ethnic Studies program,
2. Admission of more underrepresented minority students,
3. An Ethnic Studies Research Center,
4. A multicultural student center,
5. Student participation in the decision-making process in Ethnic Studies programs, and
6. No punishment of students arrested for their civil disobedience protests

The chancellor, however, refused to meet with the student protestors as long as the occupation persisted. After a ten-hour occupation, with several students being injured, the police arrested and cited 43 students.

As the chair of Ethnic Studies, I had consistently expressed my concerns regarding the steady decline of its faculty strength and course offerings. In fact, in the budget statement I submitted to the administration the year prior, I warned of the eventual demise of the department if the budget cuts persisted and the positions of retired faculty were left vacant. I therefore had no hesitation in supporting the legitimate protest and demands of the students. Within an hour of the occupation, I addressed the protesters and expressed my full support of their demands. Subsequently, I issued a long statement endorsed by the Ethnic Studies faculty. Separately, the African American Studies faculty also announced their support of the demands.

On April 29, 1999, the student protest expanded into a hunger strike in front of the chancellor's office at California Hall, beginning at midnight. Three days into the hunger strike, a mysterious flyer surfaced in front of California Hall after midnight, claiming that "Chairman Wang no longer supports the hunger strike" and that "he urges the students to end the strike." I was stunned and deeply hurt by the false flyer, and immediately concluded it was a Nixonian "political dirty trick," instigated by someone in the administration whose sole purpose was to provoke division between students and faculty, and among the faculty. The next morning, I angrily confronted the chancellor. In response, he apologized but offered no explanation. Later that same day, he called me to apologize again. But again, no explanation.

After five days of the hunger strike and orderly protest, the chancellor decided to remove the striking students in a surprise pre-dawn police sweep. The police moved in and arrested 80 students, tore down their tents, and removed all of their posters, banners, and picket signs. The arrested students were taken to the Alameda County Jail in Santa Rita, where many of the 1969 striking students were also incarcerated.

To the surprise of the administration, in an impressive demonstration of multiracial and multidisciplinary solidarity, several hundred students from departments and schools across the campus turned up to protest and volunteered to be arrested the next night. When interviewed, several said they did it for the future of Ethnic Studies and for their children. By then, the administration realized that it had to negotiate in good faith with the students if the protest was to end peacefully. On May 7, 1999, with the help of Professor Robert Brentano of History, then-Chair of the Faculty Senate, an all-day negotiation between the protest leaders, faculty, and administration began and concluded before midnight with an agreement signed by the chancellor, Professor Brentano, and myself. The agreement contained the following six points:

1. Eight new faculty positions in the next five years,
2. Financial support to start a research center,
3. Financial support to sustain the curricular offerings of Ethnic Studies,
4. A multicultural student center and a space for a wall mural,
5. Additional financial support for student recruitment, and
6. Leniency for students arrested.

In an interview the next day, a journalist asked me if I wished to declare victory. I declined on the grounds that the department "only succeeded with regaining what it was entitled to have: the vacancies resulted from retirement."

To help implement the agreement, the administration appointed a committee, made up of mostly Ethnic Studies faculty and chaired by Professor Brentano, to help chart the future of the department and implement the promises made by the chancellor. The Brentano report for "faculty renewal" was issued on June 12, 2000, and the commitments made in the agreement were gradually carried out over the next ten years. The positions vacated by retired faculty were slowly filled over several years; the Center for Race and Gender (CRG) was established in 2001; and the Multicultural Community Center (MCC) for students was opened in 2007. The wall mural is expected to be installed in Spring 2019, inside Barrows Hall, the site of the student sit-in to save Ethnic Studies.

On July 1, 2010, amidst the new energy injected into the department, the Asian American Studies program changed its name to Asian American and Asian Diaspora Studies (AAADS). This significant renaming was necessary to reflect the changing conditions of Asian American communities and the multilevel and multinational links with communities worldwide, as a result of rapid globalization and out-migration of Asians throughout the globe. Under the leadership of Elaine Kim, the change was made possible and finally approved after two years of discussion, consultation, and reviews.

CONTRIBUTIONS TO THE FIELD AND THE FUTURE OF ETHNIC STUDIES AND AAADS

When the field of Asian American studies was established fifty years ago, virtually nothing of substance was written about the experiences, cultures, and communities of various Asian American groups. A few books and articles, here and there, discussed the exclusionary movements directed against Chinese and Japanese and about their assimilation in the first half of the twentieth century. Most provided, at best, only partial coverage, and almost all were written for whites and from white perspectives. Like the various and successive exclusion laws enacted to keep each Asian subgroup out of the U.S., the experiences of Asian immigrants were effectively erased from the pages of American history and American studies, just like the experiences of Native Americans, African Americans, and Chicanos/Latinos.

Once the program was established, the faculty and students of Asian American Studies, like

Commemorating TWLF 50th at UC Berkeley, undergraduate Joanne Yi with t-shirt imprinted: "What Happened to Asian American Studies?" spoke about the need to fight against the cutbacks to the program. Imprinted on the back of the t-shirt: "What Happened to the Third World College," pointing out that the struggle at UC Berkeley is incomplete.

Aztec Dancers open the 50th Anniversary of the TWLF Strike at UC Berkeley.

the faculty of the other three Ethnic Studies programs, took on the task of unearthing their past, and restoring and revealing the hidden dynamism and creativity of their communities in the arts, sciences, and literature that have enriched American life. The program trained many scholars to become teachers in ethnic and Asian American studies in universities and colleges across the U.S. Their contributions fundamentally changed American studies and Americans' knowledge and understanding of Asian Americans.

For example, both Ron Takaki (*Strangers from a Different Shore: A History of Asian Americans*, 1989) and Sucheng Chan (*Asian Americans: An Interpretive History*, 1991) wrote seminal books on the history of Asian America and books on Asian American subgroups; Chan also edited more than fifty books on various aspects of Asian American history and life through Temple University Press. Elaine Kim and Sau-ling Wong established Asian American literature as a vital component and subfield of American literature and uncovered American literature in Asian languages. L. Ling-chi Wang identified and pursued civil rights issues at home and transnational links of Asian America in the diaspora, and developed a paradigm for studying Asian American history and community issues. Loni Ding helped translate the past and emerging Asian American ideas into powerful images in videos and films. Michael Omi called attention to the importance of race in the study of American society, politics, and culture. Khatharya Um wrote the definitive book on the refugees from Cambodia and helped advance the rights and welfare of Cambodian and Southeast Asian Americans from and within Southeast Asia. America's knowledge and views of Asian Americans have changed significantly with the advent of Asian American Studies at UCB.

As the twentieth century reached its end, it was fitting for the Ethnic Studies Department

UC Berkeley 1969 TWLF representatives from the Afro-American Students Union (AASU), Asian American Political Alliance (AAPA), Mexican-American Students Confederation (MASC), and Native American Students Union (NASU) and others commemorated the 50th Anniversary of the TWLF strike and subsequent generations who continued the struggle. Pictured: Maria Ramirez, Betty Kano, Jeff Leong, LaNada War Jack, Vicci Wong, Jean Quan, Veronica Macias, Ysidro Martinez, Oliver Jones, Floyd Huen, Nina Genera, Steve Wong, Harvey Dong, Eddie Zheng.

Eddie Zheng, co-director of Asian Prisoners Support Committee, was a former San Quentin prison inmate who was inspired by ethnic studies while taking classes from Asian American student volunteers. He circulated a petition to demand that prisons teach ethnic studies and was punished for it by being sentenced to 11 months in solitary confinement.

to have the Brentano report help chart its future, and to ponder its role in ever-changing race relations on campus, in the U.S., and the world of the twenty-first century. The stunning election of gentlemanly, bright, and visionary Barack Obama, the first African American to become President of the United States, brought not just tears and jubilation, but high hopes that he would help usher in a new era of civility in all aspects of American life, and lead the nation towards the gradual elimination of racism—a cancer in American democracy.

That turned out not to be the case. Partisanship turned mean spirited and vulgar as Republicans who had the majority in both houses of the U.S. Congress and Republican appointees in the majority on the U.S. Supreme Court declared an all-out war on the Obama legacy and were determined to dismantle democratic institutions, one by one, by any means necessary. Political discourse turned personal, strident, and ugly, paving the way not just for the election of Donald Trump in 2016, but for the deepening of racial, gender, and class divides, and the rapid ascendancy or resurgence of racism, ultranationalism, and international isolationism. The bully pulpit of the presidency became the source of lies, fake news, and fabricated facts, as President Trump declared the free press and law enforcement agencies as "enemies of the people." Sadly, "the law of the jungle" now governs the U.S. and dictates the U.S. approach to the international order.

In the face of such unprecedented and massive social and political upheavals, what has happened to the Ethnic Studies Department established fifty years ago to address issues of racial inequality and economic injustice? As the nation deals with pressing issues—such as Black Lives Matter, the rise of white nationalism and neo-Nazism, the #MeToo movement, mass deportation of immigrants, the Muslim ban, "The Wall," immigrant children being separated from parents, massive voter suppression, trade wars, etc.—why are the voices and perspectives of ethnic studies so conspicuously missing in the national debates? Has the University been so successful in silencing and assimilating the department and its programs that they are no longer distinguishable from other departments in social sciences and humanities across the campus? What happened to the vision, founding principles, autonomous governance, relevant curriculum, students, and community engagements? Will Ethnic Studies and AAADS survive the onslaught of budget cuts, white nationalism, and ethnic cleansing? These are timely and sobering questions we must raise as we celebrate and reflect on our role in the University, the nation, and the world.

The fiftieth anniversary of Asian American Studies at UCB is indeed a time for celebration. We have reasons to take pride in the intellectual and political gains we have made over the past fifty years. But it is also a time for self-reflection, renewal, and recommitment. The TWLF founding principles and mission have served us well. Fifty years ago, we put our education and indeed, our lives and future, on the line not just to establish Ethnic Studies and its programs, but also to lay claim to our legitimate place in this institution and this country to obtain racial equality, justice, and peace. Now more than ever, our university, communities, nation, and world have never been more urgently in need of Asian American and ethnic studies' voices, leadership, research, and engagement. The struggle that began fifty years ago must continue.

CHAPTER 5

STILL RELEVANT TODAY

CHANGING THE WORLD

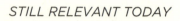

HARVEY DONG

PHOTO BY GILBERT HOM

Harvey Dong working on a graphic layout of Wei Min, Chinese Community News in 1971 at Asian Community Center.

ASIAN COMMUNITY CENTER ARCHIVES

n 1967, I had been involved in the Stop the Draft Week (STDW) protests that took place in front of the Oakland Army Induction Center. In front of the Center, thousands of anti-war demonstrators gathered to stop the processing of army inductees. There were two groups who were protesting at this time. One was a sit-in led by singer Joan Baez, which was peacefully removed and arrested by police in front of the media. A second, and much larger group, was more determined to shut down the Center and did not comply with the authorities so quickly. These protesters were attacked by police who swung their batons from above the shoulders downward. I was pretty shocked to see police officers assaulting non-violent demonstrators using nightsticks and mace in the pitch dark. The following year, another STDW took place. Many, including myself, went to the army surplus store to purchase helmets to protect our skulls from injury. Young people were determined to end the killing in Vietnam and didn't want to be drafted to fight in an unjust war.

During this time, the anti-war movement was merging with the Black Power movement, represented by the Black Panther Party, which strongly opposed U.S. involvement in Vietnam. The Black Panthers spoke at rallies connecting oppression at home with imperialism overseas. Bay Area anti-war marches had dual goals: to end the war and to free jailed Black Panther Party leader Huey P. Newton. I attended a packed, full-house "Free Huey" rally at the Oakland Kaiser Auditorium (now Oakland Civic Auditorium) that featured national Black Power spokespersons including H. Rap Brown and James Foreman from the Student Nonviolent Coordinating Committee (SNCC). There were very few Asian faces at the STDW planning meetings and Panther support rallies. At the STDW meetings, I remember two who were later active in the Third World Liberation Front (TWLF) Strike at UC Berkeley (UCB). Later I met two more STDW Asians in the UCB TWLF Strike who were members of the Asian American Political Alliance (AAPA).

My parents knew about my involvement in the anti-war movement and support for the Black Panthers. Whenever I returned home to Sacramento, I brought political literature, including Black Panther newspapers. They were a little alarmed and concerned about whether I would graduate. Sometimes there were reports of riots in Berkeley, and they wondered if I had gotten into trouble. At the same time, they knew they couldn't really do much about it because I had pretty much moved out of the house and was figuring out the world on my own. Before my mother passed away, I got to learn more about her life in China.

CHINA AND CHINATOWN

t age four, my mom was left behind in China by her parents because they prioritized boys coming over [to the U.S.] instead of girls. Her whole family was in the U.S. while she was left behind in the village in China in the care of her aunt. My mom's birth slot was given to a male cousin who entered the U.S. as a paper son. Because of the Chinese Exclusion Act of 1883, using false immigration papers was one of the few immigration alternatives.

The Sino-Japanese War, which began in 1937, ended at the same time as the end of World War II in 1945. During this period in China, my mom's teacher recruited her to be an agitator, going from village to village giving speeches and calling on people not to give up the fight against Japan. She would be the one to fire up the crowd at the rallies—a little girl getting up on a chair, raising her fist, and giving a speech. She was very proud of what she did during the war. When she came to the U.S., my mother first worked in the canneries and then later learned enough English to get a clerical job. She was involved in the California State Employees Union and wasn't afraid to give speeches at rallies.

My dad was the opposite. More reserved. He grew up in Sacramento Chinatown during Chinese exclusion and was the eldest son raised by a single mom, my grandmother. My grandfather died when my dad was nine years old, so he had a heavy burden to carry. His proudest achievement was that he finished high school level Chinese school. He was able to read newspapers and Chinese classics, and wrote letters for my grandmother to family overseas. Every Chinese New Year, my grandmother would have him write and send a letter with $50 inside to his aunt in Malaysia, who was employed as a servant. I have the address memorized: 44 Madras Road, Penang.

Harvey Dong and brother Al at home, Sacramento, CA.

My father went to City College in Sacramento and was drafted into the U.S. military to fight in the Philippines during World War II. The Allied Powers had consolidated victory in the Philippines and were preparing for a large-scale invasion of Japan when the atomic bombs were dropped on Hiroshima and Nagasaki. The atomic bombs cancelled the invasion that would have involved my father and uncle.

Through introductions, my father met my mother, and he was able to bring her over to the U.S. as a fiancée under the War Brides Act. After arriving, my mom had thirty days to decide whether or not to marry my dad, or return back to China. Coming over as a war bride enabled my mom to reunite with her parents, plus meet her five American-born siblings. They were all surprised that she was so outspoken, but in looking back at what she went through in China, it wasn't so surprising.

Our family first lived in downtown Sacramento, near Chinatown, and later, five miles away in South Sacramento. In downtown, my grandmother owned a three-unit building. She lived upstairs, we lived on the second floor, and my cousins lived downstairs. My grandmother purchased the property with savings from her cannery and fruit harvest jobs. Because of the Alien Land Laws, she could not buy the property in her own name and placed legal ownership under an American-born relative. We moved out to our own place, a newly-built home in South Sacramento. Using a GI housing loan, my father was able to skirt racial housing covenants by buying directly from a fellow veteran, a white man, who sold to Chinese.

PHOTOGRAPHS (ABOVE AND AT RIGHT) BY STEVE LOUIE, WEI MIN SHE AND ASIAN COMMUNITY
CENTER PHOTOGRAPHS, ETHNIC STUDIES LIBRARY, UC BERKELEY

At top: *Activities blackboard in the Asian Community Center with references to the April 22 Coalition Against the War and other tasks.*
Bottom: *Quotation from Chairman Mao "On Youth" posted on an ACC wall.*
At right: *A celebration gathering.*

This was the 1950s, and though there was some integration, Asians were not fully accepted. Our family still participated in the traditional Chinese social organizations. We celebrated the Chinese holidays and we attended Chinese school. Every day, the school bus would pick me up in the late afternoon and meander throughout Sacramento to bring us to Chinese school.

Although we lived in an integrated community, I grew up not really feeling accepted by the whites. I got along with white kids who lived on my block, but if I walked through another neighborhood, I would get called "ching chong" and sometimes threatened. Their parents did not teach them any better, or perhaps the children parroted their parents' views. Many of the taunts were related to the past wars in Asia, which in their minds were still going on.

When I attended my first day of junior high school, a group of white kids yelled racial slurs at me regarding the building of the railroad. I had inadvertently sat at an empty lunch table later claimed by six racist white males. They made fun of me for being a coolie railroad worker, and about how I traveled from China to work on the railroad. Seated the entire time, I ate my lunch and humility.

The next day, I avoided the cafeteria and sat alone on the outer bleachers. Several of the kids from the same group spotted me and proceeded with more racial taunting but this time, I responded differently. One of them smashed my lunch. I remember jumping on top of the lunch smasher with my hands around his neck. He panicked, yelling for help. I wasn't bothered by that person again.

Most of my friends were Asian and we hung out together for friendship and survival. Sports, dances, parties. . .and later, learning kung fu. There were a few kung fu practitioners who taught ABC (American Born Chinese) kids. I remember two I took lessons from in Sacramento. Lucky Chan was a grocery worker who taught Choy Li Fut classes behind the Chinese school during the summer. Leo Fong, a Baptist preacher and professional softball player from Arkansas, taught classes at the Firemen's Hall. My cousins organized a brick breaking club and to join, you had to break two bricks with your palm.

COLLEGE AND STUDY

I did okay in my college studies—not straight A's, but I was able to pass my classes. My parents were pretty happy that I had moved out of the house. When I was in high school, we had conflicts over how I spent my time. They would have specific ideas, and I wanted more freedom. When I got accepted to UCB, I didn't know exactly what I was getting into but welcomed the opportunity. I planned the move and packed all my stuff. I figured I'd better not bring too much just in case I flunked out and had to bring it all back. I just filled up a suitcase and moved into the dorm. I got to know people there. There were ROTC (Reserved Officers' Training Corps) army cadets on my floor. Following the example of an uncle, I joined the ROTC, where scholarships were granted to cadets to finish their upper division years.

That was my mindset in 1966. I grew up hearing stories from uncles and father about how the military got the Chinese community out of isolation. Education and housing were provided for returning GIs. The house I grew up in was through one of the GI housing loans. The realtor would not sell to us because we were Chinese, but the contractor did because he was a GI veteran like my father.

By 1967, I was opposed to the Vietnam War. I had done a lot of reading and study about why the U.S. should not have been involved in Vietnam. Cody's Books was near my dorm and I'd find books there. There were also lively discussions with fellow classmates over the war. In ROTC convocations, cadets were told by the military instructors, who were Korean War veterans, to not stop by the political literature tables on Sproul Plaza because the groups there were communists.

"If it walks like a duck, it's a duck," commented one instructor regarding the literature tables being a possible communist "front group."

AAPA NEWS / ASIAN COMMUNITY CENTER ARCHIVES

SF State TWLF picket line in which AAPA Berkeley participated, 1969.

"When Charlie comes at you, you have to be ready. We are here to get you ready," was another comment that stuck in my mind.

One time at rifle practice, a cadet hit the bullseye and stated with glee, "I just shot a Gook."

I dropped out of ROTC and attended Stop the Draft Week meetings in 1967. STDW later organized into small groups that met weekly to discuss politics. My ideas were shaped by this involvement. There was government repression after STDW and some of the leaders were being tried for conspiracy. The repression only served to bond those who participated.

When word got out that I was participating in anti-war activities, a few conservative Asian Americans in the dorms threatened me. Someone's cousin, who was in the Marines, threatened to come to campus to kick my ass. What the hell? People were dying in an unjust war and I was being threatened for opposing it? I was willing to talk to the "cousin" but the encounter never happened.

I also became concerned with issues affecting the Asian American community and began to investigate what could be done. The Black Panthers emphasized this idea of a "rainbow coalition" and the need for people of color to do work in their own communities. In fall 1968, I became active tutoring immigrant youth in San Francisco Chinatown. The project was organized by the UCB Chinese Students Club whose Social Action Committee posted notices about the project. My friend Steve Wong and I went to San Francisco Chinatown every Wednesday to tutor and hang out afterwards. We visited Leways on Jackson Street, a youth-based self-help enterprise involving a soda fountain and pool hall. Many Leways members would later radicalize to form the Red Guard Party. We also visited the ICSA (Intercollegiate Chinese for Social Action) headquarters on Clay Street to check out the youth programs that were organized by San Francisco State College (now San Francisco State University, or SF State) students.

Some of the young people we tutored were Steve's nieces. We also had relatives we bumped into who worked in the garment shops and tourist stores. This experience helped put together ideas about what later became steps towards linking Asian American studies to the community. Big changes were already taking place in the community. That same summer, a march against Chinatown poverty involved many community progressives, youth, and students. The march blasted the Chinese Six Companies (Chinese Consolidated Benevolent Association) for promoting the myth that social problems didn't exist in Chinatown. This got all over the news.

FORMING AAPA

Asian American Political Alliance (AAPA) founder Yuji Ichioka and his wife Emma Gee were civil rights workers in the American South. They wanted to bring the political activism of the anti-Vietnam War movement and the Black Power movement to the Asian American community. The term "Asian American" that we all take for granted today was coined by Yuji at a founding AAPA meeting in his Berkeley apartment back in May 1968.

Joining AAPA was the first time I was working with politically active Asian Americans who wanted to radically change the world. Around October 1968, I attended an Asian Studies 100X information session. AAPA members were working with Professors Paul Takagi and Franz Schurmann to develop a new course on the "Asian Experience in America." Professors Takagi and Schurmann co-sponsored the class but it was actually taught by graduate students Bing Thom, Ling-chi Wang, Richard Aoki, and Wai-Kit Quan, all of whom were AAPA members.

A number of meetings took place to recruit interested students. At one gathering, individuals took turns introducing themselves and what their views were about the need for Asian American political involvement. Steve Wong and I attended one such meeting where the two of us may have been among the few "newbies" present. Eyes were on us. Steve mentioned something about how he was religious and believed in a single world religion. I don't remember what I said, but it was the first time I had heard Steve's thoughts on world religion.

AAPA was diverse, with members from San Francisco Chinatown, Sacramento, the Salinas Valley, and Los Angeles. There were mixed-race members. There were members from Hong Kong who held strong anti-colonial feelings. There was Richard Aoki, a founding member of the Black Panther Party. Everyone in AAPA was focused on the idea that we needed an Asian American studies that served student and community needs. AAPA was also one of the organizations involved in the Chinatown anti-poverty protests.

TWLF strike picket line on Sproul Steps, UC Berkeley; Harvey Dong in left panel (black jacket and black rimmed glasses)

Volunteering to build a youth center in LA Chinatown.

THE IDEA OF ASIAN AMERICAN STUDIES

I became committed to the idea of Asian American studies, or "Asian studies" as it was called then. Many old-timers, such as me, automatically refer to Asian American studies as "Asian studies." That's how one can tell what period they became involved. Now, the name has been changed to Asian American and Asian Diaspora Studies (AAADS) at UCB. The idea for calling the department Asian Studies was to take back the state department-focused "Asian Studies" term, and to bring anti-colonial, anti-imperialist, and anti-orientalist meanings to it.

The Yellow Symposium ("The Asian Experience in American/Yellow Identity") was held in the Pauley Ballroom at UCB on January 11, 1969. The symposium was sponsored by the Chinese Students Club, Nisei Students Club, AAPA, and others. Students and instructors visited from other campuses, with some as far away as Hawai'i and New York. By the time the conference was over, many campus organizations, such as Oriental Concern (Sansei Concern), had also changed their names to AAPA. George Woo and Laureen Chew from SF State called on symposium attendees to support the SF State TWLF Strike, and to bring the strike issues and demands back to their own locales and campuses. Many UCB AAPA members went over to support the TWLF Strike at SF State.

On January 22, 1969, the TWLF at UCB struck for a Third World College. On March 13, 1969, a strike moratorium was called to establish an interim Department of Ethnic Studies with programs in Asian Studies, African American Studies, Chicano Studies, and Native American Studies. Negotiations were to continue towards a Third World College but this became waylaid. In 1974, the African American Studies program left the Ethnic Studies Department to form their own in the College of Letters & Science. This was opposed by many

Community protest against Chinese Times news editorial that denounced the I-Hotel struggle. From left: William Fong, Olden Ng, Mr. Jeung, Mr. Lee, Harvey Dong.

African American students and instructors, but the chancellor was successful in pulling it off. By this time, the TWLF Strike momentum was gone and could no longer exert political pressure of any significance on the university administration.

With a small budget in the beginning, Asian Studies at UCB had to be creative. Those who were paid higher salaries put their monies into a pool so that more jobs could be created. Because students were involved in the struggle to establish Asian Studies, they were passionate about making sure that it would succeed. The program was not a top-down hierarchical program, but one based on a student-advisory council that worked in conjunction with the Asian Studies coordinator and staff.

THE ELDERLY AND ALLEYWAYS

Community work was always an important component of the Third World College idea. To me, it meant learning from the masses for the purpose of serving the people. We tried to do this in different ways, with varying degrees of success. After the TWLF Strike, I worked at Self-Help for the Elderly, located on Old Chinatown Lane in San Francisco. Three of us who were involved in the TWLF Strike were now working at Self-Help: me, Steven Wong, and Victor Wong.

We did case work where we went into SRO (single room occupancy) homes to check up on elderly residents. I had the assignment of regularly checking up on an elderly Chinese man who suffered from dementia and had to remind him to take his medications. He would be yelling and cursing loudly in Portsmouth Square, and I would have to bring him back to his room to take his medication.

Conditions for seniors were bad. Kitchen facilities were limited. Dozens of tenants shared small kitchens and bathrooms. The cramped quarters led to friction. Many elderly we visited were sick and suffering in their own rooms. We were the only ones checking up on them. I remember one elderly lady in bed, crying and weeping, in need of care. Another elderly couple was more cheerful but suffered from mental issues, hoarding junk up to the ceiling.

Sam Yuen, Self-Help's director, was an affable man. He wore a vest and coat and would constantly flicker his eyes, which I think was a condition related to being overworked. To stay calm, he would fill tobacco into his pipe, light it up, and take puffs. He had to put out a lot of emergency fires related to the elderly crisis and was happy to have us former strikers as interns. We helped provide a little more reinforcement. Sam told me about how all this poverty couldn't be solved by his agency and that the problem was *systemic.* He told me that what we did during the strike, including the violence, was good. He cited Frederick Douglass: "If there is no struggle, there is no progress."

Eventually, Steven went on to teach the "Asian Communities" course in Asian Studies at UCB. Victor later contracted tuberculosis (TB) from the Self-Help job and had to quit. San Francisco Chinatown had one of the highest TB rates in the nation, as well as suicide. I stayed on at Self-Help to work on an alley renovation project with the Chinatown-North Beach Youth Council and Chinatown Neighborhood Design.

I became close with the "Team 40" youth group that was assigned the job of restoring the alleyway. The work entailed cleaning alleys, painting walls, building benches for seniors to sit on, and planting Chinese bamboo plants in large barrels. It was a challenge working with these youth. I'd organize them to paint the alley walls, only to turn around and find that I was the only one slinging the paint. After each day of work, we would hang out. Working at Self-Help allowed me to become acquainted with community youth and the elderly.

亞洲聯合中心：

我們看到我們的社會和家庭的破裂.

我們看到我們的營養不足,生肺病,自殺率高.

我們看到我們文化上的自尊被摧毀.

我們看到我們孤獨年光的一群被遺忘.

我們看到我們青年在校中反社會中受到種族歧視.

我們看到我們的父母為生活而被迫去做毫無意義的工作.

我們看到美國社會在阻止我們去得到我們生活上的需要.

我們需要適當的住屋,醫療服務,工作及教育.

我們認為：所有亞洲人必須合作,共同去解決我們社會的問題.

必須使人民了解實況,一致採取直接行動.

我們會採取一切人民認為需要的行動.

The Asian Community Center:

What We See—

    We see the breakdown of our community and families.
    We see our people suffering from malnutrition, tuberculosis,
    and high suicide rates.
    We see the destruction of our cultural pride.
    We see our elderly forgotten and alone.
    We see our youth subjected to racism in the classroom and in
    the streets.
    We see our Mothers and Fathers forced into meaningless jobs
    to make a living.
    We see American society preventing us from fulfilling our needs.

What We Want—

    We want adequate housing, medical care, employment, and
    education.

What We Believe—

    To solve our community problems, all Asian people must work
    together.
    Our people must be educated to move collectively for direct
    action.
    We will employ any effective means that our people see
    necessary.

ASIAN COMMUNITY CENTER ARCHIVES

A youth program, food program, and film series for elders were some of the many services provided by the Asian Community Center.

国际妇女节

...TE INTERNATIONAL
...OMEN'S DAY

*Harvey Dong raises his fist with Jung Sai Garment and Lee Mah Electronic workers
celebrating International Women's Day in 1974 in SF Chinatown.*

CHANGES ON KEARNY STREET

The UCB Asian Studies program found an office and meeting space in San Francisco Chinatown-Manilatown. Self-Help for the Elderly originally shared a meeting hall space with the United Filipino Association (UFA) at 832 Kearny Street, in the Victory Building, next to the International Hotel (I-Hotel). The UFA represented the I-Hotel tenants in an eviction dispute against the property owners, Milton Meyer & Co. After the signing of the lease between UFA and Milton Meyer & Co., UFA moved out of 832 Kearny Street and into the I-Hotel. Self-Help then subleased the space to the UCB Asian Studies program, and eventually moved to a new space. By February 1970, the location was solely rented out as the Asian Studies Field Office (ASFO).

Many projects originally shared that fairly large location, which had its own meeting hall, office area, large kitchen, and rooms for activities. Asian Studies classes were held at this location. Students interested in doing community field work used the office. The Chinatown Cooperative Garment Factory had a space in the location. In the evenings, many elderly utilized the office as a drop-in center. Daily meals were cooked by a Chinese chef who collected 50 cents per meal from the other community workers on the Kearny Street block: the Asian Legal Services and Draft Help, and Kearny Street Workshop.

The core of the ASFO were former AAPA members. AAPA would fold later in 1970 for a number of reasons. The intensity of strike activities was over and many members were involved in maintaining the institutional demands to legitimize Asian Studies. Others who did not agree with the outcome of the strike, in accepting an interim Department of Ethnic Studies and not a Third World College, stopped coming to meetings. Foreign-born AAPA members no longer saw a role in the U.S. and returned to Hong Kong, Taiwan, and other parts of Asia. One couple settled in Singapore, only to have all their political books confiscated by the police.

For myself and a few others, we left campus and began the next phase of the struggle by becoming more rooted in the community. There were discussions about this, and I remember being told that we shouldn't abandon what we began on campus. Some of the community youth who were in the same room when these discussions were held, were upset at proposals to drop our community work and return back to campus. I took on the position that our future was the community.

SINKING ROOTS

One of the last contributions by AAPA was the opening of Everybody's Bookstore on Kearny Street on January 1, 1970. Seed monies from AAPA members were collected to open the first Asian American bookstore in the U.S. There weren't many Asian American books in print at that time, and many of the books needed in classes had to be reprinted in copy shops. Some authors who did have printed works would bring them to resell at Everybody's. The bookstore became a community institution that challenged the more conservative community establishment.

By summer 1970, the Asian Studies Field Office eventually changed its name to Asian Community Center (ACC) to make it a more community-based organization. Programs and roots were being developed with confidence while relations with campus were no longer that amiable. The rent was being supported by elderly Chinatown residents who donated on a monthly basis. How this all started was that an ACC member went to Portsmouth Square and noticed that even during the rain, the elderly men would still sit outdoors in the park because they had no place to go. We invited them down to ACC to get away from the bad weather. Soon we had programs and activities celebrating Chinese holidays, film screenings, and Mandarin classes. There were even food giveaways arranged by Loni Ding. There would be lines of cars in front, and volunteers would assist in loading them with surplus government food.

The conservative Chinatown establishment, their media, and organizations began to accuse us of being communists. One newspaper wrote that we were "the new Red Guards." We ran a film program, and when we started showing films related to the People's Republic of China, and promoting U.S.-China relations, we began to receive death threats. Some of the seniors, concerned about the Center's safety, brought their guns to events and sat near the door. One elder in his late eighties, with thick eyeglasses, carried a .25 caliber pistol. The elders had gone through Chinese exclusion and McCarthy periods, and were hopeful that ACC would be able to survive. They encouraged us to learn kung fu and brought us around to match us with local martial arts sifus (teachers). It was funny—after an intense workout, one person would light up a cigarette to fend exhaustion.

ASIAN COMMUNITY CENTER ARCHIVES

Pooling together money to open Everybody's Bookstore in January 1970 was the last AAPA activity. Everybody's Bookstore became a community bookstore affiliated with the Asian Community Center.

THE DIAOYUTAI INCIDENT

In April 1971, the Northern California Tiao-yu Tai Islands Sovereignty Defense League called for a protest rally in San Francisco Chinatown's Portsmouth Square, and all hell broke loose. The League was protesting against the U.S. giving away islands to Japan that historically belonged to Taiwan. The protest was particularly pointed at the Taiwan government (the KMT, or Kuomintang Party) for letting this happen. In response, the protest group began to receive death threats.

The Tiao-yu Tai committee was made up largely of foreign students from UCB, Stanford, San Jose State, San Francisco City College, and other locations. They asked ACC for assistance and I remember violence that took place that day. Gang members, paid by the KMT, assembled on the corner of Brenham Place and Washington, attacked speakers, seized the microphone, and swore at the audience. The protestors froze for a few seconds until a middle-aged merchant seaman countered and led others to retake the stage and mic.

The incident sealed in my mind the seriousness of what we were trying to do. It also reminded me of the conditions that many had to deal with in their daily lives. Later, retaliatory threats

ASIAN COMMUNITY CENTER ARCHIVES (LEFT AND ABOVE)

During the I-Hotel eviction, the Asian Community Center doors were battered by riot police. Days later, ACC members draped a protest banner from the roof of the emptied building to demand the city to reopen the I-Hotel for the tenants and community centers that were evicted.

were heard throughout the Chinatown grapevine. We got the word out that we were there to serve the community, and not another gang out there wanting to become "king of the hill." Eventually, the tensions dissipated. The one positive we got out of this was that no one died.

Many of the Tiao-yu Tai committee members stayed on to work in ACC. Most of us were American-born, but with the foreign students coming on board, we now had the powerful addition of Chinese language speakers and writers. Later, the new relationship helped establish Wei Min She (Serve the People), an anti-imperialist community-based organization that lasted from 1970-1977. Wei Min She, I remember, was one of the few organizations that was respectful of how people related and worked with each other, taking in member opinions—non-hierarchical and mass-based. Not all organizations were that way.

PERSONAL STRUGGLES AND HEALING

my wife Bea and I were heavily involved in the fight to save the I-Hotel and the Asian Community Center in San Francisco Chinatown. She did trade union work with the ILGWU (International Ladies' Garment Workers' Union). But in 1981, Bea suffered a horrible injury and became disabled in a wheelchair. We had to pull ourselves together, not just in terms of dealing with her health situation, but also finding some way to continue all those things that inspired us from the earlier period.

We were living in New York at the time and Bea, while walking through a subway station with her coat and a knit cap on, was shot in the back of the neck by a young 19-year-old woman. The woman was schizophrenic and had been hearing voices telling her to shoot a Chinese man. She had taken a gun from her mother's closet in Louisville, Kentucky, and got on a bus to Newark, New Jersey. The young woman was loitering around the subways station when Bea happened to pass by.

Bea was paralyzed from the neck down—C6 and C7 paralysis. I was working when I got the phone call. Someone from the hospital had found my contact information in Bea's purse. They said that she had been injured. I didn't know what that meant. Did she get hit by a car? They told me to please come down to the hospital. I went, and that's when they told me what had happened. We figured she would eventually recover, but after a couple of weeks, one of the interns said that she wouldn't—it was a long-term paralysis because her spinal cord had been severed. The head doctor was never direct with us about her not being able to recover. I figure he didn't want to dash our hopes.

Bea was 29. We had gotten married seven years earlier in 1974 at San Francisco City Hall. I remember that was the same year as the Jung Sai Garment Workers Strike. Bea was an officer in the garment workers union and had gone there to find out what the labor dispute was about. There were some fifty Chinese immigrant women being harassed by the police at the picket line, so Bea stepped in to help. A Chinese woman striker had been hit by a company truck and couldn't move. The police accused her of faking it and this angered the picketers. The police arrested 54 people, including Bea. She bonded with the workers after the arrest and developed very long-term friendships with them.

I guess you can say that the person who shot Bea was a victim of the system, just as much as Bea was a victim of the shooting. I don't feel any anger at the unstable young girl who shot Bea. It had to do with the lack of institutional support for the mentally ill. Of course there are a lot of "what if's": What if Bea hadn't been there? What if she had had alternative transportation? All these things run through your mind when you experience something like that, but it's always after it happens. It's one of those things that stay with you because the injury is permanent. I think we try to cope by staying busy, and running Eastwind Books of Berkeley, after we

Harvey Dong and his wife, Bea, (pictured in front) host an author event for the book Beyond Lumpia, Pansit, and Seven Manangs Wild: Stories from the Heart of Filipino Americans, *at the bookstore they own and operate, Eastwind Books of Berkeley.*

purchased it in 1996, was a good healing mechanism for us.

I was also involved in building the house that we currently live in. I took it upon myself to learn construction. I attended construction school at Laney College and learned carpentry. The program had its students build affordable homes in West Oakland. I tried my best to turn something horrible into something more positive. I became friends with other carpentry students, and we all went into house-building and construction around the time of the 1989 San Francisco earthquake.

Bea and I have three kids. We ended up living downstairs at her folks' place in Oakland, across the street from Highland Hospital. Later we moved to her grandma's old building in Oakland Chinatown, right across the street from Harrison Railroad Park. They used to have old trains there. We lived there for five years or so. Our two youngest children went to Lincoln Elementary School. The oldest went to Westlake Junior High, then McChesney Junior High, and then Oakland High.

My instructor from Laney College, Ozzo Morrow, was an African American man who was paralyzed in a wheelchair from a construction accident. Ozzo would come and hang out with us when we were working on building our house. He would joke with us. He wanted to form a partnership to do other construction jobs in the Oakland area. He and Bea used to sit there and supervise from their wheelchairs. A few years afterwards, Ozzo passed away as the result of health complications related to his disability. I was honored that he proposed to the Laney College administration that I be his replacement as instructor of Construction Technology.

Harvey Dong bringing students to Angel Island in 2009.

TEACHING & PUBLISHING

Right now, I'm still at Eastwind Books of Berkeley. Since 2002, I have also been lecturing a number of UCB classes: "Asian American History," "Asian American Communities and Race Relations," and "Chinese American History." In 2016, I received the Ronald Takaki Teaching Award for American Cultures from the college.

I would say that it's important for the next generation of activists, for people interested in making changes in society, to have a history from which they can base their work. When we were involved in the 1960s and 1970s, we were searching for information. Whatever we could find, especially when we went to the community and talked to a lot of elders, helped us develop the movement at that time. When we worked in San Francisco Chinatown, people were actually really happy to see us. They welcomed us. They warned us about repercussions from the establishment. And they wanted to incorporate what we were doing into what they were doing—though their views tended to be more on the nationalistic side. So while we had differences with them, we also saw ourselves as a continuation.

Ideas and theories are really important to study and focus on. But what's even more important is the application of those theories—making contacts with people, listening to people, and learning to be good listeners; and being able to see yourself as a part of the community, as opposed to being an elitist.

In 1996, one of the first events we had at Eastwind Books was an Al Robles poetry event. In the store window, we had a photo display about the I-Hotel struggle. Little did we know, the owner of the property was the son of a San Francisco real estate developer. All of a sudden, we got an eviction notice! I suspect that the eviction had something to do with our support of the I-Hotel. I found a news clipping in which the owner's father had spoken at the San Francisco Board of Supervisors meetings, calling for the eviction of the I-Hotel tenants. It was very suspicious, but we didn't know for sure. We lost the original location, but in 1998 we were able to move into our current location around the corner.

Everything seemed to be going along well with sales. But then in 2007, the economic recession hit us, combined with the rise of Amazon's online bookstore. The bookstore took a big hit—a decline of more than 50 percent of its sales. We couldn't afford to pay for a full staff. We used to have two or three people working at the same time, but now we have a hard time surviving with even just one staff person.

It's been an uphill battle to survive, and we've had to be creative. We had to think on our feet. Right now, things are still shaky. We are trying to build a broad base of support in the community by having author readings and fundraisers. We have even published a few books under Eastwind Books of Berkeley. *A Village in the Fields* (2015) is a novel about the United Farm Workers of America by Patty Enrado. She was the daughter of farmworkers. It took her nine years to write the book. She sent out 65 requests to agents, but got rejected by all of them. So we worked with Patty at the recommendation of Evangeline Buell from the Filipino American National Historical Society (FANHS).

Another FANHS book we published was *Beyond Lumpia, Pansit, and Seven Manangs Wild* (2004), an anthology of Filipino American writers. Our other publications include *Stand Up: Archive Collection of the Bay Area Asian American Movement, 1968-1974* (2008), and the republishing of *The Forbidden Book: The Philippine-American War in Political Cartoons* (2004). We currently have two publications that are in the works, one about the TWLF Strike at SF State by Juanita Tamayo Lott and another about the TWLF Strike at UCB by strike veterans.

Eastwind Books is actually a location people can go to and find the broadest selection of Asian American fiction and non-fiction literature. We're in a unique situation because we are very urban, central, and near many different college campuses—UCB, SF State, Laney College, Berkeley City College, and Zaytuna College. Classes on Asian American and Asian Diaspora Studies at UCB, and Asian American Studies at SF State, order through us. Students are a big part of the customer base, but there are a lot of people from out of town—researchers from Japan—who just drop by, different people who are interested in Asian American and Asian diaspora studies, in ethnic studies, and fiction and non-fiction literature.

UC Berkeley joined with SF State professors and students to support the 2016 SF State hunger strike against cutbacks in Ethnic Studies. From left to right: Cynthia Ledesma (ES UCB Graduate Student), Abraham Ramirez (graduate student, UCB Ethnic Studies); Harvey Dong; Larry Solomon (Professor, SFSU Race and Resistance Studies); Ariko Ikehara (graduate student, UCB Ethnic Studies); Wesley Ueunten, (Professor, SFSU, Asian American Studies); Dan Gonzalez (Professor, SFSU, Asian American Studies).

PRESENT AND FUTURE

Today, I'm surprised, and not so surprised, that there's been an increased interest in the Asian American movement. It's a sign of big changes to come. Recently, there were two researchers from Okinawa—an internal colony of Japan. They wanted to look at how the Asian American movement related to African Americans, and how solidarity was built. All of what we have being trying to do—accumulating and building Asian American studies and making resistance central to that—is still relevant today: people changing the world, people wanting to change society, and people wanting to learn from the past.

What are the legacies of the past that are applicable to people today? There were social movements in the 1960s and 1970s, and even in the 1930s, that can be built upon for future generations. It is important to dialogue with each other and to be rooted in the community. I don't have a blueprint—only some experiences and mistakes over the past fifty years. But what has been tried before is full of lessons that we now have forever to learn from for the future.

STAND FAST AND DON'T GO QUIETLY INTO THE NIGHT

LILLIAN FABROS

LIZ DEL SOL

In Castroville, CA, checking artichokes, 1976.

For years I did not want to be interviewed about my past political activism, primarily because I don't believe that my role as an individual was that important in the bigger scheme of things. In some sense, perhaps my impact might have been convincing other people to become involved, as I was probably one of only two Filipinos who initially participated in the Third World Liberation Front (TWLF) Strike. People who knew other Filipino students would say, "Why don't you talk to them?" I would go spend hours talking to these students, who later became leaders in the Filipino movement. Looking back, there are some key lessons that have governed my individual and community responses to racism, class differences, and the need for community organizing and services.

MILITARY CLASS

Growing up, I was more aware of class and status differences than racism. My father had immigrated to the United States in 1920 and enlisted in the U.S. Army during World War II, and subsequently earned his U.S. citizenship. He was in the Second Filipino Regiment, one of two U.S, all-Filipino regiments sent to the Philippines to fight against the Japanese. He met my mother while he was in the Philippines and eventually brought her, my brother, and me to America in 1948. He was still in the military when I was in elementary school.

When my father was stationed at Fort Carson in Colorado, the army kids went to a newly built school, with brand new equipment and young enthusiastic teachers. But the following year, it was decided that the new school should only be for officers' children. And because my father was only a sergeant, I now had to attend school at an old army barracks, with very little equipment and outdated textbooks. One teacher even told us outright that he wasn't going to try hard to teach us much because we weren't going to go anywhere in life. I really hated class differences.

SALINAS VALLEY

In 1959, my father was transferred to Fort Ord near Salinas, California, where he originally had lived and soon after was discharged from the Army. My mother became a farm worker, as did my father, because there were no other jobs available for Filipinos in Salinas. Starting in the sixth grade, my brothers and I would work in the evenings after school and weekends bunching green onions. In the summer we picked tomatoes, lettuce, strawberries, etc.

In high school, I knew I was going to get out of Salinas because I was going to attend college. It was my way to escape, but there were a lot of other people who couldn't escape from these low-paying jobs. It was so unfair. My Filipino relatives and friends could rarely get non-farm work employment, because all the jobs went to white folks in Salinas. An image still remains in my mind today, one from the last days I worked in the fields of an older Filipino man married to a younger Filipino woman. They had two little kids and lived in a motel, paying $15 a day for the room. You were lucky if you could make $15 to $20 a day in the fields. That's how he lived, and he was never going to get out of that hole.

Occasionally, college students would come down and try to organize the farm workers in the Salinas Valley. This interaction taught me early on that organizers had to be from the community itself in order to be effective and long-lasting. These college students would tell us that it was really stupid of us to be working for such little money. We would get 50 cents for picking a large bag of tomatoes. The college students tried to organize us, but they themselves couldn't last a week in the fields because it was so physically demanding. If you could at least last the first couple of weeks in the fields, you might get used to the hard labor. But they couldn't, and so we had little respect for them. We felt that if you couldn't physically cut it, you shouldn't be telling us we're stupid for being out in the fields, since many of us didn't have a choice about it. Those students always had a way out: they could go back to college or their regular jobs. Although I was rooting for them, it was always a disappointment that they'd only come for a short while and then leave. When you organize, you have to organize from the bottom up with people from that community, or you have to be able to stick it out and last.

One summer, a young woman offered to give me a ride home from Gonzales and to Soledad to pick up something at my grandmother's house where I was living. We lived in a cow shed attached to an old wooden barn where the horse stalls had been converted into little bedrooms for the Filipino workers. I waved her to come inside, thinking the cow shed was pretty good since it had a separate bedroom, a little living room, and its own kitchen. Instead, she stood outside looking appalled and wouldn't even come in. I was so hurt and embarrassed. A couple of days later she left without a word. Whether or not someone lived in poor surroundings, I learned to never disrespect hospitality when people welcome you into their house.

UC BERKELEY AND ANTI-WAR ACTIVISM

hen we heard the news about what was happening with the Civil Rights movement marches in Selma, Alabama, a small group of students and adults held our own small support march in Salinas. Some of us asked ourselves, "If we are more capable or smarter, why can't we get a job?" The answer was all seemingly tied to race and class injustice. My tenth-grade U.S. history teacher was amazing and encouraged us to use our minds and to analyze what was going on. I had once believed what I'd been taught— that the reason good things happen is because God was on our side! But the racial riots, murders, civilian massacres in Vietnam, and violent action by police couldn't be explained away by simple rhetoric. That was in 1963, and my history teacher already knew the war in Vietnam was wrong.

There was just so much happening at UC Berkeley (UCB) and the Bay Area at the time. My best friend's sister was going to UCB during the Free Speech movement, and we would visit her. My cousins lived a block away from Haight-Ashbury and growing up we saw the changes in that neighborhood. By the time I went to UCB in 1966 there was the Student Nonviolent Coordinating Committee (SNCC), Students for a Democratic Society (SDS), and other left-wing groups organizing on campus. My friend Vicci, also from Salinas, participated in a lot of the anti-war demonstrations. In October 1967, we both were arrested at a "Stop the Draft" demonstration in Oakland. It was the first demonstration that turned violent, due to the police throwing tear gas and attacking demonstrators. I didn't tell my parents about my arrest. But the names of the people arrested were published in the *San Francisco Chronicle* and *San Francisco Examiner*, and so the news of our arrests eventually made it down to Salinas.

PARENTS PHOTO COURTESY OF LILLIAN FABROS; CHILDHOOD PHOTO BY ALEX FABROS

At left: Parents of Lillian, Alex, and Josefina Fabros, at a dance at the Filipino Community Center, 1951. *At right*: Lillian age 4-1/2, 1952, dressed for a Filipino dance performance at the Filipino Community Center, Salinas, CA.

Asian American Political Alliance (AAPA) marching in the Free Huey Newton/Black Panther demonstration in front of the Oakland courthouse, July/August 1968.

About thirty people were arrested in the demonstration and arraigned at the Oakland courthouse. The courtroom was packed—standing room only—with attorneys, observers, reporters, police, and, of course, prisoners. The judge looked out at the young crowd and said, "Are there any parents here? Oh, I see some parents in the back. Come on down. You can sit in the jury box." Everyone turned around, and there was my father, together with my mother and great-uncle. They were the only parents who showed up.

My father was strongly in favor of the Vietnam War, and my older brother was serving as a Marine in Vietnam at the time. Because of my family's military background, I knew there were going to be heated arguments when I got home. When my parents showed up at the court-house and sat there, all I thought was, "Ugh, how embarrassing." When we were being walked out back to jail, I had to run through a gauntlet of people, thinking, "Are my parents going to yell at me?" Then my father quietly said, "If you need anything, call me." That's all he ever said. He never said anything like, "This was a stupid. How could you shame us?" No. Instead, he said, "If you need anything, call me."

Of course, it took me many decades to really appreciate his support. It's just too bad I didn't appreciate it at the time, and didn't really understand parenting like I do now as a parent of four. In fact, it had been decades since I thought about the demonstrations, until one day my daughter in sixth grade said she had to write a paper about an immigrant family and she had chosen the singer Joan Baez. I told her that Joan Baez had been arrested during a sit-in at the Oakland "Stop the Draft" demonstrations, and that she had been released from the county jail just as I was entering it.

THE FORMATION OF AAPA

In spring 1968, my roommate Vicci and I got a phone call inviting us to participate in a meeting for Asian Americans. When asked how they got our number, it turned out that we had signed an anti-war petition and our information had been taken from it. I became very wary of signing petitions after that. Yuji Ichioka had called the meeting and sub-sequently, the Asian American Political Alliance (AAPA) was formed several weeks later at UCB. The group was comprised primarily of Chinese and Japanese, and two Filipinos. During the summer of 1968, Yuji was spearheading an effort to repeal the 1950 McCarran Internal Security Act and wanted AAPA members to sit out in Sproul Plaza on campus to collect sig-

Above: Lillian Fabros manning the AAPA anti-McCarran Act/Concentration Camps table at a Free Huey Rally at Defemery Park, Oakland, CA, July 14, 1968. **Below**: An anti-invasion demonstration march in Berkeley, April-May 1970; Asian women head the march, with Lillian on the right.

natures. Yuji and I had intense discussions about the Japanese American concentration camps. I said to him, "The Japanese invaded the Philippines and had real concentration camps, not at all what Japanese Americans experienced in America." We talked about the differences between Japanese Americans and the Japanese, and about the common struggles of Asian Americans. If Japanese Americans could be incarcerated, maybe other Asian Americans could too. Ultimately, I wound up sitting at the table in Sproul Plaza, encouraging people to support repealing the McCarran Act.

The following year, there was a lot of support from AAPA for the farm workers in Delano, where Filipinos had initiated and spearheaded the 1965 grape strike. We had students go out and talk to other Japanese, including Japanese farmers, trying to get them to support the Filipinos and Latinos who were on strike. If Filipinos could support the repeal of the McCarran Act because it could affect any community of color, then other Asian Americans should try to convince the Japanese and Chinese to support Filipinos as having a common cause. Chinese, Japanese, and Filipinos have a common history of oppression in America, despite the model minority myth America imposed on them, and that some Asian Americans perpetuate. This was an example of the intersection of class and race, where sometimes the oppressors can also be people of color.

When I was arrested in 1967 and sent to Santa Rita Jail, I met a woman who subsequently formed a group called "Honkies for Huey." In summer 1968, there were a lot of demonstrations to support activist Huey P. Newton and the Black Panthers. Later I met the Panthers, Bobby Seale, Eldridge Cleaver, and other political activists at the woman's house. I also met Richard Aoki, a Japanese American founding member of AAPA, and a member of the Black Panther Party.

During Huey's trial, AAPA joined demonstrators to march around the Oakland courthouse. I made a sign that read "Kalayaan (Tagalog for freedom) for Huey," which appeared in the *San Francisco Chronicle*. And based on that, a number of Filipino students from San Francisco State College (now San Francisco State University, or SF State) came over to check out the Filipino activist from UCB. These Filipinos were the same ones who would later participate in the SF State Strike in fall 1968. Subsequently, the Filipino activists and I met with the San Francisco Philippine Consulate General. The Consulate General told me the FBI had done a background check on me—which they had shared with him—and he wanted to know what "a nice Filipino girl" like me was doing being involved with the Panthers, the TWLF Strike, and demonstrations. It was just amazing how much detail he knew about me.

LESSONS FROM THE TWLF STRIKE

Occasionally my kids would ask about my experience at UCB and Asian American Studies. It's history to them—What was the experience like? What did I learn? Was it scary? What was the point? My youngest daughter even commented how students marched through her college campus during finals, and it seemed disruptive and alienated students more than getting them to support whatever the action was.

For this book, I was asked what or whether I regretted anything about the 1969 UCB TWLF Strike. In 2009, at the fortieth anniversary of the strike, I gave a speech on "Life Lessons Learned from the TWLF Strike"—which I didn't realize until much later. These were basic principles of community involvement and radical organizing that have held fast for me during and since the strike. I want to encourage the next generation of Asian American activists, especially given the current political situation and racist attitudes in the U.S. I realize, however, that in order to do so, we need to remember and record the history of the struggle for

Lillian Fabros is seen in a February 1968 Third World Liberation Front picket line at Bancroft Way and Telegraph Avenue in front of UC Berkeley.

PHOTOGRAPH BY STEVE LOUIE, WEI MIN SHE
AND ASIAN COMMUNITY CENTER PHOTOGRAPHS,
ETHNIC STUDIES LIBRARY, UC BERKELEY

*International Hotel anti-eviction march
through San Francisco Chinatown. From
the first eviction announcement in 1969 to
the eviction in 1977 and the I-Hotel building
demolition in 1979, there were ongoing
mobilizations bringing together students,
community residents, and labor union
supporters to save the I-Hotel, preserve
Manilatown, and to defend the community
centers located on the I-Hotel block on
Kearny Street in San Francisco.*

recognition of the contributions that Asian Americans have made to this country.

Lesson 1: Build Coalitions Before You Need Them

It is essential to build coalitions with like-minded groups before you need their help. Otherwise it comes off as opportunistic, and questions will arise about whether you will reciprocate in supporting them after they've supported you.

AAPA started the basis for coalition building among the different Asian groups. In the months and years to come, Filipino Americans would come show their support against anti-Japanese American laws, and the children of Japanese American farm owners would show their support for Filipino farm workers striking for fair wages. Likewise, members of AAPA began supporting and building relationships with other minority groups. By the time the TWLF Strike began in January 1969, AAPA had strong relationships with the Black, Chicano, and other groups.

If these connections had not taken place before the TWLF Strike, it is doubtful that such a strong alliance—based on mutual respect and trust—would have been forged. Reflecting back, the strong sense of solidarity with, and among, all the Third World groups and progressive supporters before, during, and after the strike, accounts for why many have continued to work together years after. Importantly, each of the groups in the TWLF kept their own identity, had equal rights in decision-making, and were not subsumed or swallowed up by the coalition.

Lesson 2: Race Matters

It was important then—and it is still important now—that race absolutely matters. Even fifty years ago, Asians were touted as the "model minority." The Chinese and Japanese were seen as having overcome racism. As a result, it was sometimes difficult to convince other Asians and Asian Americans to support the TWLF Strike, as many did not feel that they were being discriminated against, and so there was no need for a Third World College. Ironically, many of these same Asians did not know that Japanese Americans had been forced into U.S. concentration camps during World War II. No race has "made it," until all races have made it.

Lesson 3: Class Matters

It is very difficult for individuals from privileged backgrounds, including those of color, to truly understand the barriers faced by people of lesser economic means. UCB students may aspire for better economic status, but some of the worst oppressors of Asians have been our own people.

Lesson 4: Women Hold Up Half the Sky

During my speech, when I mentioned that "women hold up half the sky," there was loud agreement from the audience. Asian women were at least half, if not more, of the Asian students actively involved in supporting the TWLF Strike. This was in sharp contrast to the Black and Chicano student groups, where women were far fewer. Asian women's dedication has proven to be true in multiple endeavors afterwards, as advocates for civil rights, directors of service organizations, etc.

Lesson 5: Organize, Organize, Organize

It is difficult for individuals on their own to bring about change. However, you can never stop

TION NATIONAL CONF.6/1976

COURTESY OF LILLIAN FABROS

Pacific Asian Coalition in San Jose, CA, June 1976. Lillian Fabros is in the first standing row, in a black t-shirt.

organizing because the gains you achieved can disappear and the momentum can be lost, as we've seen lately. Organizing means working with a broad spectrum of supporters to build a multitude of strategies and programs. But is compromise with integrity ever possible? Being involved with change through large movements is a big switch when having to focus on change through small efforts. Yet I've often been surprised that creating small projects or working with a small group can snowball into larger efforts.

Lesson 6: The Journey is as Important as the Goal

It is arguable that because the strike ultimately ended in a moratorium, there was no victory for Third World students. For me, the victory was the jumpstarting of Asian American activism over the past decades. I have lifelong friends, men and women, who I marched with on the picket lines back in Berkeley. These friends have gone on to work against racism in different ways over the past five decades. The strike coalesced in a longing for justice that expressed itself in multiple personal and professional endeavors.

Lesson 7: Find the Goal You Are Passionate About

It is really all about sustaining your commitments by linking goals to your work. In the '70s there was a push for working in the community, even to the point of working as laborers with troubled youth, other disenfranchised folks, and the "lumpenproletariat." I recall vividly instances of well-meaning activists awkwardly, and probably ineffectively, trying to relate to youth, to organize or unionize workers, etc. Yet despite this philosophical or political mantra, many did not remain in the community to continue their initial work. This reminded me of what happened when I was younger in the fields of the Salinas Valley. We need a broad range of skills—writers, researchers, doctors, union organizers, etc. People who remain committed can help their communities —when they remember their roots. There are different paths to furthering justice.

SPIES AND LIES

S o, you've been accused of being an FBI or CIA informant, spying on the activities of the Filipino anti-Marcos movement in America and the Philippines. Now what do you do? There was an event that happened to me that's different from what happened to other people in the movement, and it has made me a stronger person. The fact that it happened probably saved my life by changing the course of my involvement in activism. I've rarely discussed this because I know of others who have quietly disappeared—gone quietly into the night. Movements implode—people start attacking each other. This happened in the student movement in Japan, when the Black Panthers started accusing each other of being spies or informants for the FBI, and so on. This is not to discount the incidents of groups being infiltrated by the FBI, CIA, or police, but sometimes people become manipulated by the government, or by their own paranoia or other insecurities.

In summer 1971, I was working full-time at UCB and involved with the International Hotel (I-Hotel) during the weekends. One weekend I visited my parents in Salinas and met a group of young Filipinos, primarily from the Philippines, who were holding anti-Marcos meetings. It turned out that they were based in San Francisco, and I tried with no luck to meet with them in the following weeks. Although I was heading to New York to attend graduate school at Columbia University, I had considered not going in order to work with them.

In New York, I worked with a number of Asian American activists, some of whom I had known from the TWLF Strike. In October 1971, during an anti-Marcos demonstration, I learned of rumors circulating that I was an FBI informant. I was very upfront about confronting those rumors, and called for a meeting to discuss them amongst the diverse groups. In fact, I called for a "people's trial," stating, "This is not true. Let's get this out into the open instead of all these rumors going around." Although the group initially agreed to hold an open forum, on the actual day, only a handful of people showed up. Supposedly people were afraid that I and two friends who had flown out from San Francisco would be carrying guns. The meeting was disbanded after a few minutes.

A week later, a ten-page document was distributed to various individuals and groups in the Filipino and Asian American community listing a number of unsubstantiated accusations. It stated that I had infiltrated Filipino anti-Marcos cells in the Philippines, and gave information to both the U.S. and Philippine governments. The document even stated that someone should take out a contract to kill me. Even though I had a full-time job which could be corroborated, it was said that I was able leave for the Philippines on a Friday night and fly back to the U.S. on Sunday, and do my undercover informant work in the Philippines—i.e., never underestimate the power of the U.S. government. Also, I couldn't speak Tagalog, having grown up in the U.S.; my father spoke Ilocano and my mother spoke Gaddang, not Tagalog. It was just impossible for me to respond to these irrational accusations.

When I told my fellow Asian American activists in New York about the accusations and shared copies of the document, I said, "You should know that there's this rumor that is going around about me." I had been working with Yuri Kochiyama, so I told her about the unfounded rumors. She said, "Oh yeah, we had already been warned and heard the rumors before you came. We just wanted to see how you acted. We're going to base our judgment on practice." I had already done some work with Yuri and her kids, as well as Nobuko Miyamoto and Chris Iijima. Yuri shared that she herself had also been accused of being an informant during the rise of the Black Power movement, but she continued her efforts against racism and the Vietnam War. It had been difficult for her and her family to live through those accusations.

The Kochiyama family was very supportive, and I continued working with them while I was in New York. Personally, it was absolutely devastating to learn that some people I had worked with during the TWLF Strike believed the rumors but never reached out to me to discuss them. People I had known for years, even some I had recruited to support the TWLF Strike, just stopped talking to me.

What I learned from this incident was that whenever I did any community work, I would bring up the rumors about my being an informant. In 1972, for example, I returned to San Francisco and started working with the Pilipino Organizing Committee in the South of Market area, focusing my work on an impoverished area where Filipinos lived. When I started my work there, I said to them, "Oh, by the way, you should know this about me." They said they had already been warned about me.

Ironically, I became good friends with several Filipino American members of the organization who also did community work with youth and immigrants in the South of Market. They were aware of the rumors that people in the anti-Marcos organization propagated. They even invited me to their organizational meetings. I found it ironic that I could attend so-called meetings on security, and yet no one would kick me out or confront me regarding the rumors. Comparable to the tight security for meetings during the TWLF Strike, it seemed that some members were playing at becoming revolutionaries.

The rumors followed me to Los Angeles after I moved in 1974. I worked with the Asian American Community Mental Health Center, Search to Involve Pilipino Americans (SIPA),

Pagkakaisa, and other local Filipino groups. Early on, I asked social worker and UCLA professor Royal "Uncle Roy" Morales whether he had heard about the accusations. He said, "Oh, yeah, we've been told about it. We were just checking out how you acted and what you did." I continued to work in the Filipino community, and again made friends with members of the anti-Marcos organization.

I've always looked at class background, not just race, in analyzing people and situations. A number of people who spread the rumors about me were from the upper class in the Philippines. If they felt so strongly about revolution in the Philippines, what were they doing in America? Years later some returned to the Philippines and became part of the government. There were a lot of issues and problems for Filipinos in America. That was my focus, more than what was happening in the Philippines, because we had other people fighting in the Philippines against Marcos at that time. I later wound up going more towards Asian American issues, mainly because my path to working with Filipinos got splintered by the rumors.

Eventually, about six years after the initial incident, I was asked to meet with the accusing Filipino organization in Los Angeles. I agreed to meet with the "mediator," who turned out to be someone I had met while working in the community. I learned that one of their criticisms was that I had "split" the Filipino movement. Some people believed in me and some did not. I had even unreasonably made good friends with people who would become spokespersons for the organization.

Some of the people I had known from Berkeley believed the rumors, even though these rumors didn't make logical sense, and others did not. Some said I should have just gone silently into the night. I knew really good people who left the movement because of similar accusations—i.e., for not being politically correct or other personal attacks. We lost good people who had contributed so much to the struggle. But I wasn't going to be chased out or voluntarily leave—I wanted to hold on and stand fast. The cause surpassed my individual feelings.

WHAT HAVE YOU DONE LATELY?

In 1979, I got my Masters in Social Work at UCLA, where my focus was in community organizing rather than clinical mental health. There was one well-known professor who had worked with Saul Alinsky, famous for his block organizing strategy ("Rules for Radicals") in Chicago and New York during the 1950s to 1970s. At the time, this was considered a very radical organizing approach. However, I had always questioned Alinsky's approach because such block organizing did not work for Asians, who lived in highly dispersed neighborhoods. One day, a group of students (composed of some Asians) approached me and criticized my questioning because I wasn't showing Alinsky any respect. I responded, "He may have done a lot of great work before. But what has he done lately?" Ah, the arrogance of youth.

Over the years I've constantly thought about this same question, and my own self. That's why I don't necessarily want to glorify my activist involvement in the '60s and '70s, because I have to ask myself too, "What have you done lately? What's your legacy now?" There are a number of people for whom their political activism during the '60s and the TWLF Strike is the highlight of their life.

Recently, I've been working with a Filipino collaborative to bring awareness of mental health problems and social services needs among Filipinos. In the '70s, there was a vibrant Filipino community in Los Angeles County, with many Filipino activists and community-involved individuals. Sadly, sometimes it feels as though we haven't made much progress since the 1970s because we're still having the same, if not worse, problems. Several of the community-based Filipino organizations with which I've worked have dwindled in the strength of their services.

In February 2018, we convened a mental health well-being summit where over 275 Filipi-

ABOVE PHOTOS BY LILLIAN FABROS

Top: Pilipino Artists Committee demonstration in San Francisco, 1973.

Above: Working on a door-to-door survey of Filipinos living in South of Market, Natoma Street, San Francisco, with Pilipino Organizing Committee, 1973.

At left: Lillian Fabros recently.

nos of all ages, both American-born and foreign-born, came together to learn about how our colonial mentality, brought over from the Philippines, still negatively influences our lives in the U.S. We're currently working on strategies to promote better mental well-being and organize our local communities.

In contrasting the old and the young guard, younger people must be involved in determining and planning their own services. Similar to my experiences, starting in Salinas, those whose futures are affected need to be drawn into leading the change. My father retired when he was 75 and then started a new career, becoming politically active in traditional politics and campaigning for local and state politicians. When he died at age 96, there were a number of politicians, such as former U.S. Congressman and Secretary of Defense Leon Panetta, who attended his funeral. At 75, my father found something new that energized him. And I want to be like that.

When I retire, I want to continue to bring the lessons I learned to other activities and share them working with the community. Do I have any regrets about being a progressive left-wing Filipino activist? None at all. Now I am thinking about what my next career and passion will be, knowing full well that the struggle for justice continues, and needs to be ever vigilant.

the FOUNDING OF THE UCLA ASIAN AMERICAN STUDIES CENTER

JEAN-PAUL R. DEGUZMAN

Women active in Asian American studies at UCLA and other L.A. campuses at a rest stop on Interstate 5 en route from L.A. to Fresno as they toured a slideshow presentation on Asian women, c. 1971. Standing (left to right): Carol Mochizuki, Miya Iwataki and May Chen. Seated (left to right): Patti Iwataki, Candace Murata, and Evelyn Yoshimura.

Campbell Hall Coalition march on UCLA campus, in support of the formation of the Ethnic Studies Centers, August 8, 1969.

The purpose of the Center should promote critical re-evaluation through honest research of the Oriental-American and his community. This research should serve as a foundation and impetus for community action and curricular reform. Research must not be an end in itself, i.e., a pedantic exercise, but as a means for social change.[1]

Penned towards the end of 1968, the preceding snippet from a larger manifesto captured how hundreds of students at the University of California, Los Angeles (UCLA) imagined a transformative new unit on their campus. In a year that witnessed political upheavals at home and abroad, these students demanded a sweeping experiment in bridging grassroots activism with academia. Within a year, the UCLA Asian American Studies Center (AASC) came to fruition due to the determined efforts of students, staff members, faculty, and a much larger network of community members who fought to challenge the university's Eurocentrism and elitism—boldly seeking to craft a politically relevant curriculum and research agenda that would truly serve the people.

"WE HAD THINGS TO BE CONCERNED ABOUT, TOO": THE CONTEXTS FOR ACTIVISM

Although the efforts to establish an Asian American Studies Center gained the most energy in the late 1960s, Asian Americans first left their imprint decades earlier. In the 1920s Asian American students formed social clubs, such as the sorority Chi Alpha Delta, as a bulwark against the isolation they faced from mainstream campus culture. These organizations continued after World War II when UCLA's Japanese American population returned from the internment camps. In 1962, the University Research Library became the primary repository of the Japanese American Research Project (JARP) which was instrumental in revising racist historical narratives that elided or misrepresented the wartime incarceration of Japanese Americans. Drawing on this trove, historian Robert Wilson offered the campus's first Japanese American history course in early 1968.

Despite these historical traces, UCLA was an unlikely stage for student uprisings—even though Los Angeles was the home to incredible racial conflict in the 1960s, from battles over segregation to the Watts Rebellion. A quiet commuter campus, only 12 percent of the UCLA student population in 1968 were people of color; Asian Americans comprised 1,700 of the 28,997 students enrolled.[2] Furthermore, Bruins of color faced racist acts, such as the defacement of a Mexican flag at a fraternity, or housing discrimination in adjacent Westwood Village.[3] Nevertheless, the tenor of the Third World movements would soon bleed onto the bucolic Westwood campus.

Within that context, an aggressive movement of African American and Chicanx Students developed at UCLA. Inspired by Pan-Africanism and critiques of the racial underpinnings of capitalism and American empire, African American students formed the Black Student Union (BSU) and chapter of the Black Panther Party. They advocated for an anti-Eurocentric education where the Black experience was not peripheral, but central, to intellectual inquiry. Chicanx students similarly established new organizations such as the United Mexican American Students (UMAS), and Movimiento Estudiantil Chicano de Aztlán (MEChA), amidst the kinetic landscape of the farm worker movement, and the East L.A. Blowouts for educational equity in high schools.

This burst of campus activism and the global events of the 1960s profoundly shaped young Asian Americans at UCLA. Then-student activist Mike Murase remembered that:

Advertisement published in Gidra newspaper for the Amerasian Generation Conference held February 8, 1971, at the UCLA Ackerman Union Grand Ballroom.

Student volunteers at Community Day in Little Tokyo to educate the public about the Vietnam War and the military draft, c. 1970.

Even learning about the history of Asian Americans was in the context of this …tumultuous backdrop of the Vietnam War, a struggle for ethnic studies all over the country…the Civil Rights movement, [and] the Black Liberation movement. And when you look at things globally, in all the countries, and in Africa were being politically becoming independent, that all happened in the 1960s.[4]

Morgan Chu specifically pointed to America's wars in Southeast Asia as a driving force that politicized Asian Americans:

There were nasty ways to describe the Vietnamese people and soldiers…. Others didn't separate out different Asians from those who were enemy combatants….There [were] lots of reasons why many people thought the war was wrong…but there was an added reason for me at least being Asian American, I'm thinking, "Really? I'm gonna go there, carry a rifle, and shoot other Asians? What's the reason for that?"

In response to these political tremors, several young people in 1968 formed Sansei Concern (later Oriental Concern), an organization primarily comprised of third-generation Japanese Americans. As the inheritors of the tragedies of wartime incarceration and the silence that often beset the Nisei (second generation), the Sansei faced a variety of challenges, from pressures to assimilate to expectations for achievement foisted upon them by the specious model minority stereotype. As a result, several Sansei "who have finally become concerned enough to break the bonds of apathy," formed Sansei Concern to "identify and define pertinent issues affecting the community, and…develop programs to become actively involved," according the group's president, Glenn Asakawa.[5] Another member, Carol Mochizuki, remembered that, like their peers of color, "we just felt as though we had things to be concerned about, too."

In fall 1968, Sansei Concern hosted a conference, "Are You Curious Yellow?" Drawing 125 attendees from around Los Angeles, the conference grappled with politics and identity issues. Center documents from the time credit "Are You Curious Yellow?" as a defining context for the rise of the Los Angeles Asian American movement and Asian American Studies.[6] Members of Sansei Concern went on to compose the Asian American Studies Center's proposal and launch the "voice of the Asian American Movement," *Gidra*, a monthly-newspaper magazine that ran from 1969-1974.

"IT WAS EXPLOSIVE": ASIAN AMERICAN STUDIES GAINS MOMENTUM

As demands for greater racial equity grew, UCLA Chancellor Charles Young oversaw institutional responses to the conflicts that swept across the nation by the end of the 1960s. BSU and UMAS members, buoyed by intense student protests, negotiated with administration for greater institutional access and resources.[7] Campus initiatives such as the High Potential Program (Hi Pot), established in 1968, were instrumental in diversifying the campus population and bridging the experiences of the city's communities of color with the university. Driven by pressure from BSU and UMAS, the program recruited students from communities of color in Los Angeles who may not have met traditional, biased criteria for admission.[8]

VISUAL COMMUNICATIONS PHOTOGRAPHIC ARCHIVE

Anti-war march in 1972.

Hi Pot specifically attracted young people cognizant of the inequalities their communities faced and who sought tools to effect change. The program initially targeted Black, Chicanx, and later indigenous students. It eventually enrolled Asian Americans to "provide students with a relevant education which explores the socio-economic problems of Asians in America" while "demonstrat[ing] the need for effective and responsible leadership in making the necessary social changes."[9]

The most comprehensive plan by administrators was the Ford Foundation-funded Institute of American Cultures which included constituent units for African American Studies, Chicano Studies, American Indian Studies, and Asian American Studies. Chancellor Young declared that these "organized research units" (ORUs) "would contribute to the understanding and resolution of national social problems," and that "Los Angeles offers an unusual geographical opportunity to serve these four cultures."[10] Activists, however, readily acknowledged that fears of campus unrest, similar to that at San Francisco State College, would erupt at UCLA and motivated these structural changes.

By the end of 1968, a steering committee comprised of faculty, students, and community members, chaired by pioneering Nisei social welfare professor Harry H.L. Kitano, articulated the need for a campus unit dedicated to Asian Americans.[11] Faculty desired research support, students envisioned a center that would create a politically relevant curriculum, and community representatives sought "interaction between themselves and the university."[12] These different perspectives, which often intersected, informed the proposal for UCLA's Asian American Studies Center, spearheaded by undergraduates, such as Suzi Wong, Dinora Gil, and Laura Ho.

The alchemy of this moment transformed students' political consciousness. Eddie Wong recalled the sentiment of "being Black is beautiful and Yellow is cool." Students were "moving from Oriental to Asian American, [which was a] big self-empowerment, self-identity thing. That was the thrilling thing: there's a whole other community of people I felt I could belong to." Murase spoke about how students educated themselves through study groups that tackled the writings of Mao and Malcolm X, or "rallies and demonstrations [with] a teach-in where people learn and [where] the speed at which we got politicized and our consciousness was raised [was] just very quick." Vivian Matsushige recalled the formation of a Marxist-Leninist study group for Asian American women, which illustrated the need for women-only spaces in response to patriarchy beyond and within Third World movements.

As students educated themselves, Center supporters fought to articulate the relevance of ethnic studies amidst critiques that the innovative field lacked the rigor of traditional disciplines. Due to model minority discourse, advocates had to disabuse administrators of the assumption that, according to one department chair, "the University has never had to go out of its way for Oriental-Americans for the very simple reason that they are a very superior group!" Or, according to the chair of the Committee on Budget and Interdepartmental Relations, Asian Americans "seem to have integrated themselves to a greater extent than have other minorities."[13]

Authors of the Center's proposal however argued that "[a]t UCLA in particular Asian-Americans [sic.] form the largest minority on campus, and the University must respond to their legitimate needs and demands."[14] Reflective of the need to gain administrative approval in the bureaucracy of the research university, the proposal emphasized the dearth of accurate scholarly literature about Asian Americans.[15] Only later in the proposal did the authors recognize the need to connect UCLA to the larger population. "Contrary to popular belief," the proposal bluntly stated, "Asian-American [sic.] communities have problems." The authors highlighted disparities in employment, mental health, and crime that the model minority myth conveniently erased. "Concrete solutions," according to the authors, "often lie beyond the reach

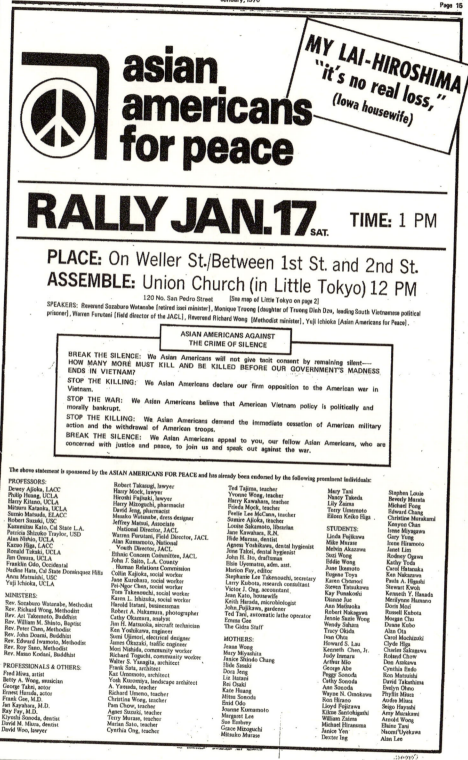

asian americans for peace

MY LAI-HIROSHIMA "it's no real loss," (Iowa housewife)

RALLY JAN. 17 SAT.   TIME: 1 PM

PLACE: On Weller St./Between 1st St. and 2nd St.
ASSEMBLE: Union Church (in Little Tokyo) 12 PM

120 No. San Pedro Street   [See map of Little Tokyo on page 2]

SPEAKERS: Reverend Sozaburo Watanabe [retired issei minister], Monique Truong [daughter of Truong Dinh Dzu, leading South Vietnamese political prisoner], Warren Furutani [field director of the JACL], Reverend Richard Wong [Methodist minister], Yuji Ichioka [Asian Americans for Peace].

ASIAN AMERICANS AGAINST THE CRIME OF SILENCE

BREAK THE SILENCE: We Asian Americans will not give tacit consent by remaining silent—— HOW MANY MORE MUST KILL AND BE KILLED BEFORE OUR GOVERNMENT'S MADNESS ENDS IN VIETNAM?

STOP THE KILLING: We Asian Americans declare our firm opposition to the American war in Vietnam.

STOP THE WAR: We Asian Americans believe that American Vietnam policy is politically and morally bankrupt.

STOP THE KILLING: We Asian Americans demand the immediate cessation of American military action and the withdrawal of American troops.

BREAK THE SILENCE: We Asian Americans appeal to you, our fellow Asian Americans, who are concerned with justice and peace, to join us and speak out against the war.

The above statement is sponsored by the ASIAN AMERICANS FOR PEACE and has already been endorsed by the following prominent individuals:

PROFESSORS:
Dewey Ajioka, LACC
Philip Huang, UCLA
Harry Kitano, UCLA
Mitsuru Kataoka, UCLA
Sumio Matsuda, ELACC
Robert Suzuki, USC
Kazumitsu Kato, Cal State L.A.
Patricia Shizuko Traylor, USD
Alan Nishio, UCLA
Kazuo Higa, LACC
Ronald Takaki, UCLA
Jim Omura, UCLA
Franklin Odo, Occidental
Nadine Hata, Cal State Dominguez Hills
Anna Matsuishi, USC
Yuji Ichioka, UCLA

MINISTERS:
Rev. Sozaburo Watanabe, Methodist
Rev. Richard Wong, Methodist
Rev. Art Takemoto, Buddhist
Rev. William M. Shinto, Baptist
Rev. Peter Chen, Methodist
Rev. John Doami, Buddhist
Rev. Edward Iwamoto, Methodist
Rev. Roy Sano, Methodist
Rev. Masao Kodani, Buddhist

PROFESSIONALS & OTHERS:
Fred Miwa, artist
Betty A. Wong, musician
George Takei, actor
Ernest Harada, actor
Frank Gee, M.D.
Jan Kayahara, M.D.
Ray Fay, M.D.
Kiyoshi Sonoda, dentist
David M. Miura, dentist
David Woo, lawyer

Robert Takasugi, lawyer
Harry Mock, lawyer
Hiroshi Fujisaki, lawyer
Harry Mizoguchi, pharmacist
David Jeng, pharmacist
Masako Watanabe, dress designer
Jeffrey Matsui, Associate National Director, JACL
Warren Furutani, Field Director, JACL
Alan Kumamoto, National Youth Director, JACL
Ethnic Concern Committee, JACL
John J. Saito, L.A. County Human Relations Commission
Collin Kajioka, social worker
Jane Kurohara, social worker
Pei-Ngor Chen, social worker
Tom Takenouchi, social worker
Karen L. Ishizuka, social worker
Harold Itatani, businessman
Robert A. Nakamura, photographer
Cathy Okamura, analyst
Jim H. Matsuoka, aircraft technician
Ken Yoshikawa, engineer
Sumi Ujimori, electrical designer
James Okazaki, traffic engineer
Mori Nishida, community worker
Richard Toguchi, community worker
Walter S. Yanagita, architect
Frank Sata, architect
Kaz Umemoto, architect
Yosh Kuromiya, landscape architect
A. Yamada, teacher
Richard Umeno, teacher
Christina Wong, teacher
Pam Chow, teacher
Agnes Suzuki, teacher
Terry Murase, teacher
Marian Sato, teacher
Cynthia Ong, teacher

Ted Tajima, teacher
Yvonne Wong, teacher
Harry Kawahara, teacher
Frieda Mock, teacher
Feelie Lee McCann, teacher
Sumire Ajioka, teacher
Louise Sakamoto, librarian
Jane Kawahara, R.N.
Hide Murase, dentist
Agness Yoshikawa, dental hygienist
June Takei, dental hygienist
John H. Ito, draftsman
Elsie Uyematsu, adm. asst.
Marion Fay, editor
Stephanie Lee Takenouchi, secretary
Larry Kubota, research consultant
Victor J. Ong, accountant
Jean Kato, housewife
Keith Harada, microbiologist
John Fujikawa, gardener
Ted Tani, automatic lathe operator
Emma Gee
The Gidra Staff

MOTHERS:
Jeane Wong
Mary Miyashita
Janice Shindo Chang
Hide Sasaki
Dora Jeng
Liz Itatani
Rei Osaki
Kate Huang
Mitsu Sonoda
Enid Odo
Joanne Kumamoto
Margaret Lee
Sue Embrey
Grace Mizoguchi
Mitsuko Murase

Mary Tani
Nancy Takeda
Lily Zaima
Terry Umemoto
Eileen Keiko Higa

STUDENTS:
Linda Fujikawa
Mike Murase
Melvin Akazawa
Suzi Wong
Eddie Wong
June Ikemoto
Eugene Toya
Karen Chomori
Steven Tatsukawa
Kay Funakoshi
Dianne Jue
Ann Matsuoka
Robert Nakagawa
Jennie Suzie Wong
Wendy Sahara
Tracy Okida
Ivan Ohta
Howard S. Lau
Kenneth Chen, Jr.
Judy Inmaru
Arthur Mio
George Abe
Peggy Sonoda
Cathy Sonoda
Ann Sonoda
Wayne N. Omokawa
Ron Hirano
Lloyd Fujizawa
Kikue Santohigashi
William Zaima
Michael Hiranuma
Janice Yen
Dexter Ing

Stephen Louie
Beverly Murata
Michael Fong
Edward Chang
Christine Murakami
Kenyon Chan
Irene Miyagawa
Gary Yung
Irene Hiramoto
Janet Lim
Rodney Ogawa
Kathy Toda
Carol Hatanaka
Ken Nakazawa
Paula A. Higashi
Stewart Kwoh
Kenneth Y. Hanada
Merilynne Hamano
Doris Mori
Russell Kubota
Morgan Chu
Duane Kubo
Alan Ota
Carol Mochizuki
Clyde Higa
Charles Sakugawa
Roland Chow
Don Asakawa
Cynthia Endo
Ron Matsuishi
David Takashima
Evelyn Ohno
Phyllis Miura
Audre Miura
Seigo Hayashi
Amy Murakami
Arnold Wong
Elaine Tani
Naomi Uyekawa
Alan Lee

Rally announcement by Asian Americans for Peace, which appeared in the January 1970 issue of Gidra newspaper.

169

of the university, but the university can render its service in the form of ideas and ideals."

As administrators reviewed the proposal for the Center, students pushed for classes to uncover the buried histories and contemporary experiences of Asian Americans. Without an ORU in place yet, the first classes were conducted under the experimental Committee for the Study of Education and Society (later, the Council on Educational Development, or CED).[17] A working group of faculty and students, including many Sansei Concern members, won approval for "Orientals in America," and recruited Nisei activist-historian Yuji Ichioka to teach it in spring 1969. A UC Berkeley graduate student, Ichioka helped found the Asian American Political Alliance and coin the term "Asian American."

Unlike the traditional university lecture, Ichioka, along with teaching assistants Laura Ho, Mike Murase, and Stewart Kwoh, drew upon the expertise of dozens of organizers and community figures as teachers. Blending lectures, panels, and discussions, individuals such as Kibei activist Karl Yoneda addressed topics such as Asian American labor. Actors from East-West Players, including Beulah Kwoh, George Takei, and James Hong, spoke about the performing arts. Scholars like Stanford Lyman delivered academic lectures on structural racism.

Intent on linking campus endeavors to the fabric of community organizing, representatives of Yellow Brotherhood, the Oriental Service Center, the Japanese American Citizens League (JACL), and the Filipino-American Council served as guest speakers. Reverends Masao Kodani, whose Senshin Buddhist Temple served as a gathering space for Asian American artists, and William Shinto addressed Asian American spirituality. Illustrating the cross-racial solidarity so important to the Asian American movement, the course also welcomed UMAS and BSU representatives.[18] This format reflected the multifaceted nature of the movement and pragmatism given the lack of textbooks and other classroom materials. "Orientals in America" generated energy within students to continue to fight for a permanent Asian American Studies Center.

A few months after Ichioka's class, the UC President's Office formally approved the creation of the Center in August 1969.[19] China historian Philip Huang served as the Center's Director. Ronald Takaki, a young Assistant Professor of African American history and Center supporter, endorsed Huang, lauding his "informed and imaginative leadership" in developing the "fine center proposal."[20] Despite Huang's support, the academic demands he faced, along with student criticisms that he steered the Center too far away from the community, meant that within a year, he relinquished the directorship to Alan Nishio, the Center's Student and Community Projects coordinator.[21]

Nishio's appointment as an interim Director signaled the extent to which student factions prioritized community engagement as an integral part of the Center's identity and the power of students in management. Elsie Uyematsu became the Center's first full-time staff member; with additional employees including a variety of undergraduate/graduate students serving as researchers, teaching assistants, and administrative workers. Staff members and students sought an egalitarian model, to the point that early salaries were collectivized. An executive committee, chaired by student Suzi Wong, steered major decisions. Reflective of student and community buy-in, the committee was comprised of eight students (selected by students), four community representatives (from local Chinese, Japanese, Filipino, and Korean enclaves), four faculty, and two administration members.

Campbell Hall housed the Ethnic Studies Centers and became ground zero for UCLA's Third World movement. The relationship between the different centers and constituents was complex. Mary Uyematsu Kao, a UCLA student who would later become an AASC staff member, remembered that each ethnic community fought their respective battles, while Murase suggested that administration deliberately met with groups separately to blunt the power of student solidarity. Kenyon Chan similarly recalled how administrators held up Asian Americans and the AASC as models to undermine the demands of other Ethnic Studies Centers. Nevertheless, the major groups came together over protests against budget constraints or efforts to destabilize the centers. According to Kao, "Campbell Hall was peopled by Black Panthers, Brown Berets, Yellow Brotherhood and American Indian Movement," many of whom were Hi Pot students. "To have all these. . .revolutionary people of color in Campbell Hall, it was explosive."

A campus protest in response to the bombing of Cambodia in May 1970 furthered the reach of politicization. "The whole campus was in an uproar," according to Kao, who remembered phalanxes of over 250 police officers marching under the massive Bunche Hall. She continued: the "columns of cops just marched right into [protesters] and just start clubbing people. Presumably I guess they wanted to clear the area. But I [saw] people jumping over hedges. It was just pandemonium." Along with her sister Amy Uyematsu, Kao went to Campbell Hall to find their mother Elsie, who barricaded herself in her office.

These violent clashes led administration to issue a state of emergency, "the first such declaration in UCLA's history," according to the *Los Angeles Times*.[23] Asian American activists Colin Watanabe and Steve Tatsukawa were among 74 individuals arrested by police.[24] Undeterred, a student coalition soon gathered to coordinate future actions; Morgan Chu chaired the often-chaotic meetings. The fervor of this political moment was infectious. Students along with supportive faculty viewed the war as one more reason for the need to build a unit that would center analyses of power in relation to Asians, Asian Americans, and U.S. imperialism.

"RELEVANCY TO CONTEMPORARY PROBLEMS": BUILDING A NEW CURRICULUM

A central part of the AASC's mission was the development of an interdisciplinary curriculum to capture the Asian American experience. Professor Kitano noted that students expressed interest in a program grounded in "relevancy to contemporary problems" and the "practical application of learned material."[25] In fall 1969, courses included "Orientals in America" (taught by Franklin Odo), "Koreans in America" and "Chinese in America" (by Linda Shin), "War Relocation Experience" (by JARP director Joe Grant Masaoka), and "Comparative Analysis of Asian American Community Organizations" (by Alan Nishio). Remarkably, 150 students enrolled in those five courses alone illustrating the hunger for Asian American studies.

The following year, new topics included Asian American public health, the history of Asian Americans and racism, and Chinese American labor.[27] In 1972, through the efforts May Chen and Karen Ito, the Center offered its first class on Asian American women, featuring a series of guest speakers who spoke about the triple oppression of racism, sexism, and classism, a framework now known as intersectionality. Given how new the courses were, instructors ranged from students to community activists.

The dearth of classroom texts compelled Odo and students such as Amy Uyematsu, Eddie Wong, and Buck Wong to compile an anthology of interviews, student research, poetry, and essays from community organizers into *Roots: An Asian American Reader* (UCLA, 1971). Other Center-sponsored collections published in 1976 include *Counterpoint*, edited by Emma Gee, and *Letters in Exile: A Pilipino American Reader*, compiled by students in Casimiro Tolentino's "Pilipino American Experience" class. These publications made invaluable contributions to research on and teaching where there had been either works that severely distorted Asian Americans, or no scholarly literature whatsoever.

Yuji Ichioka speaking at an "Asian Americans for Peace" march and rally in Little Tokyo, Los Angeles, January 17, 1970.

As early as 1970, Center faculty and students sought an Asian American Studies major. Although a full-fledged Asian American Studies or Ethnic Studies bachelor's degree was not feasible due to the administration's intransigence, the Center worked with Department of Asian Studies faculty to establish an interdisciplinary undergraduate degree program in East Asian Studies, with a concentration in Asian American Studies. The program was approved in October 1970.[28]

Some viewed the combination of East Asian Studies (a traditional discipline dominated by white male faculty who studied Asia) with Asian American Studies (an insurgent field oriented towards social and political change) as a fundamental misunderstanding of the latter. Nevertheless, since Chancellor Young stated, "I'm not certain if a degree is necessary," when asked about the possibility of an Ethnic Studies major in 1969, the collaboration was necessary.[29] Ultimately, "its purpose," according to the program's 1974 guide, was "to provide undergraduates a general education on East Asia and/or Asian Americans so that they can pursue graduate study in one of the social sciences or humanities disciplines which deal with East Asia or Asian Americans; it also trie[d] to prepare students for careers involving residence in East Asia or community work among Asian Americans." [30]

Despite the steady growth the Center enjoyed by the 1970s, its curriculum remained precarious. The CED abolished its subcommittee on ethnic studies and under the leadership of an antagonistic dentistry professor in 1974, the committee denied reapproval for various Asian American Studies (and Chicano Studies) courses, including a two-quarter "Introduction to Asian American Studies" and "Asian American Women," which formed parts of a core curriculum. Other innovative courses that fell to the whims of the CED included Tolentino's "Pilipino American Experience," "Religious Institutions in the Japanese American Community" (by doctoral student Nobuya Tsuchida), and "Education in the Chinatown Community" (by educator Buck Wong).[31] Reflective of a deep-seated dog-whistle used to silence ethnic studies, the committee questioned the intellectual merit of the courses.

The decision, which involved no consultation with the Center, sent shockwaves throughout the national ethnic studies community. The *Daily Bruin* and the Chicanx student newspaper, *La Gente*, published articles that covered the case, called for abolition of the CED, and favored independent Ethnic Studies.[32] The Student Support Committee for Ethnic Studies organized a campus rally in February 1975 to highlight the issue, while professors, including the faculty advisory committees of the Center and the East Asian Studies Program and the entire Department of Sociology, voiced their support. Bowing to the intense pressure, the CED withdrew their objections a few months later.[33] Despite this struggle, continued student activism and growing faculty support later led to a graduate program that culminated in a master's degree in Asian American Studies, the first in the nation. The cultivation of new generations of academics was necessary to develop Asian American studies as a formidable site of inquiry and action.

BEYOND "MARGINAL" AND "IRRELEVANT": BUILDING A RESEARCH AGENDA LOCALLY AND NATIONALLY

The development of an assertive research agenda reflected the Center's origins as an ORU and a stated desire to decolonize the university. This was necessary since "Asian-Americans [*sic.*] particularly have too often been dismissed as 'marginal' or 'irrelevant' to the mainstream of American life and society," according to the Center's proposal.[34] The maturation of the Center's research took place as it gained greater institutional stability in the 1970s and 1980s under sociologist Lucie Cheng Hirata, the first full-time Director.

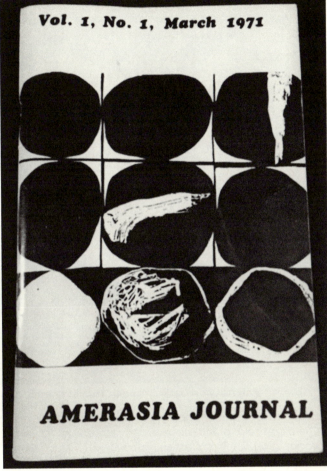

Vol. 1, No. 1, March 1971

AMERASIA JOURNAL

AMERASIA JOURNAL

The cover of the first issue of Amerasia Journal (1971).

*Students from UCLA's Ethnocommunications graduate film program documenting
the Pioneer Project's field trip taking Japanese American seniors to Lancaster, CA, to
view wildflowers in bloom, c. 1971. (From left to right) Duane Kubo, Alan Ohashi, Steve
Tatsukawa, and Mike Murase were staff members of Gidra. Duane, Alan, and Steve of
Ethnocommunications were also founders of Visual Communications, along with Bob
Nakamura and Eddie Wong.*

A major step in developing research was through publications. Founded by Yale undergraduate students Don Nakanishi and Lowell Chun-Hoon in 1971, *Amerasia Journal* was the first interdisciplinary academic forum to publish research on Asian Americans. Later that same year, the Center became the journal's publisher. Meanwhile Ichioka produced a variety of scholarly publications that tapped into the extensive JARP and other Japanese language sources. His work resulted in *A Buried Past* in 1974, and his 1988 *magnum opus, The Issei: The World of the First Generation Japanese Immigrants, 1885-1924.*

The Center also sought to establish a national network to develop the field of Asian American studies. With the Asian American Studies Program at the University of Southern California, the Center hosted the first national conference on Asian American studies in April 1971. This gathering provided a space to reflect on the development of research and curriculum, organize future actions, and bring younger scholars into the field. Workshop topics included wartime incarceration, migration patterns, contemporary communities, psychological issues, U.S. foreign policy in Asia, and a discussion about *Amerasia Journal*. Hawai'i Congresswoman Patsy Takemoto Mink, a Sansei Democrat, and well-known advocate for women's rights and peace, keynoted the conference.[35] While academic output was part and parcel of the university enterprise, students on and off campus demanded to be at the "center" of the Center.

"WE DIDN'T WANT TO BE QUIET ANYMORE": STUDENT ACTIVISM AND COMMUNITY ENGAGEMENT

ccording to the Center's first annual report, it "sponsors and supports a variety of student projects, encourages student involvement in the Asian American communities, and generally seeks as much as possible to bring the university's resources to bear on community problems."[36] Eddie Wong reiterated this attitude:

> That was one of the hallmarks of the early days of Asian American studies is that it was a whole idea that the campus should not just be an ivory tower. Education should be in service to…communities that were poor, disenfranchised, and without power…We were at an elite college, even though it was public, and we were accumulating skills, but for what reason? Was it just going to be for individual advancement, or did we owe it to a larger social purpose?"

Similarly, Alan Nishio, as the Center's first Student and Community Projects coordinator, oversaw efforts to bridge students and community-based activism. He recalled that "I was also an advocate for the continuing role of students in the Center, and the Director at that time saw Asian American Studies as a research unit and scholarly activity."

Tutorial programs offered many AASC students a foray into community service. The Oriental American (later Asian American) Tutorial Project established at Castellar Elementary School in Los Angeles's Chinatown in January 1969 exposed children, many of whom were English language learners and had no classroom exposure to Asian/Asian American histories, to culturally responsive curricula. By December, the program included over 100 tutors and a branch at California State College, Los Angeles.[37]

The Center also supported an adult English as a Second Language tutorial project. Adult education was significant since, as programs tutor and Castellar teacher Helen Chu pointed out, "in addition to the lack of English, [immigrants] also didn't know how to qualify for food stamps, social security, [or] whatever was available to them." As a result, "being able to be there [for them], being able to speak the language, really helped them out." Meanwhile, Center

Visual Communications co-founder Alan Ohashi teaches a darkroom class to children from the community in 1972. Ohashi's background as a visual artist and photographer informed his stewardship of the organization's photographic exhibits and publication. Transitioning into architecture, Alan has run his interior and environmental design firm, Ohashi Designs, since the mid-1990s.

students, working with Asian American Hardcore, an organization that engaged with gang members and incarcerated youth, took Asian American studies courses to the California Youth Authority Institution to provide an alternative education to confined Asian Americans.[39]

Gidra served as a grassroots conduit between Center students and on-the-ground activism.[40] According to Mochizuki, *Gidra's* goal was to "make the community aware that [Asian Americans] didn't want to be second class citizens. . .We didn't want to be quiet anymore." The newspaper was anti-hierarchical and published essays on Asian American identity, critiques of the nation's war machine, coverage of local issues such as redevelopment in Little Tokyo, and stories that exposed Asian Americans to other Third World movements. Reflective of the tensions between racial and gender liberation—men often sidelined women in movement activities—so *Gidra* dedicated a special issue to women and the interlocking forms of oppression they faced.[41]

Like *Gidra*, the genesis of Visual Communications (VC) was intertwined with the Center. As early as 1969, student filmmakers Betty Chen, Duane Kubo, Eddie Wong, and Robert Nakamura started to sift through the JARP collection for photographs as the Center sought to develop an educational program using visual media. Incorporated by Kubo, Wong, Nakamura, and Alan Ohashi as a nonprofit organization in 1971, and with an office adjacent to *Gidra*, VC produced educational curricula and collected still and moving images of the Asian American experience. Given the paucity of accurate representations of Asians and Asian Americans in mainstream media at the time, VC's early organizing, which included a traveling photographic exhibition, "America's Concentration Camps," portrayed the complexity of the Asia American experience.

Asian American Studies Central was located next door to VC and *Gidra*, and aided burgeoning Asian American Studies classes and programs with financial support from the Center. Led by Ron Hirano and Kenyon Chan, the organization, according to Chan, produced "sample course proposals, held workshops on teaching Asian American studies, provided guest lecturers" and was "instrumental in starting the Asian American Education Commission within the Los Angeles Public School District which fought for the inclusion of Asian American curriculum in K-12 [education]." The group also contributed to the national Asian American studies conference along with the Center at UCLA and USC.

For some students, their engagement with community organizing was transnational. Many Sansei students famously protested the U.S.-Japan Security Treaty. Meanwhile, Filipino Americans, many of whom did not fit into the Yellow Power rubric dominated by East Asians, formed Samahang Pilipino. In addition to campus activities, they protested the brutal dictatorship of Philippine president Ferdinand Marcos through the Los Angeles chapter of the Kaptipunan ng Demokratikong Pilipino [Union of Democratic Filipinos, or KDP]. According to Florante Ibañez, "mainly younger Filipino Americans and ex-patriots from the Philippines, who were escaping martial law, or had prices on their head, or were being searched by the Marcos dictatorship for elimination," established the KDP. Through study groups and protests, KDP members brought attention to the abrogation of civil liberties in the Philippines and America's role in supporting Marcos.

The Center also overlapped with Asian American student organizing through the Asian Radical Movement (ARM). Eddie Wong recalled that "It just so happened that the acronym Asian Radical Movement means ARM, and to a lot of people that means armed rebellion, or armed resistance. And so, we said like hey, that's kind of cool. You know, that's kind of badass, and, hey, we'll go with it." In one flyer, the ARM acronym signified "Ally, Rally, Move!" and, defiantly, "Attack Racist Motherfuckers!!" [43] These were not just words, however. As a Marxist and anti-imperialist organization, ARM rallied against America's wars in Southeast Asia and protested chemical weapons producer Dow Chemical.

ARM members also advocated for proletarian causes, such as the case of Charles Bargain-eer, an African American Associated Students UCLA (ASUCLA) dining services employee, whom the university unfairly dismissed. As Suzi Wong recalled, "This cafeteria worker was not Asian American, or even Asian, but it was the principle of fair treatment at work and calling UCLA to have integrity about that." ARM (with Students for a Democratic Society) staged a sit-in at the Associated Students office in November 1969, which resulted in several arrests that included Wong, her brother Eddie, and Laura Ho.[44] The university pressed charges against Ho, whom ARM raised up as "an Asian student worker [who] has been fighting back for a long time...[who] saw that the only way to make effective change is through a united movement of all Third World peoples, students, and workers."[45] The Center supported Bargaineer by embla-zoning "JOB SECURITY FOR ASCULA CAFETERIA WORKERS" across its December 1969 newsletter, as well as in letters of support for the students who faced police persecution.[46]

In spite, or perhaps because, of this activism, tensions over the Center's identity as an academic unit versus a bridge between the university and the community existed. Just some four months after the Center was established, Helen Brown, a long-time Filipina American activist, "expressed concern over the strong academic stress of the Center and hoped for the continuance of more community programs over and above the *Gidra* and Tutorial programs."[47] Although clearly invested in community work, Ichioka recognized the importance of main-taining a clear academic orientation for the Center. In debates over leadership, he stated that the "Center has to have an academic program, that if it becomes a social service agency, [it will be] a dead end. In the search for a Director, he expressed his views on the advantages of having an academic man....He would be better able to deal with the administration and the other academic units on campus."[48]

Nevertheless, in what she called "A crude but glorious outline," Vivian Matsushige argued in 1972 that "I would like to see the Center become a 'Community Advocate'...[and] consider that its primary responsibility is to the Asian community and not the university. We should actively develop and maintain a constant working relationship with the same."[49] Such a vexing issue did not have an easy solution and the Center continued to navigate a treacherous terrain to balance the demands of academia and social action through the subsequent decades.

CONCLUSION

The seeds that the founders of the Asian American Students Center planted in the late 1960s took root over the generations that came after. Despite assaults over issues ranging from affirmative action to the very existence of ethnic studies, the Center persists. So too has the student activism that created the Center. In the 1980s and 1990s, students took to the streets over struggles including apartheid; equitable working con-ditions in Los Angeles; the UCLA Chicano Studies hunger strike; and fighting for the tenure case of Don Nakanishi, the *Amerasia Journal* co-founder whom the UCLA Graduate School of Education later denied promotion. In the 2000s and 2010s, efforts to disaggregate data to better represent Asian American and Pacific Islanders and raise visibility for neglected and emerging communities, catalyzed a new generation of student activists. That articulation of a more accurate and genuine portrait, while putting Third World solidarity into action, harkened back to the motivations of the Centers earliest students.

Moreover, the Center continues to germinate the ever-changing field of Asian American studies. The Center for EthnoCommunications, founded in 1996, is a revival of the campus film school's program for filmmakers of color that attracted some of the earliest Center stu-dents in the 1960s, and produced new generations of subversive visual storytellers. Today, the

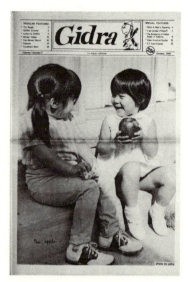

A sampling of Gidra covers, ranging from the first edition in April 1969 to an anniversary edition in 1999.

AASC partners with an Asian American Studies Department, which it worked to establish in 2004, that offers B.A. and M.A. degrees, a Pilipino Studies concentration, and study opportunities throughout Southern California, Hawaiʻi, and Guam.

Fifty years ago, when that collective of students met to articulate the words that began this essay, little did they imagine the transformations that would come about five decades on. Newer generations today have reconfigured the boundaries of "community change" and "curricular reform," but that bold experiment that those past students demanded lives on.

NOTES

1. Student Steering Committee Statement, December 15, 1968, Box CM-019, UCLA Asian American Studies Center Management Files [hereafter AASC-CM].
2. William Trombley, "12% From Minorities, First UCLA Racial Census Shows," *Los Angeles Times*, November 22, 1967; "Minorities' Enrollment Up at UCLA," *Los Angeles Times*, December 1, 1968.
3. Jacqueline Tasch, "The Long Road Home," in Claudia Mitchell-Kernan, *Forty Years of Ethnic Studies at UCLA* (Los Angeles: UCLA Graduate Division, 2009), 15.
4. All quotations from student activists are drawn from the Collective Memories Oral History Project or miscellaneous correspondence.
5. Glenn Asakawa, "The Sansei Concern," August 15, 1968, in Box Res-017, UCLA Asian American Studies Center RES Files [hereafter AASC-RES]
6. Asian American Studies Center Staff and Students [hereafter AASC Staff and Students], "A Report on the Asian American Studies Center at UCLA," September 20-21, 1969, in Box 142, Folder 5, Yuji Ichioka Papers, Special Collections, Charles E. Young Research Library, UCLA [hereafter Ichioka Papers].
7. "UCLA Establishes American Cultures Project for Ethnic Research," UCLA Office of Public Information press release, n.d., in Franklin D. Murphy Papers (Collection 363), Special Collections, Charles E. Young Research Library, UCLA [hereafter Murphy Papers].
8. Barbara A. Rhodes, "UCLA High Potential Program, 1968-1969," UCLA Special Education Programs, c. 1970.
9. Chris Rimlinger, "Young Grants Hi Pot Program Demands," *Daily Bruin*, December 2, 1969, 1; "The Asian American High Potential Program," in Box 142, Folder 6, Ichioka Papers.
10. Charles E. Young, quoted in Tasch, "The Long Road Home," 16; "Students, Faculty, Administration Back American Cultures Project at UCLA," *University Bulletin* 17:23 (February 3, 1969), 1.
11. Kitano, who published one of the first textbooks on Asian Americans released by a major publisher, served two stints as the Center's acting director during his thiry-year career at UCLA. Despite criticisms, he consistently took on administration in his advocacy for the Center.
12. Harry H.L. Kitano Memo, December 3, 1968, Box CM-019, AASC-CM.
13. "Proposal for an Asian-American Studies Center," c. 1969, 15, UCLA Asian American Studies Center Reading Room Files [hereafter AASC-RR]; E.R. Hardwick to Charles E. Young letter, June 16, 1969, in Murphy Papers.
14. "Proposal for an Asian-American Studies Center," 1. Many of the earlier documents use a hyphen between "Asian" and "American." For this essay, I drop the hyphen (as do contemporary writings) to emphasize the hybrid and dynamic nature of Asian American communities. I do not edit quoted archival material that uses the hyphen.
15. *Ibid.*, 3.

16. *Ibid.*, 17.
17. "Request for Funding of the Committee for the Study of Education and Society," 1969, in Box 142, Folder 7, Ichioka Papers.
18. "Week-By-Week Schedule: CES 103," in Box 142, Folder 7, Ichioka Papers.
19. UCLA Asian American Studies Center, "Report of the Asian American Studies Center," 1969-1970, in Box CR-005, UCLA Asian American Studies Center Records Files [hereafter AASC-REC].
20. Ronald Takaki memo to David Saxon, July 24, 1969, in Murphy Papers. Despite publications and strong student support, the History Department denied Takaki tenure. He went on to an illustrious career at UC Berkeley.
21. Ichioka served very briefly as an acting director between Huang and Nishio.
22. UCLA Asian American Studies Center Steering Committee Minutes, January 22, 1969, Box CM-019, AASC-CM.
23. Noel Greenwood, "UCLA Authorities Declare Emergency," *Los Angeles Times*, May 6, 1970, 1.
24. Mary Kao Interview.
25. Harry H.L. Kitano Memo, December 3, 1968, Box CM-019, AASC-CM.
26. "Franklin Odo," *Asian American Studies Center Newsletter*, December 1, 1969.
27. AASC Staff and Students, "A Report on the Asian American Studies Center at UCLA," September 20-21, 1969, in Box 142, Folder 5, Ichioka Papers.
28. "Guide to the Interdepartmental Major in East Asian Studies," Box CR-003, AASC-REC.
29. Quoted in Mason Stockstill and Stefanie Wong, "30 Years of Struggle," *Daily Bruin*, February 25, 1999.
30. "Guide to the Interdepartmental Major in East Asian Studies."
31. "CED Correspondence Masters" and "CED Correspondence" Folders, Box CR-002, AASC-REC.
32. "Phasing Out CED," *La Gente*, February 1975; Daniel O'Hearn, "Counter-Insurgency Pig Behind CED Cuts," *La Gente*, February 1975, 18.
33. Jeff Louie, "Asian Studies Wins approval," Daily Bruin, April 1, 1975; J.C. Ries to Lloyd Inui Letter, April 17, 1975, Box CR-002, AASC-REC.
34. "Proposal for an Asian-American Studies Center."
35. "First National Conference on Asian American Studies," Box Res-017, AASC-RES.
36. AASC, "Report of the Asian American Studies Center," 1969-1970, AASC-REC.
37. Carol Wong, "The Asian American Tutorial Project," *Asian American Studies Center Newsletter*, 1.
38. "UCLA News Briefs," *Gidra*, February 1970, 10.
39. AASC Staff Meeting Minutes, July 16, 1970 in Box CM-019, AASC-CM.
40. Digitized issues of *Gidra* are available at http://ddr.densho.org/ddr-densho-297/.
41. *Gidra*, January 1971 Issue.
42. AASC Staff Meeting Minutes, July 16, 1970 in Box CM-019, AASC-CM.
43. "Noon Rally at Meyerhoff Park," in Box 142, Folder 6, Ichioka Papers.
44. David Lees, "ARM, SDS Stage Sit-In; 35 Arrested," *Daily Bruin*, November 20, 1969, 20.
45. "Noon Rally at Meyerhoff Park."
46. *Asian American Studies Center Newsletter*, 1.
47. AASC Meeting Minutes, December 2, 1969, Box CM-019, AASC-CM.
48. AASC Student and Staff Meeting Minutes, April 23, 1970, Box CM-019, AASC-CM.
49. "A crude but glorious outline of what I, Vivian Matsushige believe the enter should be [sic.]," March 2, 1972, Box CM-019, AASC-CM.

BACK IN 1969

PROTESTS, YELLOW POWER, AND THE EMERGENCE
OF ASIAN AMERICAN STUDIES

AMY UYEMATSU

Amy Uyematsu at UCLA's Asian American Studies Center, c. 1970-1971.

In the 1920s, this was the Uyematsu's home at the family's Star Nursery in Montebello, CA. Francis Uyematsu can be found on the left end.

ANGRY ASIAN GIRL, CIRCA THE 1960S

When I was a teen growing up in the '60s, I was already angry about the racist conditions I was experiencing in Sierra Madre and Pasadena. In those days, there was no website called Angry Asian Girls, no popular comic series like Lela Lee's *Angry Little Asian Girl*—but I sure qualified as an angry Asian girl who would soon join other angry Asian Americans in the Asian American movement.

I was born 1947 in Pasadena, California, and attended public schools in Sierra Madre and Pasadena. I am a Sansei—third-generation Japanese American (JA). Grandpa Uyematsu built a thriving nursery business based in Montebello, Manhattan Beach, and Sierra Madre. After World War II, my father, Francis, the eldest son, was expected to take over running of the business; and by the mid-1950s, Star Nurseries operated solely in Sierra Madre, where he moved our family.

Dad had grown up in Montebello and was attending the University of Chicago when the Pearl Harbor attack occurred. Both my Nisei (second-generation) parents were very Americanized—they didn't try to teach my sister Mary and me Japanese or other cultural traditions like Japanese dance. Unlike other Sansei kids, our folks never forced us to attend Japanese language school on Saturdays. And sadly, we couldn't really talk to our grandparents, with the exception of Grandpa Morita, who was one of the few Issei (first-generation) who spoke fluent English.

Much as I wish I could understand Japanese, I realize that my Nisei parents were imprisoned during World War II and probably thought it was safer for us to assimilate. Along with some 120,000 Japanese American Issei and Nisei, my mother's and father's families were sent to internment camps. My mom's side (Morita), went to Gila, Arizona; and my father's side (Uyematsu), went to Manzanar, California. Growing up, my parents were like many Nisei who spoke very little about the camps. Years later, when I was in my thirties, my mother, Elsie, told me how, as a young teen, she was sent away on a train at the Pasadena station, describing how humiliating and painful it was.

Sierra Madre, a small town nestled against the San Gabriel Mountains, was a tough place for non-whites. There were only a handful of JA and Mexican families—no African American families that I was aware of. Back in the 1950s and '60s, Sierra Madre was very conservative, with a strong John Birch Society chapter. I was used to kids calling me "Jap" and pulling up the sides of their eyes while laughing at me. My elementary school teachers wouldn't stop them from yelling out "Jap" in the classroom. There were still many who considered Japan an enemy nation which bombed Pearl Harbor, and it was common thinking that Japanese Americans, even Sansei like me, were more Japanese and foreign than American. In the sixth grade, my friend Barney Barnes and I bonded over the popular Nancy Drew detective series. How disheartened I felt when he asked me who I would have sided with during World War II.

UYEMATSU FAMILY COLLECTION
AND PASADENA CITY COLLEGE

UYEMATSU FAMILY COLLECTION

Above: *In 1921, Amy's grand-mother, Kuniko Uyematsu, at the family's Star Nursery. Kuniko wrote tanka poetry and was a member of a tanka club.*

Above right: *In 1928, Amy's father, Francis Genichiro, stands next to Amy's grandfather, Francis. Sitting on the couch in a kimono is daughter Alice, who later died of tuberculosis in her early 20s at Manzanar concentration camp.*

Bottom: *In 1935, Amy Uyematsu grandparents' family, with Amy's father, Francis, standing in back.*

UYEMATSU FAMILY COLLECTION

In 1957, Amy Uyematsu's family at home on 207 Altadena Dr. in Pasadena. From Left to Right: Sam (in a white t-shirt), Elsie Morita Uyematsu (Amy and Mary's mother), Amy, Kuniko, Marian, Francis, and young Mary.

Above: In 1942, the Morita family stood in front of their J. Morita Store at 70 N. Pasadena Ave. the day before they left for incarceration. From left to right, mother Reiko, youngest Helen, 2nd son Richard, Elsie (age 15), oldest William (who just returned from Berkeley), and father Jiro. The family lived in the two-story building behind, to the left of the photo. Jiro did not believe they would be evacuated, as this was America. A White neighbor persuaded Jiro to let him run the store but he gave up after a few months. The store was closed. The Moritas continued to make mortgage payments from the Army pay of their sons. The family went to Tulare Assembly Center and Gila River Camp.

At right: Upon return from camp and Nebraska, the family returned to Pasadena Avenue in the 1940s. Reiko had a stroke but recovered.

MORITA FAMILY COLLECTION (ABOVE AND BELOW)

Above: Amy Uyematsu; her son, Chris Tachiki; and mother, Elsie Morita Uyematsu are seen with Morita family members around the Mishima Plaza plaque in Pasadena. Left to right: Dr. Ron Matsunaga, Bill Morita, Mark Matsunaga, Helen Morita Matsunaga, Reiko Morita. Behind are Marsha Matsunaga, Laura Matsunaga, and Jed Matsunaga.

Middle: From Throop College, Jiro Morita served in World War I. As a veteran, he became a naturalized citizen in 1936 and purchased his home and store.

Bottom: Jiro and Richard Morita left Gila River to work for a family, 1943. Jiro did gardening and Reiko did housework. The brothers came to visit before going overseas with the 442nd RCT I Company. Bill and Dick were roommates with Francis Uyematsu while attending University of Nebraska. Dr. Richard Morita is Professor Emeritus of Microbiology and Oceanography at Oregon State University Corvallis.

A couple of other incidents really stand out. Our first home in Sierra Madre was a rental house on Mariposa Avenue. The Jewish neighbors who lived a few doors down across the street had a cross burned on their front lawn. When my parents decided to build their own home on the Star Nursery property bordering Fairview Avenue, the surrounding neighbors circulated a petition to prevent my parents from doing so. While the petition failed, this act reflected the hostile racial climate of where I grew up.

In junior high, several of the girls I used to pal around with dropped me and acted like they didn't know me. In ninth grade, I had a drama teacher who bluntly told me not to try out for the school play (presumably because I was Asian and all the roles were given to white students). By the time I attended Pasadena High School, I felt angry and isolated. Our mother was aware that my sister and I couldn't have a normal social life like other teen-aged girls. She drove us on Sundays to the Japanese Presbyterian Church located in East Pasadena so we could meet other Sansei and have a bit of a social life (Sunday school and basement church socials).

One of my *hakujin* (white) friends told me a popular Sierra Madre teen was interested in taking me out, but wouldn't because I was Japanese. I did get asked out by a high school class-mate in tenth grade, not realizing that he was Jewish and probably also facing prejudice from others. All I recall of that date were the stares we got. Four years later, when I took a freshman English class at UCLA, I wrote about that horrible dance experience and how stigmatized I felt by people whom I thought were my friends.

As a senior at Pasadena High School, I took a civics class where I tried to talk about the World War II internment camps and how my parents and grandparents were "relocated" to Manzanar and Gila. Not one of my fellow students believed me. In the '60s, the camps were still not covered in U.S. history books. I think my teacher tried to support me, but I felt the sting of rejection from classmates who knew me. Years later, I was glad when the history books began to include the camps, and now with two grandsons, it's even more gratifying to have them tell me they're celebrating Nisei hero Fred Korematsu in a fourth-grade play at their San Francisco elementary school.

Entering UCLA in 1965, and so angry at white racism, I purposely avoided getting to know hakujin students, who were the majority. This included my freshman roommate, Fern Weather-wax, who was always kind to me, but by the spring semester I moved back home. While I had also been accepted at USC, Cal Berkeley, and UC Santa Barbara, my main reason for choosing UCLA was that it had the largest JA student population. In the mid-'60s, there were still very few minorities on the UCLA campus, and most of us "Orientals" (the accepted term at that time) were Sansei.

In the summer of 1965, right before I started at UCLA, the Watts Riots occurred. I vaguely remember watching the riots on my family's black-and-white television, but in those first two years of college I was much more interested in finding the social life I never got in high school. I joined Theta Kappa Phi, one of the two Oriental sororities, and spent more time on soror-ity activities than my classes and homework. My grades were just average, spending hours at Powell Library, along with many other JAs, looking for cute guys and unable to concentrate on my books. It's kind of a miracle I didn't flunk out—especially being a math major, and one of the few girls enrolled in predominantly white male courses. I recall UCLA having all sorts of political speakers at Meyerhoff Park, which I would pass every day on my way to class. I also remember seeing students picketing a campus bungalow that was connected to Dow Industries, the chemical firm supplying napalm to the U.S. Armed Forces in Vietnam.

Amy's maternal grandparents, Jiro and Reiko Morita, came to Pasadena High School in 1963 as part of the Mishima Sister-City program, in which Jiro was very active. Mishima Mayor Tazio Hasgawa of Japan visited the campus as part of the Sister City exchange.

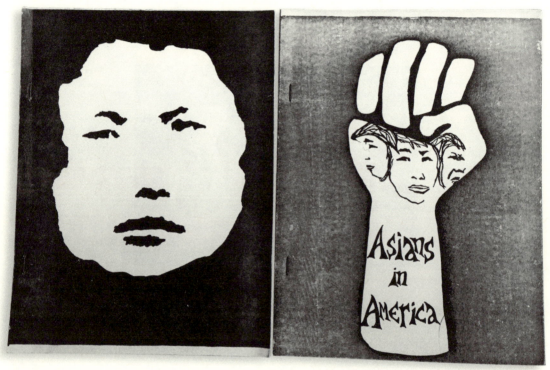

In 1970, the Center's Asian American Studies class, taught by Franklin Odo, used a two-volume mimeographed reader, "Asians in America."

THE UCLA CLASS THAT FINALLY SPOKE TO ME

968 and 1969 were transformative years for many of us. There were major widespread events in '68 that sadly included the assassinations of Dr. Martin Luther King, Jr. and Bobby Kennedy. Violent protests broke out at the Democratic National Convention in Chicago. At the Mexico City Summer Olympics, American sprinters Tommie Smith and John Carlos gave the Black Power (Human Rights) salute during the medals ceremony. On our UCLA campus, two Black Panther students, John Huggins and Bunchy Carter, were shot to death. At San Francisco State, the Third World Liberation Front, a coalition of mainly non-white students, led a massive strike lasting five months.

There were stirrings of political activity among Asian Americans at UCLA and other West Coast colleges. Locally, there was a 1968 conference called, "Are You Curious Yellow?" hosted by the student group Sansei Concern, and I'm pretty certain I attended some of these early meetings of Asian American students wanting to come together and "do something." Political concerns around racism and the Vietnam War were speaking to me and my involvement in the sorority tapered off.

By the spring of '69, during my last undergraduate semester at UCLA, I signed up for two transformative courses, "Orientals in America" and "Ethnic and Status Groups in America." "Orientals in America" radically changed—even saved—my life. Taught by political activist and JA history scholar Yuji Ichioka, it was the first and only class at UCLA that was actually relevant to me. It was called "Orientals in America" because at that time the term "Asian American" was only beginning to take hold—and interestingly, it is Yuji who was given credit for coining the term. "Orientals in America" was one of the first Asian American ethnic studies courses offered anywhere.

Attending Yuji's class was incredibly exciting for both UCLA students and people from off-campus, hungry for discussion of Asian American issues. Without any textbooks, weekly sessions consisted of lectures, guest speakers, panels, and discussion groups. I remember the lecture hall being really crowded—maybe standing room only. Each time we met, the room was charged with energy, an undeniable feeling that we were waking up, not just individually, but also as a group of young people ready to make change.

It was also a lucky circumstance that I enrolled in Sam Farber's sociology course, "Ethnic and Status Groups in America." Years later, I learned that Farber was a Marxist from Cuba. Of course, I didn't know this at the time. Farber had us read *Black Power: The Politics of Liberation in America* by Stokely Carmichael (Kwame Ture) and Charles V. Hamilton. Reading that book along with taking Yuji's class was a perfect pairing for me because it enabled me to see what was going on in the Black Power movement and gain a better understanding of our own particular experience within the broader context of America's persistent racism against all non-white groups.

Our identity as Asian Americans was rapidly changing. The "Black is beautiful" and "I'm Black and I'm proud" messages resonated deeply with our own changing self-image and self-acceptance as Asian Americans. We were tired of being called "Jap," "Chink," and "Gook." Some of us who'd fought in the Armed Forces were scared of being shot by our fellow soldiers, whose racism against the Viet Cong was generalized to all Asians. Even within the American

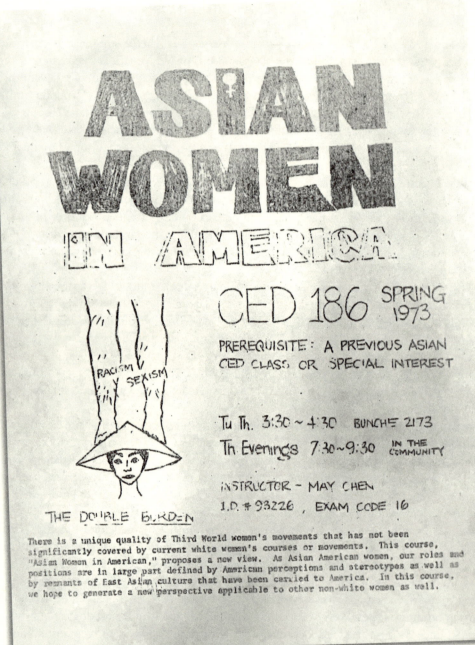

COURTESY OF UCLA ASIAN AMERICAN STUDIES CENTER COLLECTIONS

anti-war movement, our Asian American contingents were sometimes not taken as seriously. There seemed to be little awareness of the fact that the racism we faced as Asian Americans had strong connections to how Americans viewed the Vietnamese they were bombing. We were tired of being linked to immigrant hordes and the "yellow peril" exclusion policies our parents and grandparents endured. We were fed up with being characterized as silent and meek.

My long-held personal rage was finally finding a home, and my girlhood experiences could now be understood within the history of racist policies and attitudes toward Asians in America. We were finally examining our pasts and ongoing conditions in our communities from our own point of view. Instead of being either ignored completely in the history books or seeing our images grossly stereotyped and distorted by the majority culture, we were determined to uncover our true stories, to learn what really happened, and to articulate an Asian American perspective. I don't think I was alone in feeling that Yuji's "Orientals in America" class was truly life-changing.

OUR DEMAND FOR YELLOW POWER

For my final term paper in both "Orientals in America" and "Ethnic and Status Groups in America," I wrote a long essay entitled "The Emergence of Yellow Power in America." Looking back, I realize what an ambitious endeavor it was. Who was I, an undergraduate math major with little background in history and political science, attempting to write a paper with such a title? But perhaps this also reflects the tenor of the times. We knew we were fighting against racial injustice, and we felt swept into something much bigger than any one person.

The movement newspaper *Gidra* emerged in April 1969. Its inaugural issue included a short article by Larry Kubota entitled "Yellow Power." When I collected research for my term paper, I used Larry's article along with Alan Nishio's "The Oriental as 'Middleman Minority'," Carmichael and Hamilton's *Black Power*, William Petersen's 1966 *New York Times* article, "Success Story, Japanese American Style," and 1960 U.S. Census data. Back in those days, students would normally go to the library card catalog to find books and articles addressing their topic. There was little available on my topic so I used whatever sources I could find—this was long before students could do research online and simply Google the subject they were writing about.

I saw the emerging Asian American/Yellow Power movement as part of the ongoing civil rights struggles which had begun in the 1950s. We were inspired by Black activists such as the Black Panthers, Angela Davis, and Malcolm X. We also saw our young movement joining international ones against colonialism and imperialism. Many of us were reading Frantz Fanon's *The Wretched of the Earth*, where he advocated that colonized people in the Third World (Asia, Africa, Latin America) needed to rise up and gain independence.

We rejected the image of Asian Americans as a "model minority"—something which we are still fighting against fifty years later. Additionally, we refuted the stereotype of Asian Americans as quiet and passive—just look at our history and see how we've stood up and spoken out. One great example are the No-No Boys at Heart Mountain Concentration Camp, who went to jail for refusing to answer questions about their so-called loyalty while they and their families were imprisoned behind barbed wire by the U.S. government.

Student activist Mike Murase included my term paper in the October '69 issue of *Gidra*. A few weeks later, part one of the essay got published in the *L.A. Free Press*. Philip Huang, who was Acting Director of the newly formed Asian American Studies Center (AASC), hired me that same month to join the staff as a research assistant. I guess my writing was decent enough

PHOTO BY MARY UYEMATSU

Amy went on a cross-country road trip in 1973 with her sister Mary and their friend Lynn Yamashiro Taise. They visited Asian American movement people in Denver, Chicago, Detroit, and New York City. On the bookshelf are copies of Roots: An Asian American Reader *and* Asian Women.

for him to think I might be able to do research and writing for the Center.

At the end of my Yellow Power term paper, I included three poems I'd written during the course. I was undergoing so much personal change that an essay alone could not convey all the emotions I felt. I must admit I was more excited by Mike Murase's August '69 publication of those poems than my essay, never imagining that I would continue to write poetry the next five decades that followed. The pages of *Gidra* were filled with poetry and art by young activists, making *Gidra* all the more important in documenting the Asian American (AA) movement. For my own evolution as a writer, those monthly printed poems in *Gidra*, as well as the early political poetry I was reading by Lawson Inada, Janice Mirikitani, Nikki Giovanni, and others, were inspirations. Asian American themes continue to be a primary impetus in my work; and I even venture to say that anger and a "yellow power" mentality fueled the writing of my first book, *30 Miles from J-Town*, and are still expressed in my poems today.

EARLY DAYS IN ASIAN AMERICAN STUDIES

The ethnic studies programs, which began in the late 1960s, were the result of many college campus struggles, primarily organized and led by determined minority students. In the fall of 1969, four research units opened at UCLA—the Asian American Studies Center (AASC), the American Indian Studies Center, the Bunche Center for African American Studies, and the Chicano Studies Research Center. With limited budgets and resources, each center wanted to offer ethnic studies courses and produce publications that reflected the true histories and ongoing issues of our respective communities. Being able to fight inequities through education would prove to be thrilling, challenging, and fulfilling.

I joined the AASC staff about a month or two after it opened. My mother Elsie was the Center's very first staff member. According to my mom, the committee that chose her was impressed by the fact she'd read the *Autobiography of Malcolm X*—a book most other Nisei had not. In those early years, students would hang out at the Center and enjoyed talking with my mom, who was likely close in age to their own parents.

Prior to being employed by the Center, I had actually applied to IBM for a computer-related job. Computers were just beginning to take hold, and my father had urged me to pursue math because he saw such a future in computers. Attitudes toward women then, even more if you were also non-white, were backward. Women's liberation had not yet made gains on the job front. I passed the first few rounds of the math aptitude testing. But when interviewed by a male IBM recruiter, I was asked questions that aren't legal now—like, wouldn't I rather stay at home as a wife and mother? Needless to say, I wasn't hired.

In retrospect, I'm glad the computer job didn't materialize and that I was asked to join the AASC staff. The AA movement was just beginning to blossom, and I consider myself lucky to have been right in the midst of early ethnic studies. My own political activism, spurred on by the racist experiences I had growing up, could keep developing and be expressed in a variety of roles I played at the Center—in curriculum (as both a teaching assistant and later a co-instructor), in research, and in publication.

Since this was an entirely new field with no precedents, we had enormous freedom. At the time, I didn't realize what a rare opportunity this was to create. We were pretty much inventing our roles and programs as we went along. There was an idealism, purpose, and willingness to work long hours, knowing we were fighting racial inequality and improving how Asian Americans are viewed and treated. The idea of self-determination was highly valued in the movement, with Asian American studies providing one way we could redefine and empower ourselves.

My new boss, Alan Nishio, was just a few years older than me. When I was given specific tasks, I was often completely on my own to figure things out. For example, my first research assignment was to discuss the need for continuing the recruitment of Pilipino students for UCLA's High Potential (Hi Pot) program. I used data from the 1960 Census, L.A. County Commission on Human Relations, and the Los Angeles Unified School District, resulting in a report, "The Filipino in the Hi Potential Program." In those days, we didn't have the arsenal of scholars like we now have now in Asian American studies, so we had to do all our own investigating.

Eddie Wong, another research assistant, and I were teaching assistants (TA) for Franklin Odo's introductory class, "Asian American Experience." We were hired part-time, both of us still students. Being a TA was super exciting for me. None of us were "experts" so we could discuss and debate topics freely and passionately. There was a lot of collaboration between Franklin and the students in deciding on guest speakers, films, and community panels as we planned courses that had never been taught before. When Franklin developed a class linking U.S. policy in Asia to how we are treated here, he asked students to assist him with research and writing up the class proposal. These challenging, and what we considered vitally important, tasks,were done collectively and often with a credentialed person (someone with a master's or doctorate degree) working closely with activist students.

Decision making at the Center was also done collectively and was deliberately set up to **not be** top-down authoritarian. There was a strong commitment to serve our Asian American student population, and early on, that became a major issue. We had a Coordinating Committee that consisted of the Center director, along with reps from each Center program (curriculum, resource development/publications, student-community programs, and administrative support). One of the biggest Center "struggles" I witnessed was over the hiring of the Student Community Programs coordinator. Those of us on the student "side" packed the meeting where the two major candidates spoke at. We were determined to have the more progressive candidate be selected. AA activists, both on and off campus, wanted to make sure the AASC didn't become an irrelevant academic institution with weak or no ties to our students and local communities.

BEFORE XEROX MACHINES AND COMPUTERS

hen Franklin taught that intro course, we had no formal textbook. There simply weren't books at the time that covered the topics we wanted, so we gave our students a two-volume mimeographed reader that was stapled together. Students today probably have never heard of the term "mimeograph." When we needed to have many copies of a page or article, we used an inexpensive duplicating device that forced ink through a stencil onto paper. It was commonly used in offices and also by school teachers. I still have copies of "A Reader on Asians in America." The title page carries the date October 1970, and in Franklin Odo's "Preface" the text is called "experimental." It contained an eclectic, wide-ranging assortment of articles from various books and newspapers (primarily *Gidra*). We included scholarly pieces (such as Alex Saxton's "Race and the House of Labor"), along with controversial work (like Dinora Gil's "Yellow Prostitution" and Ron Tanaka's "I Hate My Wife for Her Flat, Yellow Face"). We even required students to read work by well-known political writers, such as Noam Chomsky and Jean-Paul Sartre, in order to deepen their perspectives of the war in Indochina.

Sometime in 1970, Alan Nishio appointed me to be publications coordinator, with the initial task of producing a book for Asian American studies classes. Our editorial committee consisted of Franklin Odo, Eddie Wong, Buck Wong, and myself (previously Amy Tachiki). We used the mimeographed readers as a starting point and brainstormed about additional content for the three sections: "Identity," "History," and "Community." Our book was going to include documents from the movement, such as I Wor Kuen's "12 Point Program and Platform," and interviews with Philip Vera Cruz, Pat Sumi, and other key Asian American political figures. This early phase of planning content and doing interviews was the most enjoyable for me. In the "Identity" section I was in charge of, we added poems by published authors like Lawson Fusao Inada and Al Robles, as well as undergrad students like Violet Rabaya and Marie Chung.

Once we agreed on content, the time-consuming production phase began. First, we had to type up the text. Besides myself, I think we hired several students to use IBM Selectric typewriters and, if memory serves me, we corrected mistakes with liquid white-out and made duplicate copies using carbon paper. After the text was typed up, our design team pasted up the copy and laid out each page—something that computer desktop publishing has made so much faster and simpler. The designers were Kathy Glascock (an off-campus Sansei artist a few years older than the rest of us), along with three UCLA students—my sister Mary Uyematsu, Eddie's sister Donna Wong, and photographer Bob Nakamura.

The book went to press in 1971 and was called *Roots: An Asian American Reader*. I believe that Eddie or Franklin came up with the title. Our book, and *Asian Women*, published the same year by a UC Berkeley women's collective, were the only two Asian American studies books available. For several years, they were the standard texts used in Asian American studies classes. After so much work and effort was put into the making of *Roots*, I don't remember there being too much feedback. Years later, I learned that *Roots* has sold around 50,000 copies and had ten to 12 printings, which was good to know.

THE *LITTLE RED BOOK* AND STUDENT ORGANIZING

While I was on staff at the AASC, I was also a member of the Asian American Student Alliance (AASA). From 1970 to 1972, I was a graduate student in education and working toward a master's degree along with a teaching credential. I spent most of my time however doing Center-related tasks and attending political meetings and rallies. I often skipped my graduate classes, but I was still conscientious enough to turn in the final required papers. What surprised me was how my liberal professors, even giving me good grades when, instead of focusing on the course topics, I turned in essays on my anti-war involvement and the unique perspective of Asian Americans. I saved one of those papers, and am still amused by my writing on "Asian Mobilization against the War" and my name beneath the title.

I think there have been several iterations of AASA at UCLA. Looking back at the AASA minutes I still have from 1972, I can see how much our members wanted to share our strong anti-war beliefs with other AA students on campus. We also tried to have study groups where we could read and discuss what was then termed Marxist-Leninist-Mao Zedong Thought. Many of us carried Mao's book of quotations (the *Little Red Book*), and in our minutes, it is evident that we were influenced by his thoughts on "criticism/self-criticism." It was typical for AA movement organizations, like AASA, to talk about strengths and weaknesses, evaluating our group efforts, while also being self-critical of our individual roles.

Besides study groups, the AASA put out a newsletter and offered film screenings and discussions, mainly focused on the war. Perhaps the biggest AASA event I helped with was a program called "Put Your Foot in Your Mouth." The line-up included conga players, Kasamahan dancers, and the popular movement trio Chris Iijima, Joanne Miyamoto (now Nobuko), and Charlie Chin. Proceeds from the event were given to a group called "AMMO Vietnamese Supply Drive." One of our continuing concerns (and sometimes frustrations) was our ability to bring in larger numbers of AA students on campus.

Asian Americans for Action, with out-of-town visitors, summer of 1973. Sitting from left: Visiting feminist from Japan, Mitzi Sawada, Amy [Tachiki] Uyematsu, Lynn [Yamashiro] Taise; standing from left: Elsie [Uyematsu] Osajima, Yuri Kochiyama, Min Matsuda, and Aiko Herzig-Yoshinaga.

ANTI-WAR PROTESTS I WILL NEVER FORGET

There were thousands of protests, rallies, and sit-ins during the 1960s and '70s. The causes ranged from civil rights to women's liberation, ethnic studies to gay rights, and demonstrations were against the war in Vietnam. In my own experiences, there were two protests that are seared into memory.

One protest was at UCLA in the early '70s. Thousands of students were gathered on the grassy lawns between the boys' and girls' gyms to hear anti-war speeches. What stood out in my mind weren't the speeches, but the chaos and panic of the crowd afterwards fleeing in every direction when the police had come on campus. Many of us were worried because of previous rallies where the LAPD SWAT Team had used force against protestors. I ran towards Campbell Hall, where I worked. Just outside, I saw a cop hitting a young Latino student. Though he was curled in a fetal position on the ground, the cop wouldn't stop bashing him with his baton.

The second protest I'll always remember was in the summer of 1973. My sister Mary, friend Lynn Yamashiro (now Taise), and I had traveled cross country and were staying in New York City. We went to an anti-war march in Times Square. Shortly into the march, the NYPD's mounted police were rushing toward us to break up the crowd. Everyone started running, and I wasn't fast enough to escape into a restaurant or business, like others. One cop on horseback came after me. Even though I was crouching against a storefront, he still rode his horse right up to me and then had the horse rise up on its hind legs and kick me. Fortunately, I wasn't injured and was able to get to the subway. Years later, I learned that this particular policeman had the reputation of being a bully.

Also memorable about that cross-country trip was meeting members of Asian Americans for Action, including several Nisei women activists like Mary (Yuri) Kochiyama and Aiko Herzig-Yoshinaga. We attended a Chinatown Health Fair on Mott Street organized by students and volunteer doctors (similar health programs were being offered by movement groups on both coasts). One night I went to the Apollo Theater in Harlem to hear singer/poet Gil Scott-Heron, who I already knew from his song, "The Revolution Will Not Be Televised." In cities like Chicago, D.C., and Denver, we met and stayed with other young Asian American movement activists. In those days we would crash at movement contact's apartments, even those we were meeting for the very first time.

THE RAUCOUS, INSPIRATIONAL, UNSTOPPABLE REVOLUTIONARY '60S

While it's a little hard to accept the fact that I'm a 70-year-old "baby boomer," I feel incredibly lucky to have been young during the '60s and consider the 1960s and '70s one of the most important political and social periods of American history. On the political front, it was easy to get involved and become an activist with so much occurring daily, both nationally and internationally. The early '60s civil rights struggles in the South had mushroomed into all sorts of minority resistance groups, ranging from Black Power groups like the Black Panthers to the Brown Berets, Young Lords Party, Asian American Political Alliance, and American Indian Movement. Anti-war and free speech movements were widespread at universities; environmental, women's rights and gay liberation groups were springing up; and the New Left was emerging with a definite socialist and Marxist-Leninist perspective. We were affected by the revolutions and socialist movements occurring outside our borders, often inspired by the freedom struggles occurring in the Third World.

Accompanying the tumultuous political events were immense cultural changes. Hippies and

COURTESY OF AMY UYEMATSU AND JOYCE NAKO

PAAWWW (Pacific Asian American Women Writers West) began around 1976 and was a LA-based support group of Asian American writers for over 25 years. The group included novelists, playwrights, poets, journalists, and actresses.

Front left to right: Amy Uyematsu, Akemi Kikumura Yano, Joyce Nako, Naomi Hirahara, Emma Gee, Momoko Iko

Middle row left to right: Pam Tom, Velina Houston (behind Joyce), Cecilia Manguerra Brainard, Ardis Nishikawa

Back Row left to right: Jude Narita, Fe Koons, Wanda Coleman (who wasn't a member but was good friends with members and did a reading with the group at least once), Chungmi Kim

the counterculture movement, marijuana, Woodstock, psychedelics, the Beatles (whom I saw at the Hollywood Bowl in 1964), sexual freedom, Motown, Andy Warhol and pop art, America's moon landing, on and on. Guitarist Carlos Santana describes the era this way: "The '60s were a leap in human consciousness. Mahatma Gandhi, Malcolm X, Martin Luther King, Che Guevara, Mother Teresa, they led a revolution of conscience. The Beatles, the Doors, Jimi Hendrix created revolution and evolution themes."

So when I look back at my own political transformation in the late '60s, it was almost inevitable to be swept into the "mind-blowing" and radical climate of the times. I am grateful to have been at UCLA's Asian American Studies Center right when ethnic studies was starting. How lucky we were to have the freedom to develop new classes and books. At the time, I didn't fully realize what important work we were doing. And I owe so much to the Asian American movement for helping me develop a worldview that continues to guide me and help me better understand complex political and social conditions.

It was also gratifying to be part of the anti-war struggle and actually see the war end. I am glad to see so many of today's movements—environmental, #BlackLivesMatter, the 2017 Women's March, #NoBanNoWall, the Parkland High students' #NeverAgain, among others—in this current reactionary period. When I was involved in the '60s, America was also very divided—around the war, civil rights, youth rebellion, and more. Yet the divisions and ultra-right extremism we're experiencing now in 2019 feel harsher and more dangerous. In 1974, the year my son was born, Nixon was impeached, and there were congressmen of conscience, both Democratic and Republican, who united against him. That is no longer the case. What worries many people my age is whether the gains we fought so hard for—including voting rights, affirmative action, a woman's right to an abortion—will be taken away.

As a former high school teacher, I am dismayed by what our young people aren't learning in public schools and colleges. The humanities and arts keep getting cut back, with the resulting damage to our children's ability to create and imagine. In this age of "fake news," we need to be critical, skeptical, and thorough in our information gathering—especially in this age of Google when we can go online and be bombarded by all sorts of crazy websites with biased and sometimes incredibly false claims (such as lies that the Holocaust never happened or that Sandy Hook was a hoax). For me, in order to develop a critical point of view, you need to talk a lot about the issues, observe, read, and trust your gut for what you know is true. I think it's hard for many people to be able to stand up for what they believe—even if it goes against the majority, even if it means you might get some flack or make some enemies. But to make positive change, we've gotta stand up. If there's anything at all we learned from the movement days, it is this fact: Stand up for truth and speak out against injustice. This may be the most valuable lesson I gained from my involvement, and it's a belief which I continue to adhere to.

Corny as this may sound, I still have faith in "Power to the People." Younger students in Asian American and other ethnic studies need to remember it took months and months of struggle and protest before universities allowed these programs to be created. One of my favorite slogans from marches, and still heard in today's demonstrations, is from a Chilean song used before the 1973 overthrow of the Allende regime, "¡El pueblo unido jamás será vencido!"—the people, united, will never be defeated. This was true in 1968 and 1969 when Black, Brown, Yellow, and Red students closed down San Francisco State as they led the Third World Liberation Front Strike. This is just as necessary and true today.

Bassist Taiji Miyagawa accompanying Amy when she gave a poetry reading for her first book, 30 Miles from J-Town, at the Japanese American National Museum in 1993.

Amy and Taiji Miyagawa at the Los Angeles Times Festival of Books in 2006 for her third book, Stone Bow Prayer.

CHAPTER 9

COMMITMENT TO SERVICE

*PILIPINO STUDENTS AND THE BEGINNINGS
OF ASIAN AMERICAN STUDIES*

CASIMIRO TOLENTINO

EARLY LIFE

my father was a retired disabled veteran of the U.S. Army and a recipient of the Congressional Medal of Honor given to Filipino World War II veterans in 2016. My father was a Lieutenant initially in the Philippine Scouts, which was incorporated into the U.S. Army. He survived the Bataan Death March, which rendered him with many debilitating chronic diseases. He remained in the U.S. Army as a dentist. My mother and her family lived in the mountains of her province to escape the Imperial Japanese Army. My parents met when my father was stationed in my mother's province. They moved to Quezon City, and my mother became a high school home economics and physical education teacher.

I was born in Manila, Philippines in 1949, and was an American citizen because my father was part of the U.S. Army. My siblings were also all born as American citizens. I have an older brother who attended UCLA and became a chemist and a Captain in the U.S. Army. Among my three sisters, they became a chemist (a UCLA grad and Asian American Studies Center alumni), an insurance officer, and a nurse, respectively. My mother had to undergo naturalization when we migrated to the U.S.

In 1959, when I was ten years old, my family migrated to Los Angeles, California. This was a very difficult and traumatic experience for both of my parents. Our family did not have close relatives here. My father had distant cousins—extended families from his home province—but my mother had no one. Because of California's discriminatory licensing regulations, my father was not able to practice as a dentist. His foreign training was not acceptable for licensing in California. Similarly, my mother was unable to teach due to her Philippine educational credentials. I still remember my mother crying every night for her family and friends back home. My father held two jobs till he died at the age of 65, as a clerk with the State of California and a postal worker for the U.S. Postal Service.

My mother stayed at home and was the neighborhood babysitter. Our home was filled with about ten kids almost every day for ten years. When my youngest sister enrolled in high school, my mother at the age of 55 went back to college at Cal State Fullerton to get her California teaching credentials and a Master's in Special Education. She spent the next 24 years teaching special education classes for the Downey Unified School District.

My first school in America was Magnolia Elementary School in the Pico-Union area of Los Angeles. I was placed in the English as a Second Language (ESL) track, got pulled out for ESL classes about twice a week. It was my first time to be in contact with other folks of color. My friends were Black or Hispanic, and I don't recall ever making a distinction, except that I was just some kind of Asian person in their eyes. Filipinos were not part of their experience until I arrived.

Our landlady, Mrs. Langlois, was kind and generous to our family. I recall my father answering an ad for a one-bedroom apartment and we could see our future landlady shaking her head no when we arrived. She looked at us waiting outside of our car and asked my father if we were his kids. He said yes and she rented the apartment to us because she liked that we were "well-behaved" children. She baked cookies for our school bake sales and my mother would

UCLA School of Law Graduation portrait of Casimiro Tolentino, 1975.

Casimiro Tolentino at an anti-war rally in Los Angeles in 1970.

share Filipino desserts. Mrs. Langlois and her husband lived in a back house and shared many stories of her growing up during the Great Depression in L.A., including selling apples and ties on the Venice trolley.

We lived for a short while in South Central, then moved to Montebello for junior and senior high school. I enjoyed high school because I had a great English teacher and learned to read books avidly. She would buy "banned books" to share with her students and made literature come alive. I was part of a "college track" program, and we had blocks of time for English, history, social studies, and "free period."

AT UCLA

Since my brother went to UCLA, I was also predestined to attend. My parents had hoped for me to become a doctor or an engineer. My first major was engineering, which lasted a quick two quarters. I changed to zoology because I had a great biology teacher in high school and was part of a track to go to medical school. I enjoyed zoology because of both the subject matter and teachers. I was also active in helping a life sciences student support group, and slowly became involved in community service as a tutor for the UCLA Tutorial Project. I eventually became a Coordinator, Trainer, and the Director of the Project—an unusual area of participation for a south campus, hard science major at UCLA. I tutored Black and Chicano kids at Broadway Elementary School in Venice, coordinated trips, and subsequently ran a summer school for six weeks supported by foundation grants.

My work with the UCLA Tutorial Project extended to the Asian American Tutorial Project (AATP). I was encouraged by fellow students who were undergoing a growing consciousness as Asian Americans, Pilipino Americans, and in general as a person of color. The Civil Rights movement and anti-Vietnam War movement were seminal in my growing consciousness. Although the Vietnam War was in Asia, there were initially very few Asian American voices. The "Asian American Experience" class I took, campus demonstrations, sit-ins, and teach-ins inculcated in me the need to learn about more about the Asian Pacific American and Pilipino American experience. I still recall Franklin Odo, my "Asian American Experience" professor, lecturing on Pilipino history for one class session lasting 45 minutes, and yet other APA groups were covered over many more lectures. I asked him why there was such a dearth of history, and he replied that there was a minimal amount of written Pilipino American history available.

It was at that point that I began to study and research the Pilipino experience in America. I learned about the pensionados; the farm workers in the Central, Salinas, Coachella, and Imperial valleys; the Alaskeros in the Alaskan canneries; the plantation workers in Hawai'i; the stewards in the Navy; and the waiters, bartenders, and servants in cities such as Los Angeles, San Francisco, and Stockton. I learned about American history and its interactions with people of color from Professor Ron Takaki's American history class. His lectures were the first of many history courses that I would take in fulfilling UCLA's course requirements.

PILIPINO AMERICAN CONNECTIONS

I continued to work with the Asian American Studies Center (the Center) in developing an Asian American Unicamp, and slowly came in contact with other Filipino American students that started showing up during my senior year. One person was Florante Ibanez, who was not a UCLA student but worked at the Center as a library assistant, and met at various community events such as for SIPA (Search to Involve Pilipino Americans). Florante learned that I was active in the various Center student projects and the mainstream UCLA community, and proposed developing a Filipino American student group. We convened our

Casimiro Tolentino teaching the Pilipino American Experience Course at UCLA. 1973.

first meeting as a potluck, and that was the first time I actually met Jennifer Masculino (my future spouse) and Sheila Tabag. We began our group by registering three student registration cards—Jennifer, Sheila, and myself. Jennifer and Sheila went out there on Bruin Walk with mimeographed flyers advertising, "Big meeting with Filipino student group." Our group didn't have the name Samahang Pilipino at that point in time yet, but about twenty folks showed up and that was the beginning.

We called ourselves, Samahang Pilipino Ng UCLA, "Pilipinos Coming Together at UCLA." A core group of about eight students had the most organized potlucks, cultural programs, and participated in the then-largest student-organized project, the UCLA Mardi Gras—a fund-raising event for UCLA Unicamp, a summer camp sponsored by the University Religious Conference. Samahang Pilipino earned about eight trophies, including best decorated booth. There were many mispronunciations of our name but this allowed us to shout back the correct pronunciation.

We participated in Filipino American student conferences leading up to the annual Filipino American Far West Convention. Founded in Seattle, the convention shared experiences growing up in America, addressed pressing issues our community, and to develop a network of activists. I coordinated the labor panel with union organizers, Silme Domingo and Gene Viernes, for several conventions. Silme and Gene were later assassinated because of their work organizing the Alaska cannery workers. Phone calls, faxes, and snail mail was our main means of communications back then, which meant we had to work on the panel several months before the convention date.

Samahang Pilipino began as a support group by bringing Filipino American students together who had difficulties adjusting to UCLA, culturally and socially. It brought together south campus (science and engineering) students to interact with the north campus (humanities and social sciences) students. With time, Samahang Pilipino became an advocate for Pilipino American history classes, recruitment of P/Filipinos, retention of UCLA P/Filipino students, and P/Filipino curriculum in the L.A. Unified Schools. Around this time, President Ferdinand Marcos imposed martial law in the Philippines. The issue of whether you were pro or anti-Marcos was a difficult one not only at UCLA, but also in the Filipino community. A cultural program with no political basis would be open to challenges, whether or not the organizers were pro or anti-Marcos. This divisiveness permeated projects and programs in the Filipino community.

Our first conference as Samahang Pilipino was in San Diego. For the first time, we saw other Filipino students who shared our experiences as sons and daughters of farm workers and the U.S. Navy and Army. We began lasting friendships and developed an informal network. There was no Internet, and thus no emails or cell phones to facilitate communications. Samahang was able to obtain office space at the Center and we used their IBM Selectric typewriters, fax machines, mimeograph, and telephones to maintain communications with the other student groups.

As the Los Angeles Filipino community learned of Samahang Pilipino, several community leaders and educators, such as Royal Morales, Ester Soriano, Helen Brown, and Dr. Milagros Aquino (Cal State Dominguez Hills) contacted us. With their organizations such as SIPA and the Council of Oriental Organizations, Samahang Pilipino members put together several teach-ins relating to the Pilipino American experiences at the Methodist Church in L.A. Phil-

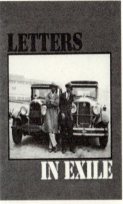

COURTESY OF CASIMIRO TOLENTINO

First published reader on Pilipinos in America edited by Jesse Quinsaat. Associate Editors were Henry Empeno, Vince Nafarrete, and Lourdes Pammit, with Assistant Editors Jaime Geaga and Casimiro Tolentino. 1973.

Casimiro Tolentino serving as Vice-Chair of the Los Angeles City Civil Service Commission. 1983

ip Veracruz spoke about the farm workers in Delano; Larry Itliong spoke of the founding of the Filipino American Political Association; and Helen Brown spoke the lack of books, literature and curriculum on Pilipino-American history at the L.A. Unified School District.

Samahang Pilipino organized the 1974 Filipino American Far West Convention. At that time, issues relating to our experience, history, and culture were covered, while the issue of pro or anti-Marcos came into the forefront. The Seattle group, who founded the Convention, walked out of the conference because they felt that the focus was no longer on the issues facing P/Filipinos in America, now instead on issues facing P/Filipinos in the Philippines. This created a divide that continued into future conventions, which eventually ended in the early 1980s.

TEACHING THE PILIPINO AMERICAN EXPERIENCE

While taking Professor Odo's class and working as a teaching assistant for Alan Moriyama's Asian American Studies class, I began to draft a syllabus for a class on the "Pilipino American Experience" in America. My research was focused on P/Filipinos in California, since I was not as knowledgeable about the history of P/Filipinos in Washington, Hawai'i, and Alaska. I prepared the syllabus during the summer before I started my first year at UCLA Law School. It was to be used by a lecturer that the Center had hoped would teach the class, but they couldn't find someone, and I was told by colleagues that there was no one to teach it except for myself.

To teach the course, I had to meet with a faculty committee who had to approve it. The committee members came from geology, history, psychology, and sociology. Some faculty had difficulty in determining what history I was teaching—Philippine history or Pilipino history in America. One member related his experience during World War II in the Philippines and believed that this was the focus of the course, to which I eventually clarified for him that it was not. Some believed that our history in America did not seem unique enough to merit a whole course. In the end however the course was approved, and I was hired by the Center as a lecturer/research assistant.

"Pilipino American Experience" consisted of three lectures a week and a small group discussion class led by my teaching assistants. One lecture each week was conducted by a speaker from the Pilipino community, which included Royal Morales, Albert Mendoza, Philip Veracruz, Helen Brown, Ester Soriano, and Dr. Milagros Aquino. The class attended community meetings and took two trips to help build the Pablo Agbayani Village, a farm workers retirement home named after the first striker who died on the picket line. Class projects included oral histories of each student's family, and original essays on the Navy, farm workers, and growing up as a Pilipino.

My relationship with the Asian American Studies Center was a collection of various push and pull factors. First and foremost, the push to the Center came as I began participating in Center student projects such as the Asian American Tutorial Project, Unicamp, and taking Asian Pacific American (APA) classes. Pulling me along was the development of my consciousness as an Asian Pacific American, and especially as a Pilipino American. I saw the Center as very Japanese-centric and considered various approaches to increase Pilipino student participation, including being part of the coordinating committee. Founding Samahang Pilipino was a pull factor, as I felt compelled to find a mechanism to bring Pilipino students and their issues together. The Center became the fulcrum for this with its support and encouragement, and Pilipino students appeared to participate more in their programs. The Center assisted Samahang Pilipino by allowing us access to its equipment, supporting our programs such as the Pilipino Youth Center in Wilmington, and sponsoring cultural programs, teach-ins, and conferences.

Another pull factor was the commitment of the Pilipino students in my class to continue learning about their own history. Many students were moved by the lectures from community speakers and wanted to put together a reader on the Pilipino experience. We were familiar with *Roots: An Asian American Reader* (UCLA, 1976), which we admired as the seminal work on APA history and wanted to do a similar project. Students wanted to use the oral histories that they had compiled from their parents and communities, and felt that it was important to share them with those outside the university. We were encouraged by our interactions with Far West Convention participants and what we were learning from each other. Friendships that lasted past graduation developed and an informal network had begun.

The Center encouraged Pilipino students to work on developing *Letters in Exile: An Introductory Reader on the History of Pilipinos in America*, the first reader on Pilipino Americans published by the Center in 1976. The readings from the Pilipino American Experience class, which I copied from various sources such as newspaper and magazine articles, and essays from the class became the basis of the anthology. The Center supported the project by continuing to hire me and Jesse Quinsaat as research assistants. It was difficult work for novice writers and editors. We had to contact copyright owners, edit each other's original essays, and compile the articles and essays that would cover everything from the diaspora to the Pilipino American experience. We were students who had different majors, ranging from engineering, to sociology, to zoology. We debated about the inclusion of certain articles such as "America's First Vietnam" relating to the Pilipino American War; on "America's Floating Plantation" relating to the Pilipinos in the U.S. Navy; and on the "Yellow Peril." There was no debate on including excerpts from Carlos Bulosan's *America Is in the Heart*. We also learned from Lowell Chun-Hoon, then-Editor of the *Amerasia Journal*, who gave us direction and guidance that we tried into incorporate in this anthology.

Letters in Exile remains a seminal publication, and many students have shared with me that it was the first book that influenced their interest in learning more about the Pilipino experience. Publishing *Letters in Exile* and organizing Samahang Pilipino as an advocacy group were additional inspirations for us continuing the Far West Convention.

LAW AND COMMUNITY ORGANIZING

After graduating from law school, I worked as a civil rights lawyer at the federal government for the then-Department of Health, Education and Welfare (DHEW) in Washington, D.C. I litigated cases on school desegregation and handicap discrimination; and wrote regulations and guidelines for the Lau decision, Title IX, and what was to be the future Age Discrimination in Employment Act (ADEA). After a year-and-a-half, I returned to California as an attorney for the Agricultural Labor Relations Board (ALRB). I worked in the San Joaquin, Sacramento, Salinas, Coachella and Imperial Valleys, litigating unfair labor practices.

The Agricultural Labor Relations Act (ALRA) provided a level playing field between growers and farm workers. It was difficult yet enlightening in learning at a very personal level about the life of both growers and farm workers. I was assisted by Philip Vera Cruz, Pete Velasco, and other Pilipino farm worker assistants of the United Farm Workers (UFW) legal department in my hearings. They helped me immensely in understanding the dynamics between the growers and unions, as well as the history and experience of the Pilipino, Yemeni, and Mexican farm workers. I eventually became the Fresno Regional Attorney, Sacramento Regional Director, and San Diego Regional Director at the Agricultural Labor Relations Board (ALRB).

I left UCLA with community organizing skills and a much better understanding of my own

Above: The Tolentino family, including Jennifer, CJ, and Cristina at the FilAmArts Festival at Point Fermin, Los Angeles, CA, 2014.

Below: Pilipino American Alumni-UCLA celebrating the co-founders of UCLA Samahang Pilipino, 2012. Left to Right: Jennifer Tolentino, Florante Ibanez, Casimiro Tolentino.

history and of Asian Pacific American history. There was a drive in me to make sure that Pilipino American and APA history was accurately portrayed and that we were advocates for issues important to us. To that end, I helped Visual Communications in becoming a nonprofit film and media organization to ensure that our stories would be told in various media.

After eight years, I moved back to Los Angeles, still working in labor law at the Writers Guild of America West. At that time, reconnecting with UCLA law school friends, such as Stewart Kwoh and Michael Eng, we organized the Asian Pacific American Legal Center (now Asian Americans Advancing Justice-Los Angeles). I served as a volunteer attorney and Board Chair. Members of the Legal Center shared the same values and goals: to be advocates for Asian Pacific Americans and to ensure our voices were heard in decisions that impacted our communities. We wanted our issues placed on the table and also resolved with our input—a national voice.

Using the organizing skills we learned at UCLA and our experience with the Asian American Studies Center, the Legal Center advocated for Asian American issues by organizing a working legal advocacy group with the help of law students and APA attorney bar associations. Our first major case involved the murder of Vincent Chin, a Chinese American who was mistakenly identified as Japanese in Detroit and, because of his presumed ethnicity, was beaten to death by two white Americans who scapegoated the Japanese for their loss of autoworker jobs. We organized rallies and legal guidance for the Chin family and supporters. The case coalesced the APA community and provided a focus on APA issues. Subsequent cases involved the El Monte Garment workers, and the community uprising in 1992 that affected the relations between the Black and Korean communities in Los Angeles following the Rodney King verdict. We were a national voice for our communities.

I continued to help Visual Communications develop as an advocate for APA issues in the media as a board member. I also continued community work in organizing the Pilipino American bar associations in San Diego and Los Angeles, and to organize the National Association for the Advancement of Philippine Arts and Culture (FilAmArts) as a volunteer curator and board member.

In the mainstream community, I was active with the local United Way, ReBuild L.A., and various civic organizations. I was appointed a Commissioner for the Los Angeles City Civil Service Commission in the 1980s, the Los Angeles City Fire Commission in the mid-2000s, and am currently a Commissioner for the Los Angeles County Sheriff Civilian Oversight Commission. Professionally, I continued as a civil rights attorney as the Assistant Chief Counsel for the Department of Fair Employment and Housing for ten years, and as an Administrative Law Judge for the State of California for 19 years.

In retrospect, I engaged with many civic organizations, in addition to APA groups, to make sure Pilipino American and Asian Pacific Americans were able to sustain our collective voices. I am proud that some the groups that I helped have remained strong and self-sustaining. The hardest dynamic is making sure that a strong foundation in leadership and mission is maintained. Samahang Pilipino continues to be a leading student organization at UCLA; Asian Americans Advancing Justice-Los Angeles is the leading APA voice on issues of immigration, human rights, and civil rights; and Visual Communications is a vital APA voice in the entertainment industry.

In general, many of us who were alumni of the Asian American Studies Center kept in touch because we shared the same values in advocating for the APA community, and wanted to organize our communities to reflect those values. Today, we support and maintain community advocacy groups and continue to organize conferences, teach-ins, and many other activities to educate our communities.

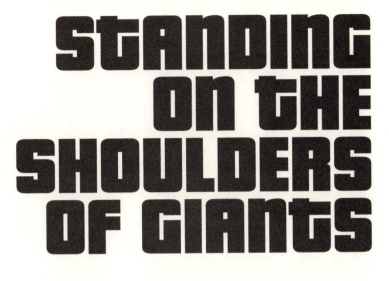

CHAPTER 10

STANDING ON THE SHOULDERS OF GIANTS

NEW VOICES IN ASIAN AMERICAN STUDIES AND ACTIVISM

HOLLY LIM

Holly Lim at 2016 OACC Eddie Huang-Jeff Chang Authors in Conversation.

FAMILY BACKGROUND

I was born in the Philippines. My mom and dad are both Filipino, but my dad is also part Chinese. My mom has a little bit of Spanish in her background as well. I came to the United States with my mom when I was around four years old. Eventually, my brother joined us, but my dad stayed in the Philippines. He and mom are divorced, and now he lives in Nevada.

For most of my life, I grew up in a single parent home. My mom was a nurse. She speaks really good English but experienced a lot of racism. For instance, she had the necessary education and the experience, but was often overlooked for promotion. I didn't really understand those dynamics until I attended UC Riverside (UCR) where I took ethnic studies courses.

My mom's family is from Ilocos Norte. She's Ilocano and grew up on a farm. For them, freedom meant getting a higher education and coming to the United States. In order to do that, my mom and her siblings moved to Manila, to Quezon City, and got their degrees. One by one, they started coming to the United States, thanks to the 1965 Immigration and Nationality Act (Hart-Cellar Act)! One by one, the siblings sponsored each other, and then their parents. Eventually in the late 1980s, my mom and I were able to come here.

We first landed in Los Angeles, and lived mostly in the downtown area for the first couple of years. Then we moved to Montebello and then to Pico Rivera. Even though that's where our home was, I interacted a lot with friends in the San Gabriel Valley area. I grew up mostly with Latino kids in elementary school. In high school, I got to hang out with other Asians. For a good part of elementary school, I thought I was Mexican, actually! I realized in the sixth grade that "I'm actually not Mexican. I'm Asian!" I went to St. Benedict Elementary School in Montebello, and then to Ramona Convent Secondary School in Alhambra—a mix of both Asian and Latino cultures.

Initially, it was hard adjusting, assimilating. I didn't have teachers that looked like me. I didn't have a lot of friends that looked like me, either. My only source of ethnic or cultural resource/reference was my family, which I thought was more than enough. But it was also good to see that in the classroom and with your peers, and I didn't fully get that until I was in college.

HIGH SCHOOL YEARS

I went to an all-girls, Catholic private college prep school. My mom worked really hard as a nurse. In my family, education was a huge deal, and my mom sacrificed herself so that I could have the best education possible. Ramona Convent was hard academically. I actually think high school was a lot harder than college, but it prepared me for so much in that way.

Although it was a Catholic school, and all-girls, Ramona Convent was not with the Catholic archdiocese at the time, and so I think my religion teachers were able to teach us religion in a different way. All of my religion teachers from ninth through twelfth grade were "divorced from the church"—former nuns or priests. One was gay, and another came out after I graduated. This was the setting in which learned about religion and Catholicism. My sense of social justice actually stems from my religion teachers, because they taught from a perspective of love and social justice.

Holly Lim, while growing up in the Philippines (above)
and in California (below).

Because it was an all-girls school, there was a minor women's studies-based curriculum. I took a summer computer class, which was pretty rare for a girl in 1999, to take one class before getting into high school. I had to make a website on a woman in science and her accomplishments. That wasn't a normal type of education for a young girl. It wasn't ethnic studies, more like feminist studies—social justice, women's empowerment, and women's consciousness type of topics.

COLLEGE YEARS

Even though I signed the paper that said, "I commit to UC Riverside," I feel like it was fate—that UC Riverside chose me. I really wanted to go to Loyola Marymount because I went to a high school where we were cranking out a bunch of folks who went there. However, I ended up going to Riverside because my family couldn't afford Loyola. Even with scholarships and other resources, it just wasn't enough. I didn't want to get into really bad student loan debt.

If I could somehow turn back time and got acceptance letters to Harvard, Stanford, any Ivy League, UC Berkeley, or UCLA, I would probably decline them and still go to UC Riverside, which propelled me into ethnic studies and leadership. I had two cousins who had attended Riverside: Rod Daus-Magbual, who was also in ethnic studies, and his brother. I relied on the networks I had—my social capital— because my cousins had gone there. They connected me to a few people who introduced me to Asian Pacific Student Programs (APSP), where I felt home in this sea of 15,000 students.

When you're in a new environment, you don't know whom to trust. If Rod said, "You can trust Joe Virta," I felt like I could trust Joe, who was the Director of the Asian Pacific Student Programs office. Joe was really a mentor to me. APSP hired student coordinators to handle different aspects of the program. There were program coordinators for the API Women's Mentor Program (APIWMP), part of the Peer Mentor Youth Program. I could go into these different program spaces and feel connected to people; that connection to others who looked like me, and going through similar things like me, felt like home. Yet home sometimes never feels perfect, posing challenges for me that helped me grow into the leader that I didn't know I could be.

I volunteered with APSP for a while. They offered me a program coordinator position of APIWMP. That's what got me into ethnic studies. That fall, Dr. Jodi Kim was teaching "Asian American Women." As a coordinator, I didn't know enough at the time to be leading and creating programs for API women, so I took the class. That was the start. After one class, I took another. It eventually turned into a minor. I really used what I learned at APSP and Katipunan Pilipino Student Organization.

I was also a part of an informal student organization called, Pilipino Studies Collective (PSt), and formally co-founded Collective when we officially registered as a student organization with its own budget. Between watching TV and during commercials, we talked about Tagalog classes and how much we needed more of them. We daydreamed about what we wanted. These dreams were the reason why I was able to take Tagalog and Filipino American studies classes at UC Riverside.

When I was in the Philippines, I spoke Tagalog. I often heard Ilocano among my family, but no one really taught me the language. Before I came to the United States, my mom had told my preschool teachers and everyone around me to only speak English. She was planning for us to come here and she didn't want me to feel out of place with an accent.

I wanted to get back to my home language when I went to UC Riverside. One of the first classes I took was for Tagalog. When I told my family about it, the reaction from my elders was, "We're in the United States. You speak English perfectly. Why would you want to go backwards?!" I thought I was going to get more positive reactions like, "Yes! We're so happy that you want to speak the language."

PSt was also part of this statewide collective of other campuses that wanted more Pilipino studies courses, like at UC Irvine and UCLA. In my third year, I was really passionate about re-instating Filipino studies courses at UCR, which hadn't been taught in five years. People forgot about them.

It was me and someone I called *kuya* (older brother), who had a shared interest in Filipino studies. It was me and my family: my *kuya* and my *adings* (little siblings)—we created our own constitution and by-laws. We did a grassroots campaign where we got several hundred signatures and submitted it to Professor Dylan Rodriguez, who agreed to teach a course. I was expecting a much longer campaign, but we got it done in one semester! It was really important for me to see that organizing as a collective could get you the results you hoped for. I enrolled in all of the Filipino studies courses afterward.

For me, social capital means having the networks and people who can provide resources, opportunities, or open doors. An example of that would be my cousin Rod and his girlfriend at the time, Arlene Daus-Magbual, now Assistant Dean of Asian American and Pacific Islander Student Services at San Francisco State University, who both attended UCR. They left a great impact with the way they conducted leadership development, were involved in APSP, and led the high school mentorship program that supported youth who ended up going to UCR. One of these youth was Jocyl Sacramento. Arlene was in student government, so that influenced and encouraged Jocyl to be involved, too.

When I first started at UC Riverside, Jocyl was the external vice president of the student senate. She chose me to be one of her interns. One of the first things that Jocyl said during the Proposition 54 campaign was "We're going to make coffins." We were going to do a visual demonstration, at the center of campus, of all the things that could die if Prop. 54 were to pass. Prop. 54, the way I understood it, was a legalized way of racial profiling. It was the cherry on top of Proposition 209, which banned affirmative action in California.

The older students didn't want to have Prop. 209, part two. There was a lot of energy among student organizations statewide to ensure Prop. 54 didn't pass. As the external vice president, Jocyl sat on the board of the University of California Student Association (UCSA). One of their top three issues was working on the "No on Prop. 54" campaign. All of the UC campuses were doing some sort of demonstration that day, and that was my introduction to student government: "We're going to make coffins because we don't want Prop. 54 to pass."

That same day, Jocyl said, "You're going to make a class announcement about registering people to vote, and why they should vote 'no' on Prop. 54. You're going to go into the largest lecture hall on campus to make an announcement, and advocate for this." I had signed up for student government thinking I was just going to make signs and get shuffled around where I would be needed, not working on a political campaign. I didn't expect that, but I'm glad that that's what happened because that's where my passion now lies.

Lim learned how to connect legislative advocacy and community organizing through the United States Student Association national network, working with other student leaders in Washington, D.C., in 2004 (above). As co-chair of USSA's Asian Pacific Islander Caucus in 2006 (below), she helped mentor and support API student leaders.

GROWTH, LEADERSHIP DEVELOPMENT, AND THE STUDENT BODY PRESIDENCY

When I started out, I really didn't intend to seek leadership in student government. I was just trying to do something; I didn't think I was going to be student body president one day. Post-Prop. 54, after the doing grassroots work of talking to students, registering them to vote, and educating them, we hosted "Grassroots Organizing Weekend" (GrOW) with the United States Student Association (USSA), the counterpart of UCSA. GrOW did trainings geared towards leadership development for young people, and taught us how to do grassroots organizing. They created scenarios for us, and we would role play. It culminated in the ultimate scenario, where we would be going to a meeting to ask a decision-maker to make a favorable decision.

I always thought of myself as a supporter in the background. It was Jocyl and Catherine Cu who had organized GrOW on campus, but said, "Holly, you're going to be our spokesperson." There was a lot of self-doubt. When I was really young, I remember watching an episode of the TV show *90210*, and the character Brandon Walsh had become student body president of the university. The first thought that came into my head was, "I could never be like Brandon."

At first, I didn't want to be the spokesperson because I thought, "What could I possibly say to a powerful decision-maker?" When I spoke and then said things that I had no idea I could say during the role play scenario, it surprised the person playing the decision-maker, and it surprised a lot of people in the room, too. I was probably the most surprised. I later came to the self-realization that I had a voice.

What had started at UCR developed this passion within me around leadership development. It's a lot of the reason why I'm at Public Allies today, and why I'm doing the work that I'm doing. It's been fifteen years since those role play scenarios, but they still carry a lot of weight for me today.

It's similar to how my team and I run Public Allies. We get a lot of resistance like, "That's not me. I'm not going to do that." We push, and then ten months later, we're graduating our allies. There's a purpose to making them uncomfortable. One of the things that I ask allies is, "Are you uncomfortable or unsafe?" People tend to conflate the two. "If you're uncomfortable, but you're growing, then let's keep doing that. If it's really unsafe, let's not do that." Looking back at those times when I was uncomfortable, I just had to allow that to happen in order for me to grow.

After the GrOW training, I began to think, "I could do this!" and ran for student senate. I actually ended up becoming the external vice president. When you're in that role, you have to sit on the board of both UCSA and USSA. I became a part of a network of badass people of color student organizers and leaders. One example was Gregory Cendana from the national Asian Pacific American Labor Alliance (APALA). We were on the board together. The campaigns that UCSA and USSA had set forth were aligned with what I was passionate about—access to higher education. Another important campaign was the DREAM Act (Development, Relief, and Education for Alien Minors Act), both in California and nationally. Although I wasn't undocumented, I felt an allyship in being an immigrant.

I had this solidarity with student organizer leaders, not just from California, but from all over the country. I had this network that really helped me to navigate leadership, because leadership for a woman of color was very difficult. It was difficult for me when Jocyl and Catherine, people who were my models, had left. I was it—the leader. People were looking to me now, and it could be lonely. So it was important that I had the network within UCSA and USSA.

I was elected student body president from 2006 to 2007. I have this aura of humility that people don't quite equate with leadership. A lot of people didn't expect me to become student body president. Eventually, that became my master's program thesis: Why is it when it comes to Asian women, we are thought of as incapable of leadership? Why are there so few of us? Before me, there was only one other Filipino student body president at UCR, and she was the first in the entire UC system. Filipinas have had a long history in California, but it amazes me how very few of us—Asian women—are in top leadership positions, even when it comes to student government.

I felt like my accomplishments weren't just mine, but also belonged to the people that I worked with. Our student center was being remodeled and they were tearing down buildings with student fee money. The administration wanted to purchase a trellis and palm trees. I proposed putting the student money back into the programs. There was a lot of resistance from the administration, so I ran on a slate on UCR's parliamentary system where the students elected their senators, and the senators elected their officers. I ran on a slate for three years. My first year, I got seven senators in, including myself. The next year, I got ten. My last year, I got a supermajority of all of the officer positions, except for one.

Because of that coalition building, I was able to gain support for putting the money back into the student resource centers to be more accessible. UCR always prided itself on being a diverse campus, but I thought it was a shame that our programs, that served students of color, women, and LGBT folks, weren't getting adequate resources to serve this large student body.

I organized a meeting with the administrators in a large space and packed the room with a hundred people all wearing green t-shirts. Green for yes—let's spend this money on our student programs! That summer they did the renovations, and APSP, instead of being located in the back of the building, was now in the front with windows. It's a huge space now. The others student programs used to be cramped in the corner, but were now more accessible!

My greatest accomplishment was being the voice that I didn't know I could be, and using the power that I had as a decision-maker in a position of leadership. . .to move something that I was passionate about, and that I knew would benefit the community, not just when I was there at UCR but also for future generations.

COMMUNITY ACTIVISM AFTER GRADUATION

Before I graduated, UCSA offered me a position as a field organizer and collective bargaining coordinator. I accepted it because I just wanted to organize. That was at the heart of what I wanted to do after graduating.

It was challenging for me because I was coming from a position of power to now being a field organizer serving students. I needed to heighten and elevate the voices of students. I was really lucky to have landed in that position, because for a 21-year-old to be running a statewide campaign on the California DREAM Act, or a youth registration drive, was rare. During my second year, when we did a voter registration drive, we registered between 35,000 to 40,000 students. I was now mentoring and coaching the next generation of student leaders. That was the position that cemented for me that leadership development was something that I wanted to do professionally. I wanted to keep doing campaigning or organizing, too.

UCSA is based in Oakland, and it's what brought me to the Bay Area. That was a transition too for me, since I never lived that far away from home before. I had family in Daly City, but for the most part, I had to get readjusted to not being in school, to working, and to a new environment. It was good for me. Whereas Riverside didn't feel quite like home, Oakland had that home feeling for me. That's partly why I haven't left and have been here since 2007.

UCSA and USSA were the networks that allowed me to continue to do the work I was pas-

At UC San Diego, Lim trained students to register voters and educate and engage the campus community in 2007.

sionate about; even after student organizing was technically done for me. It gave me a job here. I went to quarterly conferences where I met students who were doing similar things. UCSA and USSA helped me to develop a community in Oakland, working with Asian Pacific Islander Youth Promoting Advocacy and Leadership and Filipino Advocates for Justice. My UCSA friends were my network of support, and were involved in the community. We still have potluck dinners together to talk about issues and provide support, both personally and professionally.

I stayed with UCSA for two years. I could've stayed longer, but it was my philosophy that I wouldn't have had the experiences, new knowledge, and new skills as an organizer if the person before me had not left. It was this tradition of only doing the position for two years and making room for the next generation. When I left, it was 2009 and the Great Recession was going on. It was hard to find a job, so I was unemployed for a while. I did some work with Job Corps and realized it wasn't for me. One of my housemates was great friends with Lailan Huen, the daughter of Jean Quan, the former mayor of Oakland. Lailan and her family were looking for someone to be the day-to-day campaign coordinator for Jean's mayoral campaign. I interviewed with them and they gave the position to me. I started around the summer of 2010, and had just turned 25.

Even while I was at UC Riverside, I was always rooting for the underdog. Anyone I had on my election slate were people that always got overlooked. Even during the entire mayoral campaign, Jean was one of the top contenders, but was constantly being overlooked for someone like Don Peralta—a white man with resources and part of the good ol' boys network. What I learned was that community is really important, and that it was her family and her community that propelled her forward.

You can't do leadership alone. You need to have a community backing you. I learned this at UCSA: I'm not here to work *for* you; I'm here to work *with* you. That is the mentality I still continue to have. It's what propelled me to pick the title for my master's program thesis: "That's What She Said!: Narratives of Asian American Women Leadership." I starting noticing that a lot of the narratives being told about Jean were similar to the stories that I heard when I was UCR student body president. I finally made the connection that it wasn't just me, but that there were external factors causing these narratives to happen.

I was the second Pinay student body president at UC Riverside. Jean was the first Asian in Oakland, and the first Asian woman, mayor of a major U.S. city. But why only now? California has been around for a while. And our institutions have been around for a while as well. During my mid-twenties, that's when I started thinking about the parallels between my personal story and Jean's campaign.

ASIAN AMERICAN STUDIES AT SF STATE

was getting a lot of pressure from my cousins to go to San Francisco State University. They talked a lot about their master's program. Within the five years after I had graduated from UCR, Rod and Arlene would ask, "When are you going to grad school? When are you coming to State?" Dr. Allyson Tintiangco-Cubales, a professor in the Asian American Studies Department, would ask from time to time too. I was also getting pressure from my mom.

It was really helpful to have people be supportive of me furthering my education. I just wanted it to be on my own time. I was waiting for something to make grad school meaningful for me, and that happened with the narratives about Jean Quan and how they were similar to my experience. I asked myself, "Where could I go to study this? Where can I get the most support?" There weren't any Asian women's programs available to my knowledge, and so I went into Asian American Studies at SF State. If I was going to talk about women leadership, I wanted to talk and learn about that from women leaders.

My master's thesis confirmed my theory, that stereotypes around Asian American women were contradictory. You're either too tough—the "dragon lady"—or too soft—the "lotus flower." That's a recipe for crazy-making, because if you do one small thing, it could either make you look too aggressive, or too submissive. It's really hard to navigate that. When I was student body president, I got a lot of "Holly, you're not tough enough." But then there would be other situations where I would get, "You're too harsh, Holly."

During Jean's campaign, people said the same things like, "You're going to be too soft on crime. But, Jean, smile more." What did they want her to do? I felt the same. What did I have to do to please everyone? We really shouldn't have to please everyone, but part of the story was this crazy-making that happens from expectations of people, based on stereotypes, of what Asian women are supposed to be. Those expectations get exacerbated in positions of leadership. A lot of it is racially and gender-charged with racism and sexism.

COMMUNITY ACTIVISM POST-SF STATE

After graduate school, I had a hard time finding a job. I had all this energy—I had just written this thesis and was really passionate about it. I wanted to practice it. For me, my thesis wasn't something that I was just going to put on a shelf in the library and let die. For me, it was about praxis. That's the thing about ethnic studies and community work—knowledge is important, but practicing to apply that knowledge in the community is the essence of why I do ethnic studies.

It was frustrating after SF State to not be able to do that. I did nonprofit work, but it wasn't until I was hired at the Oakland Asian Cultural Center (OACC) that I was able to do more programming. But still, I wasn't doing leadership development work. What I tell my Public Allies now is, "If you're ever lost, figure out what your North Star is." For me, my North Star had always been leadership. So I was feeling pretty lost. I was wondering, "How can I get back to leadership?" I didn't have to be in a position of leadership, but I could be in leadership development. I didn't find that until I joined Public Allies.

After OACC, I worked for Asian Health Services (AHS) as the executive assistant to Sherry Hirota, the CEO and who been at the helm of AHS for almost forty years. Sherry has this great leadership style, and has a lot of respect from her peers. How can other Asian women, or women of color, build that influence or network, so we that can move our communities? Sherry had that ability. If something was important to the community, Sherry was able to elevate that. That was one thing that I learned from her: How do I replicate that influence, not just for yourself, but also how I teach that to others?

The challenge in nonprofits is always is funding. Part of it, too, is balancing what people are used to. I'll often come into spaces where people think, "This is how we've always done it." But you also have energy from new folks who have innovative and creative ideas. I've noticed that folks who have been there longer aren't open to hearing about the innovations that are possible that can strengthen the overall organization. That's where there is tension.

Through Urban Habitat's Boards and Commissions Leadership Institute, I'm learning to apply a just transition framework developed by Movement Generation. That's how I see social change moving forward, the idea that transitions are going to happen. What I like about that just transition framework is that it's regenerative, instead of extractive. In a capitalist society, we like to extract, take, and throw away. What might be coming next is: How do we regenerate? How do we center people? How do we center the earth? Before, I used to be very radical.

In Filipino spaces, it's like, *Kapitalismo, ibagsak!* (Overthrow capitalism!) That was my social change back in my early twenties. Now, it's not that I'm accepting capitalism, but thinking about it more in terms of just-transitions.

At Public Allies, I am the site director. We value social justice and equity, and firmly believe that there needs to be a pipeline of diverse young adults, working in nonprofits and government agencies, to ensure that social justice, and equitable practices and solutions are part of the process. Former First Lady Michelle Obama co-founded Public Allies in Chicago, and directed the Chicago chapter. In a weird way, I'm kind of doing her former job for the Bay Area.

One of the things that has came up a lot for me, all throughout UC Riverside until now, is imposter syndrome—believing that you are a fraud, and that you somehow persuaded a group of people into giving you a job or a position, or being allowed into a school. During the first week at SF State, I actually went into Allyson Tintiangco-Cubales's office and I said, "I don't think I can do this. I think I'm going to quit." She looked at me and said, "You're one of the most capable people who *can do this.*"

That was how I was first introduced to imposter syndrome, and it's a common theme that comes up a lot in the Public Allies space. We're trying our best to figure out programming and training to support allies or fellows on how to navigate imposter syndrome. At the core of it is coaching young people to be adults with a mind frame and mindset of equity and social justice. We're replicating a lot of what I learned in GrOW—finding your voice, how to practice that, and how to continue this commitment to the community, social justice, and equity.

LEGACY OF THE THIRD WORLD STRIKE

Ethnic studies classes and community work go hand-in-hand. I could not do community work if I didn't have ethnic studies. And, I couldn't do ethnic studies without community work. Both had to happen in order for me to be on the path that I ended up being on. If I only did ethnic studies in the classroom, I wouldn't be applying what I was learning. I wouldn't be putting a critical lens to what was happening in decision-making spaces. If I was in community spaces and didn't have the context of ethnic studies, I couldn't do the programs that I was trying to run. I couldn't run the API Women's Mentor Program without understanding API women's history and experiences. For me, the two had to have happened at the same time.

The "Asian American Women" course I took gave me the context to provide stories outside of the classroom setting. Not everyone wanted to take ethnic studies, but people wanted to connect with people who looked like them or had similar experiences. In a way, we were making ethnic studies accessible to folks.

In spaces of government, if it wasn't for ethnic studies, I wouldn't look for representation. Now I count how many women, Asian folks, and people of color there are. Ethnic studies taught me to ask, "Whose voices aren't at the table? Whose stories aren't being mentioned? How can we elevate those voices?" These decisions impact a lot of people.

The core of ethnic studies and social justice is this idea of care. How do we care for one another? How do we care for ourselves? How do we care for the earth? That was the same message that I got from my high school religion teachers—the values around how you care for everyone. That has carried on to my leadership framework. In my thesis, I redefine leadership as caring for others and doing something about it. Leadership sometimes feels inaccessible to a lot of people who think of it as a foreclosed space for them, similar to how I thought I could never be like Brandon Walsh.

There's that saying, "We stand on the shoulders of giants." After the Third World Liberation Front and their strike, the folks coming afterwards are standing on their shoulders. That's how I

Lim delivered the 2015 keynote speech at the 25th anniversary of UC Riverside's Asian Pacific Student Programs celebration and linked arms with some of her mentors, including Dr. Arlene Daus-Magbual, Director of Asian American and Pacific Islander Student Services at SFSU (2nd from left), her cousin the Honorable Rod Daus-Magbual, Daly City City Councilmember and Director, Pin@y Educational Partnerships, (3rd from left) and Professor Grace Yoo, former chair of Asian American Studies, SFSU.

connect to the folks who started ethnic studies. I feel like I have this responsibility to continue that legacy—not in a savior complex way. More so because ethnic studies has done so much in opening my mind, doors, and opportunities; I want to continue doing that for generations to come. The giants gave me my torch, and I'm lighting the torches of my allies, and my students, encouraging them to do the same. Part of my leadership and teaching philosophy is that it's not about the leader, but about leadership. Movements can't be sustained by just one person, or by just the leader. Movements are sustained by leadership, and that's why leadership development is important to me, because we're passing that on.

NEW STRATEGIES

Learning happens inside and outside of the classroom. For ethnic studies, more needs to be done outside of the classroom. How do students practice what they're learning? There's this tendency sometimes with some students to get stuck in the theory. Ethnic studies happened because of the praxis: balancing theory and the practice is important. When people think of movements, they think of national ones, something that needs to be on a national or global scale, in order for anything to happen in this nation, our communities, or our lives. What I'm learning is that what happens at the national or global level first starts at the local level. I like to think of short-term, intermediate, and long-term strategies. I haven't quite grasped yet what the long-term strategy is, but for me, the short-term strategy should focus on the local level, getting more of us in local leadership spaces—on commissions, in local politics. Before anything reaches the national level, it has to start locally. That's why part of the strategy is to organize locally, and to elect and appoint progressive folks of color in local politics.

CHAPTER 11

HONORING COMMUNITY RESILIENCE & RESISTANCE

NKAUJ LAB YANG

Nkauj Iab Yang, speaking at the Southeast Asia Resource Action Center (SEARAC) Inaugural Equity Summit, October 2018.

FAMILY HISTORY

my parents are both Hmong and came from Laos because of the war there. Often-times, people forget that during the American War (Vietnam War), there was a war in Laos at the same time. My dad, who was only a teenager during that time, served as a soldier for the CIA Secret Army. I don't remember how old he was, maybe 14 or 15. When the war in Laos ended in May 1975, my parents were already married and decided to flee with my grandparents to Thailand. They were there for a few months and then they resettled in the United States, specifically in the Tenderloin in San Francisco. They were sponsored by a church in San Francisco and that's how they resettled there.

From there, my parents decided to move around and find their family. They moved to Texas and found family there. They also moved to Minnesota where they were able to reunite with my grandparents, and then they eventually settled in Colorado for a few years, where most of my siblings and I were born. I have five brothers, and I'm the youngest—a girl. I was born in 1984. Then in 1986, we decided to move to Sacramento, California, where I grew up.

Growing up in North Sacramento in Del Paso Heights was definitely trying times. We lived in a low-income neighborhood with a bunch of other communities. At that time we didn't know then, but after going to college, I learned and realized that in low-income communities, we all struggle and are all fighting each other for crumbs.

When I was in the K-12 school system, it was a struggle. I definitely grew up knowing that something was wrong. I definitely grew up with a lot of discomfort. I grew up watching a lot of violence, both inside and outside of the house. A lot of times, the violence inside the house was around financial struggles, and I just never knew how to put it into words. It wasn't until I came to UC Berkeley (UCB) and I took my first Asian American studies class that I found those words.

UC BERKELEY

I think it was ASAMST 20A, "Asian American History" with Harvey Dong where I started learning about Asian American history. For the first time in my life in a school system, I was able to learn about Southeast Asian history, even though it was just a bit of it. Still, it was the first significant moment in my life where I was able to finally feel like, "Whoa! Somebody sees the struggle that I went through." Through that class, I was able to finally have the appropriate context, the appropriate words, language, and knowledge to understand why I grew up the way I did. I understood that I had the power to create change. Taking "Asian American History" changed my life.

I came to UCB as an intended Political Science major, but once I took "Asian American

Yang, advocating for the disaggregation of Asian American Pacific Islander (AAPI) data in Sacramento, CA, in 2016.

Top: Yang and other REACH! coordinators in 2005. REACH! stands for "Retention and Empowerment of Asian Pacific Islander Youths Considering Higher Education." Their community work targeted high school students, especially those who are underrepresented, low-income, and non-college tracked.

Bottom: Yang at the second annual UC Berkeley Southeast Asian Student Coalition Summer Institute, Berkeley, CA, June 2003. Photo credit: Michael Tran

History," I decided I was going to be either an Asian American studies or ethnic studies major. I decided to be an ethnic studies major because I felt like there was a way for me to really be able to learn about other communities. To be honest, Asian American studies by itself didn't always speak to me as a Hmong American. It was important for me to be able to learn more about the Asian American studies curriculum, but it was also important for me to learn about other communities and see how I'm able to connect and really build solidarity with them, whether it's culturally or in terms of the struggles that we face as people of color.

When I arrived at UCB in Fall 2002, I knew immediately that I needed to find a community. I was really thankful to REACH!, the Asian and Pacific Islander Recruitment and Retention Center on campus, for reaching out to me right away. There were other organizations as well, but I definitely resonated more with REACH!, especially because there were other Southeast Asian students that were a part of it and doing outreach to neighboring Southeast Asian and low-income Asian American communities. I knew this is what I wanted to do, because back in high school not a lot of people reached out to me and my friends, and so I wanted to make sure that I could reach out to as many young people as I could. I wanted to do that so that they know that there's a life outside of their neighborhood, a life outside of their city, and that college is also an option for them. So I decided to become involved with REACH! and served as a coordinator each year for one of the programs.

There was another organization called the Southeast Asian Student Coalition (SASC) that helped to really politicize me. When I got involved with SASC, I started to learn about the deportation of Cambodians that was happening at that time. I also learned about Cambodians who came here as refugee children and grew up in the streets the same way I did in the '90s. Back in the '90s, we had a lot of wars against low-income folks. We had war on poverty, war against immigrant communities, and also the "three-strikes" law. There were just so many different policies that really criminalized low-income folks, including Southeast Asian communities who were criminalized not only by the state of California, but also the U.S.

I learned about how Cambodians were impacted by all of those different policies in the '90s, and also how Southeast Asians were impacted. They came here as lawful permanent residents but still had their rights taken away because they might have some sort of criminal offense. "Criminal offense" was very widely defined and so I felt that it was wrong. So I stood with SASC and we demonstrated on campus. We were involved with other community organizations in Oakland, and also nationally.

I didn't realize that I was going to be that involved. But because I cared so much about my family and my community, this was one of the fights that really brought me into community organizing and community activism. So since then, I've really just been committed to learning about the various issues that impact not just Southeast Asian American communities, but also Asian American communities, communities of color, low-income communities, and immigrant communities, and what it means to really be able to fight for our rights.

I definitely think that being an ethnic studies major, together with my on-campus involvement, helped to shape me for my professional career. I definitely took a risk by taking "Asian American History," not really knowing what I was going to get myself into. That class helped me to contemplate what it meant to be Asian American.

Growing up, I always identified as Asian American or Hmong. I never even knew to identify myself as Hmong American. So it was really interesting growing up saying that I was Asian American and not really knowing the origins of that political identity; I didn't even know what Asian American identity means. So I was really thankful to have taken "Asian American History" and learn about the origins of the term "Asian American," which came from Asian American organizers in the '60s. Before that, I had no idea we were called "Orientals." Now I had the understanding that Asian American was actually a political identity, and today it's just a very common identity.

I also learned about the various struggles that Asian American ethnic groups have gone through historically in the U.S., and making connections as to what this Asian American history means to me as a Southeast Asian American. My parents came here in 1975, I was born in the 1980s, and I grew up as a Hmong person. I was able to understand that sometimes there were differences between Southeast Asians and other Asian American and Pacific Islander communities, but we were also treated as a community or a group in the U.S. I was able to understand that there were a lot of divisions, but that we needed to fight harder to ensure that we were united and understood our differences and that having differences is not necessarily a bad thing.

So that was really something that helped to me expand my understanding as an Asian American. I learned to not just fight for myself or my community as a Hmong American. I was able to understand what my struggles were as a Hmong American, as a Southeast Asian American, but also as an Asian American and a person of color. And I got all of that understanding from taking Asian American and ethnic studies classes. I also learned about the Third World Liberation Front (TWLF), the struggles of the '60s and '70s, and the connection of Asian Americans being in solidarity with the Black Power movement and the Black Panthers. The beauty that came out of it—the way various communities inspired each other. It wasn't just about Asian Americans being inspired by other communities, but also about other communities being inspired by Asian American activists.

And then to learn about the 1999 Ethnic Studies hunger strike and how folks were still carrying on the struggle. The fight really inspired me to determine what my role was going to be. If ethnic studies and Asian American studies had such a big impact on me, what was my role? I knew I needed to continue to be involved in the community, but I also needed to really sharpen my game and my education. I always need to be knowledgeable about a situation, but always first and foremost, need to be knowledgeable about the experience of the community. What are they feeling? What are they going through? What are their anxieties? By combining community and education together, we can develop real solutions to move us forward.

Attending UCB was a beautiful opportunity for me. I know that we have a lot of criticism about these systems, these institutions. And I have my own criticism too. But at the same time, without UCB, I would have never met Harvey Dong and taken an Asian American studies class. I would have never been an ethnic studies major. I would have never learned about REACH! or SASC. These things really pushed me to continue to be involved in the community, and shaped me and my foundation to be both "book smart" and "street smart," and to always have the community in my heart. That's how I chose to live my life moving forward.

PARENTAL EXPECTATIONS

My parents weren't that much different from other Asian American parents in terms of what they wanted and hoped for their children's careers. I know that they wanted the best for us. I know that they didn't want to see us struggle like the way that they struggled. So I'm really grateful that my parents pushed me hard. And when I say hard, it was really hard. But I have no resentment towards them because I felt like without them pushing me that way, I would not be as resilient as I am today. But my parents definitely had the same goals as others, wanting me to be a doctor, lawyer, or engineer, something that made money.

Originally, I wanted to be a political science major and was considering being a lawyer. But as I mentioned, after I took my first Asian American studies class, I knew what my calling was, and that was to serve the people. My parents weren't happy about that. I think they were still hopeful that I would come out of UCB as a different major, but it didn't happen. I knew that once my heart was set, I was going to be an ethnic studies major for the rest of my life. My parents were not happy, and I think it was more so because they didn't want to see me struggle. They wanted to make sure that I had a career that would provide me with more than sufficient income for me to live comfortably. And we know that sometimes serving the community doesn't always bring income.

My dad was definitely the first person in my life who taught me about getting involved with the community. So although he was disappointed, I knew that he understood my passion to serve the community because he too was about serving the community and making sure that the community knew what was happening. When [the community] didn't have language access, he was one of the first Hmong in Sacramento to do a Hmong radio show to make sure that folks who didn't speak English understood the current local and national news. He wanted to make sure folks felt connected and not isolated. So I'm really thankful to my dad for teaching me those values and I carry them to this day with me.

YOUTH TOGETHER

After I graduated from UCB, I was really appreciative to land a job with an educational justice organization in Oakland called Youth Together. People always say that it's really about your networks, and it really was. Because of my involvement both on campus and off campus, I was able to meet really amazing community advocates and leaders. And when I say off campus, I'm talking about folks in Oakland, folks in Richmond. As a community, we're always observing each other and looking out for each other. So I was really thankful that there was a job opening, and would've never known about it if I didn't know Jidan Koon, who said, "Hey, Youth Together is looking to hire; you should definitely apply." And so, I gave it a shot and landed the job at Youth Together, which provided me with that substantial training ground to be a community organizer.

My role at Youth Together was to raise educational justice at Berkeley High School. That in itself was its own challenge. It really deepened my understanding and experience with building solidarity with other communities. It wasn't just about serving the Asian American community, but also low-income people of color, or students of color in this case, and ensuring that we were addressing the inequities in education that they faced at Berkeley High.

That's what I was able to do immediately after my years at UCB. It really set the tone in terms of my ability to do community engagement and community organizing, working with young people, and providing them with the tools and skills needed to utilize their voice and to validate their experience and the discomfort they felt when they knew something was unjust. I wanted to be able to provide them with the appropriate language to articulate the issues they were going through, and develop possible solutions to those issues. That was something that I wanted to do, because as a young person, I felt that discomfort. I felt that unjustness, but didn't know how to articulate it. I didn't know the right words to say because I just didn't know what was happening.

Top: Yang with Banteay Srei and The Spot youth in Oakland, California after an intergenerational Southeast Asian American cooking and storytelling session. 2016.

Bottom: Serve the People, Bay Area celebrating the completion of the first ever Rites of Passage cohort. Oakland, CA, 2009.

SERVE THE PEOPLE

Being at Youth Together was great. It also made me realize that there is still an under-representation of Southeast Asian young people being served and their stories being heard. Oftentimes, Southeast Asians are a much smaller community. The smaller you are, the more marginalized you become. Myself and a good handful of colleagues who were also doing community organizing work, including Jidan Koon, Somnang Chan, Mike Tran, and Tony Douangviseth, came together and realized that we needed to do something about serving Southeast Asian young people. We needed to provide the necessary space for them to be one hundred percent themselves and not feel like they had to sacrifice any piece of being a Southeast Asian young person to be a part of a space, and that their voice matters. So we developed a space and we were able to create a grassroots organization called Serve the People in Oakland.

During our early years, it was beautiful. We started in 2006 and it kept going. We were able to get around fifty to sixty young people to be a part of our grassroots organization. We really politicized them and provided them the space to own their Southeast Asian experiences, whether it was the struggles that they were having at home, at school, or in their neighborhoods. We wanted for them to just feel like, "I can fully embrace who I am as a Cambodian American, a Mien American, a Vietnamese American, or even mixed ethnicity or race." Because oftentimes, we don't have that kind of space.

When I moved to Sacramento, we also started Serve the People there for a couple of years. But there's always a struggle with doing grassroots organizing—it's something that you do on top of your regular work. It's volunteer work and there's no funding. So because we were having folks transition in and out of the organization, we eventually decided to fold the organization. But when it did exist, it was beautiful. You had folks just really be able to not only feel empowered, but also take initiative and really fight for themselves and each other.

HEALING PROCESS

It wasn't until "Asian American History" that I felt like I was truly starting my healing process. Everything just started to make so much more sense. And so I think that fueled my drive to want to keep learning and growing, and being a part of the community so that I not only could serve the community, but also heal from all the hurt that I experienced as a young person. The more I started working with young people, though, the more I started realizing that it wasn't just about healing the hurt that I experienced as a young person, but really about healing the community and the generations that came before me.

Healing is not something that we talk about as Hmong Americans or as Southeast Asians on a regular basis. So when we were part of Serve the People, healing was such a big element in our curriculum. We built a space for young people, and ourselves, because we were still trying to process and understand who we were as young community activists/organizers. We were really able to tell our stories. We bonded with and validated each other, so that our stories weren't just something that we kept to ourselves, but they were also something we could share with each other. We were able to understand that it wasn't just something that each of us was individually experiencing—my brothers and young people who came after me are experiencing it too. We identified that it was something that we needed to change, that it was not okay for young Southeast Asians to grow up and feel all of this pain, violence, and hurt. Through Serve the

People, we were able to provide a family for each other and really start our healing process.

I think sometimes healing can be super abstract. What does healing even mean? But for me, through Serve the People, part of our healing was being able to make sense of our narratives, to build them, to get them out there, get our stories told and seen. That's part of our healing and I think Serve the People did exactly that. If we didn't do anything else, we were able to provide a healing space for young folks—for them to start seeing that there's people out there that see them completely, see their stories and hear their voices—see that their experiences matter, and that it's not something that's made up. And that's what Asian American studies did for me. Asian American studies saw me. My story was not made up, and it made me feel powerful.

BANTEAY SREI

After Youth Together, I became involved with Banteay Srei, a Southeast Asian nonprofit organization that serves young Southeast Asian women impacted by sexual exploitation. Sometimes people ask, "Why did you get involved with Banteay Srei?" For me, I knew that the Southeast Asian American community was already a very marginalized community, and that Southeast Asian women were marginalized even more so. Women-specific issues are not always addressed.

A story that I don't tell too often is that I felt like there wasn't a lot of love in my life. And so as a young teenager, I sought love through a boyfriend. I think sometimes even to this day, we have a lot of young Southeast Asians who may feel that way—that love is something that is missing in their lives, which may or may not be true. For me, growing up as a teenager, I didn't know that my parents were showing me love by providing a roof over me, and ensuring that I always had food to eat. I equated love with what I saw on TV. I grew up watching *Full House* and thought, "Yeah, my parents don't hug me. They don't tell me they love me. We don't sit and talk, and have family dinners together." That's what I thought love was, and so I always felt like it was something that was missing. And with all the discomfort and injustice that I was experiencing, and not having the right words to articulate how I felt, I thought I was resilient, and went looking for love. And so I knew that there were predators out there—that predators would take advantage of young women who were in similar situations like I was in.

I felt that it was important for me to get involved with an organization like Banteay Srei, to be able to provide a space where young people—young Southeast Asian women—felt love, a place where they didn't always have to resort to seeking it somewhere else and were able to first and foremost find that self-love. If no one else loves you, how do you really love yourself and have that self-value? What does that look like? What does taking care of yourself look like? What does that even mean?

And so I got involved with Banteay Srei because I cared. Banteay Srei wasn't a community organizing space. It was not a community activist space. It was really a self-development space. And I think we can do all the community organizing that we want, but if we're not focused on self-development, then we're not going to be able to start our healing. We're not going to be able to truly love ourselves so that we can understand what loving others is.

SOUTHEAST ASIAN RESOURCE ACTION CENTER

I committed to Banteay Srei for four to five years. It was a challenge working with young women who are impacted by sexual exploitation. There were a lot of times when you felt really helpless. Yet, as much as I really loved being at Banteay Srei, I felt like I would be more valuable in a space where I was creating systems change again, and I found that at

COURTESY OF MICHAEL TRAN (ABOVE) AND NKAUJ LAB YANG (BELOW)

Top: Yang leading a workshop for Serve The People, Sacramento, a Southeast Asian youth organization in Sacramento, Caifornia. 2010.

Bottom: Yang meeting Richard Aoki for the first time when he spoke in Asian American Studies 20A (Asian American history) at UC Berkeley in Spring 2003.

Yang speaking out against the unjust immigration laws, deportation of Southeast Asians, and advocating to keep families together. Stockton, CA, 2017.

the Southeast Asian Resource Action Center (SEARAC).

It was a very timely opportunity, and I was able to really push for policy changes both at the California statewide level and nationally, to address education, health, and immigration issues that our communities faced. I know people have their criticisms around policy advocacy, but it is a key element in creating systems change along with self-development, direct services, and community organizing. We need all of those different elements to happen at the same time. Sometimes the ideology will clash, but we need all of them to happen at the same time for our communities to see justice and equity simultaneously.

Today, I still serve as SEARAC's California Director of Policies and Programs. One of our big wins recently was getting the state to disaggregate Asian American Pacific Islander health data. That was important to the Southeast Asian community because it all goes back to visibility—being seen—and having accurate data so that we can really have an understanding of what's happening in the community to address relevant issues and ensure that those in our communities are living quality lives.

ETHNIC STUDIES FOREVER!

After working a few years, I had to decide if I wanted to continue working, or if it was the right time for me to pursue an advanced degree. I knew that I wanted to still do something that would enhance my community engagement and systems change work. While looking to apply to various programs, I talked to folks who received their master's in social work, public health, and ethnic studies. Everyone said, "If you're going to get your master's, go get something that is career-oriented." It made a lot of sense, but my heart said I needed to do ethnic studies.

I felt I needed to do that because one of my goals was to really be able to contribute to literature about the Hmong community that was through a positive lens. Right now, there has been really great work around Hmong in education, the struggles that we face, and recommending great solutions. So I went ahead and pursued my master's in Ethnic Studies at San Francisco State University (SF State). I felt that SF State would be able to provide me with the additional skills and lens to really contribute answers to questions like, "What does healing mean to the Hmong community? What does that look like?" I am really grateful to the cohort that I was a part of, and also to the professors who taught me.

I'm still working on my thesis. It's been a few years, but it's something that's still on my mind to complete. I'm really thankful to my advisor because I felt like I needed someone who understood marginalized Asian American communities, and pushed our stories out with a positive lens; not just always look at problems and providing solutions, but also be able to say, "Our communities also have great traditional ceremonies that serve us."

I think that it's also about time we start writing about the beauty of our communities that is not often told. I think when we're looking at marginalized communities, we always want to react to the problem and figure out the solution. And so my thesis topic is about looking at how traditional Hmong funerals have served as a healing mechanism for Hmong Americans; how this is able to teach Hmong Americans their deeper history and traditions; and how it makes them closer to their loved ones who have passed and to their families and community that show up for them.

People always ask, "Why did you choose ethnic studies and not Asian American studies?" Pursuing my master's reaffirmed what I felt as an undergrad—that Asian American studies was beautiful, but as a Hmong American, there were certain things about other communities that really resonated with me. For example, in my Africana studies class, I learned about Africana

Top: *Yang, with her family, receiving Deveta Giving Circle's 2017 Courage and Leadership Award.*

At left: *With her partner and community activist Mike Tran in 2019.*

psychology, and how similar it was to how Hmong people lived our lives. I can't even say "Hmong psychology" because that doesn't exist right now in books. But that class just resonated with me. Similarly, Native American studies, and how some of their psychology or way of living resonates with how Hmong Americans have lived our lives.

In pursuing my master's in ethnic studies, I was also privileged to take Asian American studies courses with the Asian American studies cohort. It continues to remind me that, although I am Hmong American and identify heavily as Hmong American and Southeast Asian American, I am Asian American as well. It reminds me that we have a lot of work to do so that we can continue to build our solidarity within the Asian American community, and really strengthen our unity so that we can fight for the entire Asian American community—whether it's in California or on a national level.

When I was at SF State, I was very careful about who I would choose as my advisor. Wesley Ueunten was a professor in the Asian American Studies Department. I chose him because he is Okinawan, and Okinawans are also a very marginalized ethnic group worldwide. I knew that he was going to understand my struggles as a Hmong American. And he did. I was so nervous when I approached him, but he invited me into his office and said," Yeah, let's just talk story." I knew he was the right person to be my advisor—it was important for us to get to know each other before we jumped into talking about business, in this case, my master's thesis.

ASIAN AMERICAN STUDIES TODAY

Asian American studies and ethnic studies continue to be extremely important today. We need to continue to remember the history of Asian American studies, and how it was really the students and the community who stood up and fought for it and ethnic studies to exist. As an ethnic studies major and student whose life changed because of Harvey Dong's "Asian American History" class, I think it's amazing to see more folks in the community as government affairs managers and professors who were Asian American studies and ethnic studies majors. And so that myth that, "Oh, you're not going to be able to find a job because you're an Asian American studies or ethnic studies major," is exactly that—a myth. There are so many people who have come out of these programs and who are holding powerful and meaningful jobs, and creating extreme changes for our communities and really fighting for social justice.

I feel that I'm really blessed to be out in the field, and to meet so many people who have really brought the value of social justice from Asian American studies into where they work. These are the people who really create change and normalize the need, and fight, for social justice. Even to this day, as a policy advocate in California on the statewide level, I see there are movements for the public K-12 education system to seriously implement ethnic studies. At that level of education, and that age level, it is so inspiring. We know that we don't want young people to wait until they go to college—if they go to college—to be able to learn about themselves and each other. For me, college was the starting point of my healing process.

It's so important that we start implementing a K-12 ethnic studies curriculum appropriately, and that we're fighting to make sure that California is putting money into this so that young people can have the lens to really learn about themselves, develop their self-love at a much earlier age, and to learn about each other. In the Sacramento City Unified School District just this past year, there was an incident where a Chinese American student at C.K. McClatchy High School did a science project on various ethnic communities and their IQs. This student's project concluded that East Asians had a higher IQ than Southeast Asians and African Americans. There was a big blow up.

First, why did the teachers not intervene in advance? Second, it shows that our communities—even among Asian Americans—don't know enough about each other. This is why things like ethnic studies and Asian American studies need to exist—to educate. The school district brought everyone together to address the variations of history, the struggles that various communities faced. They addressed the racism that existed because of the lack of having opportunities to learn about each other, each other's history and struggles, and how we were more alike than different, but that those differences were also something to celebrate.

Asian American studies is important, even though it has constantly faced budget struggles since the existence of the TWLF. But we've made a lot of progress. We still continue to have struggles internally, with the institution, or with ensuring that there are enough folks majoring in the various programs so that we can continue them. At the same time, there is also a movement where the K-12 folks want to implement it too. So there has been a strong impact that has been made throughout the years. We can't forget the history of what the TWLF fighters stood for. It is because of their legacy that we're able to move Asian American studies beyond college institutions. That means also going through the K-12 educational system because it is so significant to our education, not just academically, but to our education as human beings, and for communities who live among each other.

Moving forward, it's important we remember to hold on to the elements of what makes Asian American studies and ethnic studies what they are. We need to continue to ensure that our communities have access to our own histories, that our communities are the ones that are writing our own histories, and that we have that element of fighting for social justice for our communities. We need to continue to be involved in the community and ensure that we don't become too caught up in what the university expects of us. We need to be able to balance playing the game with the institution, and also continue to have the core values of community and social justice.

I'm very optimistic about the future of Asian American studies. I believe that there are so many pupils of Asian American studies who are out there doing the work and fighting for the community. And I will remain optimistic as long as Asian American studies continues to remember that students and the community need to be at the core of Asian American studies programs and departments. We need to continue to expand our listening skills to listen deeply to what the students in their community are saying. That is what's going to continue to drive Asian American studies forward.

CHAPTER 12

SHARING LEADERSHIP, CHALLENGING SYSTEMS

A GROUNDED PERSPECTIVE OF ASIAN AMERICAN STUDIES

Preeti Sharma speaks at wage increase hearings, 2015.

GROWING UP

I was born in the early '80s and raised in South Florida. My parents and sister, who is a few years younger than me, are still there in the state. It's always funny talking about Florida with folks on the West Coast because they think it's some other world. In one sense, it was "strange," because growing up I was made to feel that I was different. As early as pre-kindergarten, people would ask me what kind of Indian I was. They'd make racist hand gestures, point to their heads, and ask, "Are you this dot Indian or are you this feather Indian?" From that moment on, I knew that I didn't belong.

Florida is very much a part of the infrastructure of the South, but I didn't have any of the words, language, or tools to describe my experiences of difference at that age. I was one of a handful of Indians and South Asians in my neighborhood, which was predominantly white seniors, Cuban refugees, and folks from Jamaica. To some extent the infrastructure, racism, and legacy of the South was palpable while doing everyday things like going to school, grocery shopping, and being in public places.

And then to another extent, South Florida was an immigrant and refugee kind of space, where I also felt that vibrancy of the Caribbean diaspora. It was clear that I was in a mix of these worlds and that context was a key part of what it meant to be Asian American, and South Asian American, in the South. I didn't have the tools to name or describe that context until I went to college and was directly a part of the ethnic studies, and gender and sexuality studies, curriculum.

ASIAN AMERICAN STUDENT UNION

I started at the University of Florida (UF) in 2002. During my freshman year, I didn't know what major I was going to be. I remember going through the course catalogue, crossing off a bunch of majors, and thinking, "Let me take as many courses as I can until I decide." My heart, however, was into literature, since it was a way for me to access the narratives of people of color and immigrant communities. I started taking courses in American literature and then the African diaspora, South Asian diaspora, and British literature. This was my way of pushing for representation by, and information from, people of color about their lives, their migration, and questions about empire.

At the end of my sophomore year, while passing through Turlington Plaza on the way to class, there was a loud protest being held by the Asian American Student Union (AASU) for Asian American Studies to become an official major. The feeling of excitement, tension, and the sight of my peers making demands for an important cause was incredible. Walking into the plaza, it struck me that this was what I was looking for: a community, a place to be able to

University of Florida Asian American Student Union dinner, 2005. Top left to right: Leo Esclamado, Jennifer Aldeguer, Sandy Chiu, Satish Kunisi, Mark Villegas, Linh Nguyen; Bottom left to right: Jessica Aldeguer, Theresa Jaranilla, Rupali Patel, Preeti Sharma.

recognize concerns and issues, and a way to think about my own life and history in knowledge production. I had this immediate sense of wanting to be a part of what that these folks were doing. I ended up talking to someone, who was also a part of the Indian Student Union, and asked how I could join.

A few weeks later, AASU hosted an event called, "Why Not White Studies?" It was a panel and some of my favorite professors were actually on it. At that time I was also a student leader with the Office of Community Service. I was primarily doing different volunteer work specific to the Gainesville public housing projects, which often used a band-aid approach to social issues rather than centering the residents' experiences, or addressing the root causes of affordable housing. I hadn't connected yet with some of the student organizing efforts on campus, and so I remember being a little shy at the panel. Even though I ended up seeing folks there that would later become my close friends for the next decade and a half of my life, I didn't talk to them at first. But after attending the panel, I confirmed to myself that I wanted to join AASU, and that was how I ended the spring semester.

During the fall semester of my junior year, I saw that there was an Asian American Studies class, AML 3673: "Introduction to Asian American Literature," being taught in the English department by a South Asian American professor, Dr. Malini Schueller. I thought to myself, "Let me sign up for this!" Not only was I interested in the subject matter, but there was also a South Asian American professor. While sitting in class, it turned out that 99 percent of the students there were also in AASU. I was looking for them, and they were also looking for me, because I had just taken a small leadership role with the Indian Student Union. And so, we all became friends through this course.

"Introduction to Asian American Literature" was inspiring because of the intellectual aspect of being able to read through major conversations in Asian American studies. We were thinking about Frank Chin and deconstructing the troubling constructions of the term "Asian American." We were reading Angel Island poetry and thinking about transnationalism and diaspora, alongside readings by Karen Tei Yamashita. We moved through classical texts, but also thought about them in the context of orientalism (Edward Said) and larger questions of empire. It also influenced me that almost all the folks in class were Asian American students from AASU, and who wanted to understand our place at an institution such as University of Florida and the broader geography of the South.

I ended up double majoring in English and women's studies. Both majors were able to support personal and academic questions that I had at the time. Women's studies had its attention to women of color feminisms. Through one of those courses, I remember I was able to discover Sonia Shah's book, *Dragon Ladies: Asian American Feminists Breath Fire* (1999), on Asian American feminisms in conversation, with other important work like Patricia Hill Collins's text on Black feminisms, *Black Feminist Thought*.

When I first met the AASU students, they were primarily advocating for an Asian American Studies certificate and minor program to be housed in the English department. The advisor was going to be Dr. Schueller. November was Asian American History Month, and the folks in leadership, some of whom eventually became students in the Asian American Studies graduate program at UCLA, helped to run cutting-edge student programming and build the leadership skills of many students in AASU.

The fight for Asian American studies that solidified took a number of years, and the certificate program was finally approved in my junior year. Certificate requirements included "Introduction to Asian American Literature" and other existing and new courses. Another struggle that AASU was pushing for at the time was getting an Asian American/Pacific Islander student affairs person, which they now have at the university.

AASU was also thinking broadly and helped start the Southeast Regional Conference of Asian American Leaders (SERCAAL), the first conference for Asian American student leaders in the Southeast. Folks from Virginia, Louisiana, and Georgia attended the conference. It was amazing to see how everyone worked together, and really cared about each other and Asian American issues in the context of the region. It was an incredible time to be at UF and be connected with AASU. I missed the conference that first year because it was the weekend of the 2004 presidential election, and I didn't want to miss the chance to vote. I however ended up co-directing SERCAAL the following year together with a talented co-leader and team.

We had a dynamic range of speakers, including Rinku Sen, the Publisher of *Colorlines*, for the second SERCAAL conference. In fact, we had a lot of dynamic scholars, advocates, and artists come through AASU's events: historians Vijay Prashad and the late Ronald Takaki; comedian Kristina Wong; choreographer Shyamala Moorty; and also musicians, including spoken word and hip hop artists. Ultimately, I feel like my training through my courses, the culture that student leaders had established, and what we were doing outside of the classroom, was truly something else and will never forget those experiences.

MASTER'S DEGREE AND COMMUNITY ORGANIZATIONS

In 2006, two of my good friends and colleagues, whom I admired, did some research about the Department of Asian American Studies M.A. program at UCLA. To this day, there are only two master's degree programs in Asian American studies in the entire country—San Francisco State University and UCLA. At that time, I initially imagined I would become a professor, and so I applied to the M.A. program, and a few Ph.D. programs. Luckily enough, I got into the M.A. program at UCLA.

JEAN-PAUL DEGUZMAN; BELOW: GENA HAMAMOTO

UCLA Asian American Studies cohort, 2006; left to right: Satish Kunisi, Paul Ocampo, Carrie Usui, Ronaldo Noche, Preeti Sharma, Lindsay Gervacio, Jolie Chea, Napoleon Lustre

Below*: At UCLA Asian American Studies graduation, 2008; left to right: Christine Lee, Carrie Usui, Preeti Sharma, Paul Ocampo, Jolie Chea, Ronaldo Noche*

Not only was the Asian American Studies M.A. program the right fit, it was also the best thing that could've happened to me then. I felt like a "kid in a candy shop." At the University of Florida, we created a spirit that made room for us to unpack and think through what it meant to be Asian American in the South. Coming to Los Angeles however, I saw this massive infrastructure of Asian American nonprofits built through the legacy of a West Coast Asian American movement building. I was shocked and floored at the number of multiple Asian American service agencies, and movement building social justice organizations—later known as "worker centers." I was marveled by what little I was able to understand of the scope of those organizations at that time, but any event that was going on, I was there: an arts event at Visual Communications; the East West Players Tuesday night cafe project; or a youth-led event by Khmer Girls in Action down in Long Beach.

Coming to Asian American studies from a non-California centric perspective allowed me to think about its problems, too. I wanted to understand the boundaries of the field and where it was being challenged. My brilliant program cohort members were also always invested and interested in thinking about Asian American studies from a perspective of Southeast Asian American, South Asian American, and Pacific Islander studies; and in terms of how those communities raise questions for American exceptionalism and imperialism, detention and deportation, and sovereignty. Similarly, it was incredible when I got a chance to see what Los Angeles-area community-based organizations were striving for, and how those efforts were not in the "mainstream" of rights and advocacy.

DOCTORATE DEGREE AND COMMUNITY ACTIVISM

t's been a long trajectory for me—not just getting a Ph.D.—but my own political education. The folks that I've been able to meet through various community-based and intellectual efforts have been compassionate and generative. Within the few first weeks of me coming to Los Angeles, there were a couple of special things happening. For example, it was the ten-year anniversary of the National Asian Pacific American Women's Forum (NAPAWF). I immediately emailed the Forum to ask if there was something I could do and plug into. I met a lot of incredible folks through NAPAWF's conference on developing intersectional efforts for feminist movement building, and saw the range of organizations that were in Los Angeles, as well as across the country.

I remember contacting the South Asian Network (SAN), a community-based organization for persons of South Asian descent in the Los Angeles area, focused around civil rights, health, and violence prevention. SAN is a dynamic and special organization, and it continues to be, yet its iteration at that time made it a leader for its intersectional approach as a nonprofit community-based organization. SAN tended to the needs of multiple communities in a holistic and understanding way with its programs around queer visibility, workers' rights, tenants' rights, immigration (particularly around detention and deportation in the context of post-9/11 surveillance), and health and violence prevention needs of South Asian community members.

My friends and I went to SAN's office in Artesia to ask if we could volunteer for them. I plugged into part of SAN's Civil Rights Unit, where they were focusing on workers' rights as well as tenants' rights work. I learned about the severe undercount of the Bangladeshi population in the Koreatown area, and how there was a concerted effort, in 2005 to 2006, on the part of organizers, community members, as well as UCLA Urban Planning M.A. researchers to do a community mapping. The undercount meant a lack of resources, but it was also about notions of pride for Bangladeshi residents. Based on the knowledge of community leaders, the mapping project wasn't just about numbers, but also identifying community needs.

Above: Sharma at the launch of South Asian Network's human rights report in 2010.

Below: South Asian Network Workers Rights Actions with Summer Activist Training in 2010.

The Great Recession was about to hit, and Los Angeles was also developing and strengthening its current movement for housing and tenants' rights against gentrification. Like other Los Angeles community-based organizations, SAN had started to see that folks were being pushed out or evicted from their apartments in Koreatown because of the neighborhood's "affordability" and central access to transportation.

I assisted SAN with other programs, including one for young Bangladeshi women. I worked with four bright, young Bangladeshi leaders to create a film on their community's experiences post-9/11, particularly around issues of surveillance, and also what it meant to be a youth. The film, *Status. . .Pending*, screened at the National Center for the Preservation of Democracy. Two members of the film crew got to speak in front of a crowd of over 100 people. *Status. . .Pending* was screened together with other films by formerly incarcerated youth and folks from Latinx communities. This approach of allowing youth to put out their own stories was generative because it presented young peoples' stories of race in Los Angeles relationally.

I also assisted SAN and the Los Angeles Taxi Workers Alliance (LATWA) with their campaign around medallions and how taxi workers had to buy into their own "non-worker" status as someone who leases a taxi. The debate still continues around the misclassification of taxi workers, who are seen as shareholders in their industry, but don't end up making much. Taxi workers are stuck in what the LATWA calls "sweatshops on wheels." When I graduated from the M.A. program at UCLA, I continued working at SAN as a Community Advocate for tenants' rights, and then later as a Communications Associate to support the organization's media efforts.

In January 2008, a groundbreaking strike by about thirty Nepali and Indian women took place at a popular threading salon. A couple of women leaders decided to organize the walkout because of a contract with two questionable pieces that they didn't have time to look over. One item was a decrease in folks' commission, and the other was around the inability to work at another threading salon within a radius of that salon chain. The strike was unprecedented in two ways. First, the mainstream labor movement hadn't really dealt with the private service sector in terms of small-business and immigrant-run establishments, including beauty salons. Second, this was a salon worker-led strike facilitated by conversations with SAN. The strike spoke to the buildup of an Asian American worker movement happening in Los Angeles, San Francisco, and California broadly.

A few years later, I had a conversation with one of the salon leaders and asked her about the strike and that time period. I held a lot of assumptions about what the greatest loss for her was during that time, and thought it would be income. Instead, she said that her greatest loss was all of her customers. After the salon fired her, she couldn't tell anybody that she was leaving. For her, it was about the loss of those relationships and how they were the core labor of her work. This then became the crux of the questions that I took with me as I pursued my Ph.D. in the Department of Gender Studies at UCLA.

While in the Ph.D. program, I was able to continue my relationship and mentoring from my M.A. professors Grace Hong and Purnima Mankekar. It was important for me to be able to do a project in Asian American studies, and about Asian American women, that looked at the contours of these labor movements, but also at how these movements were made up of folks who were working at salons. Given Southern California's relationship to Hollywood—where beauty culture has such a presence—I was reminded through my research how South Asian American and Vietnamese American women created and led everyday beauty culture. At the heart of salon workers' day-to-day work, is the labor that builds relationships with people as their base. A lot of those experiences at SAN and Los Angeles's immigrant, community-based organizations that motivated me then, still motivates me years later.

onversations in Asian American studies continue to change, as they should. I am still invested in a version of Asian American studies that relates to Asian American movement building spaces, including with those in community-based organizations— developing theories and visions of what liberation looks like. These conversations are not clearly just "university" and "non-university," as folks like to paint them. Ultimately, such conversations get at questions about the ways in which Asians in the U.S. have both contributed to and pushed back against different facets of U.S. empire, and what that means for the current moment of U.S. government relations within the continent and broadly.

I am also inspired by folks who are currently taking on critical refugee studies as a part of thinking about memory, trauma, war, and healing. Such scholarship compounds with folks also thinking about Asian settler colonialism in Hawai'i and the Pacific Islands, and the structure of settler colonialism in the U.S. broadly. It also relates to those interrogating facets of what it means to be South Asian American, situated in the lens and legacy of the work around orientalism, as a project of understanding empire, and different periodizations of South Asian early migration, from post-Immigration and Nationality Act of 1965 to post-9/11 surveillance. I am also interested in folks who are thinking about different valences of gender and sexuality—not just painting early periods of Asian migrants as "bachelor societies," but giving us a language to understand homosociality and different types of relationships. I'm excited to be able to participate in a lot of those crossing of intellectual communities.

I'm also excited to think about the nexus of, for me personally, in South Asian American studies, labor studies, and the culture of the global beauty aesthetic, and how that takes form in a city like Los Angeles. There are a lot of different ways that I'm hopeful to personally contribute to the field and to such questions of empire, race, class, gender, sexuality, and labor in terms of immigrants and refugees that can allow us to understand the current formations of capital.

A part of me also feels like the places where I enjoyed Asian American studies the most, were through the relationships and community that I built with other students. At the University of Florida, for example, I wanted to "do something." Those projects and efforts were not haphazard; they were very thoughtful and intentional. The Asian American Student Union at UF looked at the relationship to place, what it could ask for, and what the needs were. That was really powerful for me as a student in a college town in Florida, in the South where, what we also had was our relationships to each other.

There are also many demands on students: do your homework, go to class, do the readings, plus other external concerns. They are all important! That being said, for me, another space of possible growth has always been the connection to and collaboration with community-based organizations. Such organizations aren't just empty sites, nor are they there for people to impose something and/or give something without any thoughtfulness. I received most of my learning out of these spaces, especially in how community-based organizations are contributing to intellectual traditions and the understanding of root causes for social problems from a racial justice, immigrant justice, and gender justice lens.

For example, young Cambodian women's contributions for liberation make it possible to think about the increasing raids in Long Beach of Cambodians, and what it means in a Trump era of immigration—a legacy of Obama-era detention and deportation. Through organizations like Khmer Girls in Action, we're able to think about: How do these raids speak to the criminal justice system? How do they speak to the immigration and refugee system broadly? How do they impact folks who are second-generation refugees? And, where do sites of trauma and healing inform how to intervene in something that requires a rapid response? In other words,

Sharma at South Asians for Justice API Undocumented Cultural Show Fundraiser, 2012; top left to right: Sameer Gardezi, Muneera Shariff Gardezi, Azeem Khan, Bupen Ram, Vivek Mittal, Tanzila Ahmed, Maithreyi Shankar; bottom left to right: Khushboo Gulati, Jusdeep SIngh Sethi, Diya Bose, Preeti Sharma, Aakash Kishore, Ami Patel, Natasha Khanna-Dang.

Below*: Chinatown Community for Equitable Development photo exhibit, 2013.*

Khmer Girls in Action Yellow Lounge Show in Long Beach, CA, 2015.
***Below:** Chinatown Community for Equitable Development Fundraiser, 2016.*

community-based organizations provide venues for an analysis of, and creative opportunities to, think about what Asian American studies "is." These don't have to be traditional community-based organizations, either.

In 2012, together with a group of folks that I look up to, helped form an all-volunteer and activist-run organization in Chinatown called Chinatown Community for Equitable Development (CCED), a space where students can plug in and out of. CCED first started as a campaign against Walmart, challenging the number one global retailer as it wanted to make inroads in Los Angeles by opening up a neighborhood market in Chinatown. In contrast, there were already other grocery stores and retailers in the region that could have used investment and support to strengthen food sustainability, for example. At that time, CCED and its campaign to stop Walmart was an emergency scrambling together of bright folks, some of whom were part of the older generation of Chinatown and Asian American organizing. Today, CCED is still all-volunteer, and is challenging itself to think about gentrification in an area that is 90 percent tenants, 90 percent immigrants, and one of the lowest income neighborhoods in the city.

I would say to a young person that they can join any of these organizations in whatever way you are able to, both on and off campus. They are happy to figure out a role for you. For me, I gained the most experience through the combination of my classes and these spaces.

LEGACY OF ASIAN AMERICAN STUDIES AT UCLA

Through our courses at UCLA, we learned a little bit about the folks who demanded an Asian American Studies Center and program. I also remember reading about students demanding an Asian American Women Studies course. While looking through *Gidra*, a monthly newspaper-magazine that ran from 1969 to 1974, we came across Asian American students and other activists at UCLA, including Yuji Ichioka and Suzi Wong, fighting for these programs.

We're now in a strange moment where U.S. national memory often erases its own legacy of racism and settler colonialism. Currently, the ways in which white nationalism is being manifested, not exceptionalized, but upheld even, is intense. It is very intense. I remember seeing Confederate flags while growing up. I remember the different verbal racial harassments happening in public places. And so, this tenor of overt racism and white supremacy isn't a surprise.

There are a couple of troubling pieces from our current news cycle: how fast it moves and the idea that "facts" aren't real. Both concerns with the news cycle irk me, as someone invested in knowledge production. We can produce our own content and tell our own stories, which is still really important to me. But these national debates question facts and question knowledge, through rhetoric and also media spins. It is challenging to wake up and read about a judge who is an abuser being recommended for confirmation to the U.S. Supreme Court by a president who is also an abuser. You have to watch it to stay on top of it, but then when you watch it, you get sick.

So, how do I stay committed to telling our stories and having conversations where we can talk about how knowledge is produced? I don't know. Keeping my sanity in these trying moments is helped by going back to community-based organizations and my friends in these spaces, to be together, and to keep a grounded perspective.

There are local campaigns that push the possibilities of current concerns. I can work on Proposition 10 to overturn the Costa-Hawkins Rental Housing Act in order to bolster tenants' rights across California. I can look at folks doing local work around sexual assault and what that means on a national level, too. The work continues, despite the rhetoric and the impact from the federal level. I stay really inspired by how we can understand power through the work

Sharma helped create the video for "I am a #YOUNGWORKER," which was "part of a broader multimedia research project in June 2016 that combined data, stories, and images by and for young people. It gets to the core of what young workers face today – their struggles, their dreams, and their hopes for the future. The project also includes a young worker photo gallery exhibited at the UCLA Labor Center. You can read the report and see the photo exhibit at: www.youngworkersrising.org."

of movement building that challenges empire.

I find that the more we think about ourselves as being alone or unable to grapple with these big concepts by ourselves, I'm reminded about how isolationism is a part of the project of capitalism, if you will, or settler colonialism. What you have in Asian American worker centers, are the intentional labor of committed folks who have experienced social issues in their own lives, and who are working out how to not just make claims to the state, but to change culture and systems.

American studies, critical ethnic studies, women's studies, and queer studies have allowed us to think about knowledge production and whose voices get to be archived, and what those stories get to say or don't say for communities. There is an important role for storytelling, not just in this era of fake news and misstatement of facts, but in questioning the content we produce, how we produce it, and our responsibility to the folks that we're producing it with. Asian American studies and archives like this allow us to challenge the way that knowledge continues to be produced, and to even say that these sites of production were created as a contestation to the dominant paradigms of knowledge.

BIOGRAPHIES

LIFE STORIES

IRENE DEA COLLIER immigrated to the United States from Hoiping in Guangdong Province, China in 1953. After helping establish some of the first Asian American Studies classes and campus-to-community connections, Collier became an active leader in the Association of Chinese Teachers (TACT) and the director of Wah Mei School, San Francisco's 1st bilingual preschool, championing language equality and multilingual education in our school systems.

HARVEY DONG is a second generation Chinese American who was active in AAPA, TWLF-UC Berkeley, Asian Community Center and was active in the struggle to save the International Hotel. He currently teaches Asian American & Asian Diaspora Studies at UC Berkeley and is active in running Eastwind Books of Berkeley as a community bookstore.

LILLIAN FABROS is from Salinas, CA. She attended UC Berkeley and became a student organizer, active in the formation of the Asian American Political Alliance (AAPA) and the Third World Liberation Front (TWLF). She worked as a social worker/community organizer and attorney. Today, she is a Program Manager with Los Angeles County and volunteers in the Filipino community.

HOLLY RAÑA LIM immigrated to the U.S. from the Philippines when she was four year old and grew up with her single mother in neighborhoods of Los Angeles, Montebello and Pico Rivera. With degrees in Political Science/Law and Society from UC Riverside and an MA in Asian American Studies from SFSU, she has taught Asian American Studies at local colleges and is focused on tenants' rights and fundraising as the Board Vice President for Filipino Advocates for Justice. Today, as Director of Public Allies SF/Silicon Valley, she trains, inspires and empowers young activists as a community leader and a campaign organizer.

JEFF MORI, who grew up in San Francisco's Richmond district, worked as Executive Director of the Japanese Community Youth Council (JCYC), an organization that he helped co-found, and later as director of the SF Mayor's Office of Children, Youth and Their Families. With his unique understanding of politics and community, he also built Asian American Recovery Services Inc. (AARS).

PREETI SHARMA grew up in South Florida and attended the University of Florida before entering graduate school at UCLA. As a master's student in the UCLA Department of Asian American Studies, Sharma became involved in a wide array of Los Angeles-area Asian American community organizations, including Khmer Girls in Action, South Asian Network, and Chinatown Community for Equitable Development. Currently, she is a Ph.D. candidate in the Department of Gender Studies; her research is focused on the roles of South Asian American and Vietnamese American women in the beauty industry.

CASIMIRO TOLENTINO was born in Manila and migrated to Los Angeles at the age of ten. He became involved in the Asian American movement as a UCLA student. Tolentino has had a long career in law, working as an attorney for the California Agricultural Labor Relations Board and Department of Fair Employment and Housing, among other organizations, as well as serving as Administrative Law Judge for the State of California. His contributions to Asian American non-profit organizations have been numerous, playing crucial roles with the Asian Pacific American Legal Center (now Asian Americans Advancing Justice-L.A.) and Visual Communications.

AMY UYEMATSU, a Sansei born in Pasadena, California, attended UCLA and took part in the Asian American movement during the late '60s. During that time, she joined the staff of the UCLA Asian American Studies Center, working as a researcher, publications coordinator, and instructor; she was also a co-editor of the seminal collection *Roots: An Asian American Reader* (1971). Uyematsu became a well-known poet, while working as a high school mathematics teacher in the Los Angeles area.

NKAUJ IAB YANG is Director of California Policy and Programs for the Southeast Asia Resource Action Center (SEARAC). She works closely with Southeast Asian American-led and-serving organizations throughout California to build a statewide Southeast Asian American equity agenda. Nkauj Iab spent the last 11 years committed to youth organizing and youth development work both in Sacramento and Oakland.

CAMPUS HISTORIES

MALCOLM COLLIER is a founding member and Lecturer Emeritus of Asian American Studies at San Francisco State University. A native of New Mexico and educated in Peru, Malcolm is also active in photography, visual anthropology, cross-cultural education, and raising his grandchildren with his longtime partner, Irene Dea Collier.

JEAN-PAUL DEGUZMAN is a scholar of twentieth-century American history, with particular interests in Asian American history and Los Angeles. Earning his Ph.D. in History from UCLA, deGuzman has an extensive background teaching Asian American studies and working in public history. DeGuzman is currently on the history faculty of Windward School in Los Angeles.

DANIEL PHIL GONZALEZ has taught, researched, written, and recorded video since participating in the founding of Asian American Studies and the School (now College) of Ethnic Studies at San Francisco State University in 1969. He has been historical advisor to several print projects, films, and television programs about Asian Americans and American legal, political, and social processes, Filipino American history, and Philippines-US relations. He received his BA, International Relations, from SFSU, and his Juris Doctorate from Hastings College of Law.

L. LING-CHI WANG helped establish Asian American Studies at UC Berkeley, and taught its first course in 1969. He is a founder of Chinese For Affirmative Action and the recipient of the Association for Asian American Studies Lifetime Achievement Award. Before his retirement in 2006, Professor Wang headed the program and the Ethnic Studies Department several times. He helped create the Ethnic Studies graduate program, as well as the campus American Cultures requirement. In 1992, Professor Wang co-founded the International Society for the Study of Chinese Overseas (ISSCO).

EDITORS

HARVEY DONG (see campus histories authors above)

RUSSELL JEUNG grew up in San Francisco, CA and first took Asian American Studies at Lowell High School. After graduating from Stanford University, where he was involved with the statewide Asian Pacific Student Union with co-editors Eric Mar and Karen Umemoto, he worked for the Mayor of San Francisco. He obtained a Ph.D. in Sociology at UC Berkeley, and has written several books on Asian Americans and religion. His memoir, "At Home in Exile: Meeting Jesus Among My Ancestors and Refugee Neighbors," shares his family's six generations in California and his organizing work with refugees.

ERIC MAR is a former San Francisco Supervisor and grew up in Sacramento with his twin brother Gordon, a newly elected SF Supervisor for the Sunset District. Now an Assistant Professor at SF State University, Eric credits his Asian Pacific Student Union (APSU) colleagues, Asian American Studies at UC Davis, and grassroots community leaders from groups like the Chinese Progressive Association (CPA) for helping guide his activism. He has served as Acting Dean of the New College of California School of Law, union shop steward for SEIU Local 790, Director of the Coalition for Immigrant Rights, and President of the SF Board of Education.

ARNOLD PAN is Associate Editor of *Amerasia Journal* and a staff member at the UCLA Asian American Studies Center. Prior to joining the staff of the Asian American Studies Center, Pan earned a Ph.D. in English at the University of California, Irvine; his dissertation research is on representations of race and space in early twentieth century literature. In addition to his academic background, Pan has worked as a freelance writer on music and culture.

LISA HIRAI TSUCHITANI was born and raised in San Jose. She received her doctorate in Social and Cultural Studies in Education from UC Berkeley, where she majored in East Asian Studies and Asian American Studies as an undergraduate. She teaches courses on Japanese American history, critical pedagogy, and educational equity in the Asian American & Asian Diaspora Studies Program at UC Berkeley, where she is Chair of the Japanese American Studies Advisory Committee and Faculty Chair of the Asian American and Pacific Islander Standing Committee of the Office of the Vice Chancellor of Equity & Inclusion.

KAREN UMEMOTO was born and raised in Los Angeles and was involved in student and community organizing on a range of issues, including divestiture of university funds in apartheid South Africa, tenant organizing against evictions, mobilizing for redress and reparations for Japanese Americans incarcerated during World War II, and juvenile justice reform. She received her undergraduate degree in Liberal Studies from SF State, master's degree in Asian American Studies from UCLA, and doctorate in Urban Studies from MIT. She taught at the University of Hawai'i at Mānoa in urban planning for 22 years before returning to UCLA, where she is Professor of Urban Planning and Asian American Studies and the Helen and Morgan Chu Endowed Director's Chair and Director of the Asian American Studies Center.

Cover and book design & production:
HyunJu Chappell | Magna Citizen Studio

The front cover illustration multiplies the
movement logo, symbolizing solidarity,
of UC Berkeley's Third World Liberation Front.